THE
Tenant Retention
Solution

Editorial Consultants
Thomas W. Gille, CPM®
Joseph W. Karp, CPM®
Robert D. Oliver, CPM®
R. Bruce Smith, CPM®

Joseph T. Lannon
Publishing and Curriculum Development Manager

Caroline Scoulas
Senior Editor

THE
Tenant Retention Solution

A Revolutionary
Approach to
Commercial Real Estate
Management

Howard K. Lundeen, CPM®
Laurence C. Harmon, CPM®
Kathleen M. McKenna-Harmon, CPM®

IREM Institute of Real Estate Management

CHICAGO

This publication is designed to provide accurate and authoritative information in regard to
the subject matter covered. Forms or other documents included in this book are intended as
samples only. Because of changing and varying state and local laws, competent professional
advice should be sought prior to the use of any document, form, exhibit, or the like.

This publication is sold with the understanding that the publisher is not engaged in ren-
dering legal, accounting, or any other service. If legal advice or other expert assistance is required, the services of a competent professional should be sought.

The opinions expressed in this text are those of the authors and do not necessarily reflect
the policies and positions of the Institute of Real Estate Management. Reference to specific
products and services does not constitute endorsement by the authors or the Institute.

Sources of quotations and data are cataloged in Endnotes. Permission to reprint excerpts
from other works is acknowledged in the Bibliography.

Library of Congress Cataloging-in-Publication Data

Lundeen, Howard K., 1948-
    The tenant retention solution : a revolutionary approach to
  commercial real estate management / Howard K. Lundeen, Laurence C.
  Harmon, Kathleen M. McKenna-Harmon.
        p.   cm.
    Includes bibliographical references and index.
    ISBN 1-57203-008-9
    1. Commercial real estate--management.   2. Office buildings-
  -Tenant satisfaction.   3. Customer service.   I. Harmon, Laurence
  C., 1943-   .   II. McKenna-Harmon, Kathleen, 1946-   III. Title.
  HD1393.55.L86   1994
      333.33'87'068--dc20   95-11791
                                                                        CIP

Printed in the United States of America

1 2 3 4 5 6 7 8 9 10 Printing / Year 04 03 02 01 00 99 98 97 96 95

THE Tenant Retention Solution is dedicated
to Caroline Scoulas, Senior Editor of the Institute of Real Estate Management,
whose dedication to the work, confidence in and patience with its authors,
and willingness to contribute her own insights and
those of practitioners in a variety of commercial real estate environments
added inestimable value to the product.

Preface

Sam Walton, founder of Wal-Mart and Sam's Warehouse Club, was one of the pioneers who revolutionized retail selling, perhaps forever. His approach emphasized cut-rate retailing and rock-bottom pricing as the competitive expectation for every industry in every market—including commercial real estate.

Because of Walton, "no-frills" selling is now typical in the airline industry, computer sales, clothiers, drug store chains, and an army of other businesses. So-called discount centers, off-price centers, and manufacturers' outlet centers are merely the latest, most noteworthy examples of retailing inspired by the late Arkansas billionaire. Even today, the Wal-Mart threat continues to send shivers of dread down the backs of businessmen who could never hope to battle technologically advanced national "price merchants" successfully—at least if price alone is the basis of the contest.

The so-called "unbundled" product—generic goods that are lowest in price, marketed electronically or in a warehouse setting—establishes one pole of the competitive spectrum. At incremental gradations along the spectrum toward the opposite high-end pole are a variety of attributes that are "bundled" together with the core commodity, at once differentiating it from its peers and increasing its price. These added characteristics comprise the entire package that makes the product more valuable—in itself or as it is perceived.

The strategy for combatting "price merchants" has involved a retail revolution of its own, although one that has been infinitely greater in scope and implications than the one led by Sam Walton. This revolution has been characterized by a rudimentary restructuring of the relationship between seller and buyer. The metamorphosis has challenged vendors to personalize their approaches to customers, to incorporate the views of their clients into product design and service, and even to consider their patrons as business partners. Beginning with enhancing the caliber of service provided to customers, this retail revolution has brought about the "reengineering" of the organizational design of the processes, organization, and culture of corporations; reconstructed and enriched the relationship between the company and its employees; and embraced quality concepts that have even been exported to the Pacific Rim and transformed the economies of those countries.

Paradoxically, although this revolution was initiated and led by trailblazers who were themselves retail tenants, commercial real estate is a relative latecomer to the revolution. The realization that tenants are the mainstay, the lifeblood of leasing, is a consequence of the catastrophic overbuilding of commercial space that occurred nationally during the 1980s. Rent-paying, space-occupying tenants have been in short supply; they are a precious commodity that deserves uncommon attention.

The importance of service in customer retention is undeniable. Developing a customer focus is even being taught in business schools—for example, the Purdue University Center for Customer-Driven Quality. In *THE Tenant Retention Solution: A Revolutionary Approach to Commercial Real Estate Management,* our goal is to provide you with innovative tools to meet the challenge of creating satisfied tenants and motivating their loyalty.

A Cornucopia of Service Strategies

THE Tenant Retention Solution traces the extraordinary progression of the retail revolution and applies its lessons to the management of commercial properties. The Prologue introduces some of the specific authors whose books launched the revolution in the retailing and consumer services industries, establishing a context for the chapters that follow. Chapter 1 describes the revolution itself and suggests its implications for the commercial real estate industry, including issues of value and price and factors that are changing the demand for commercial space. Chapter 2 addresses the significance of critical incidents (moments of truth), the importance of hiring nice people to serve at the front lines, and the need to create positive word of mouth. Many of the specific strategies introduced here and in chapter 1 will be covered in depth in later chapters. Chapter 3 looks more closely at the hiring issue: Your employees are really your *internal customers,* and their job satisfaction is linked to retention of your *external customers*—your tenants.

Chapter 4 differentiates the more traditional marketing efforts aimed solely at acquiring customers (so-called conquest marketing) from more recent strategies directed to retaining customers (retention marketing). Here we explore the costs of tenant turnover and examine the potential losses that can result from poor service and negative word of mouth. In the absence of specifics regarding tenants' dissatisfaction, it is impossible to remedy problems; therefore, chapter 5 presents strategies for surfacing tenants' complaints. Chapter 6 builds on this theme with a discussion of what constitutes customer satisfaction. Here we explore the notion of service recovery—

strategies for not only overcoming tenants' dissatisfaction, but for motivating their loyalty.

Chapter 7 examines service in the context of company leadership. Here we present ways to develop a customer-focused business, working from the top down, with an emphasis on strategic planning. Chapter 8 addresses strategies for benchmarking external sources for innovative approaches to problem-solving. Here we look at the comparison grid analysis exercise and suggest additional factors that can be evaluated in an effort to distinguish your commercial property from your competition.

Chapter 9 brings together the full array of service strategies, including real world examples of how programs implemented by some management companies are already helping to retain commercial tenants. The chapter concludes with a call to action—a list of the roads to a tenant retention revolution. Finally, the Epilogue serves as a reminder that tenant retention begins even before the lease is signed.

Some Notes About Style and Presentation

THE Tenant Retention Solution is written from a very personal perspective—many of the incidents, stories, and strategies presented in this book are from our own experience. To make the text more reader-friendly, the word "we" is used throughout in referring to our experiences and opinions, and the reader is addressed as "you." We also recognize that, while commercial tenants are in fact business entities, efforts at tenant retention are primarily directed to people, and we have tried to keep this distinction in mind throughout.

The Prologue and individual chapters open with one or more quotations that focus on the topics covered. Quotations appearing throughout the text are generally set off as indented blocks of copy, preceded by an arrowhead, and the author whose words are used is named beforehand. Examples related to commercial real estate management are also block indented, but with no arrowhead indicator. The sources of quotations and data cited in the text are identified sequentially in the Endnotes at the back of the book. The Bibliography lists the service books we cited in the text and includes acknowledgment of permission to reprint excerpts. Also listed are sources that provided background information. Because the various service-related terms are defined in place or elaborated in their immediate context, we have not included a glossary.

Other Considerations

When Tom Peters and Robert Waterman wrote *In Search of Excellence: Lessons from America's Best-Run Companies* in 1982, they identified being "close to the customer" as one of eight attributes that distinguish excellent companies. They viewed their research results as confirmation that, in the early 1980s, good management existed in America as well as Japan, and many believe Tom Peters' work started the customer service revolution. While *In Search of Excellence* was a defining point for American business, it covered a broad spectrum of factors that contributed to business excellence. Later writers—Jan Carlzon, Karl Albrecht, and Ron Zemke in particular—focused on this one attribute and developed a whole literature on customer service. It is these later writers whose works have enlightened us and inspired this book.

While many of the innovative ideas described in this book have been tested by ourselves and others, we would caution against adopting some of them without first considering their consequences. In chapter 3, we point out how the language in some lease clauses can be potentially problematic, especially from the tenant's perspective. Because a written lease provides important protections for the tenant as well as the owner and the manager, we do not recommend abandoning such clauses; instead, we are suggesting that you consider finding ways to modify the lease language—with the advice of legal counsel, of course—to state the requirements in a more positive way.

There are also legal implications related to hiring practices. The value—and possible problems—of pre-employment psychological testing is discussed in chapter 3. While we also suggest the use of group interviews to help determine a candidate's "fit" with your organization, it is important to remind all personnel involved in the interview process of the need to maintain confidentiality regarding conversations with job applicants.

Finally, *THE Tenant Retention Solution* is, by definition, about tenants as customers. In fact, at commercial properties, the management company's customers include not only the tenant companies, but also their employees, suppliers, and clients. Although we point out that your owner-clients are important customers, too, we have not concentrated on owners' specific requirements such as budgeting, reporting, and forecasting within the text. (The importance of these tasks in the broader context of real estate management has been addressed extensively in other IREM publications.) Moreover, while tenant retention as a strategy may be somewhat unfamiliar to many owners and asset managers, we have found that our own owner-clients are increasingly supportive of efforts to improve tenant relations and reduce tenant turnover, especially because success in these areas is economically beneficial to their properties—both short term as regards their performance and long term in enhancing their value.

Our hope is that, as owners increasingly become sensitized to the importance of tenant relations, they will be willing to fully embrace the practical consequences of this fresh outlook toward their customers. For example, we believe that tenant retention merits budgetary considerations and dollar allocations apart from, and in addition to, those accorded to conventional marketing—which is simply business acquisition. Marketing itself has very little to do with fostering long-term customer relations; on the contrary, it only allows them to become a possibility. In our opinion, the success of retention efforts will be determined in large part by the friendliness and overall people skills of the on-site management team.

ACKNOWLEDGMENTS

Our first acknowledgment is to *The Resident Retention Revolution.* That companion volume, addressed to apartment managers, has the same fundamental underpinnings as *THE Tenant Retention Solution,* and most of the customer service strategies outlined there are similarly applicable at commercial properties.

We have each felt strongly that there is no greater priority in commercial real estate management today than building loyalty and long-term relationships—i.e., retaining clients, customers, and tenants. As stated by CEL & Associates, Inc., "Failure to know your clients/customers/tenants—current and potential—always results in only a partial fulfillment of your organization's true potential." Our research and practical experience have taught us valuable lessons about knowing customers and building loyalty—*the roads to a tenant retention revolution.*

As in any revolution, there are many individuals and institutions who refused to accept traditional ways of customer service. We gratefully acknowledge these revolutionaries:

The management and staff of the Westin South Coast Plaza Hotel who shared with us their vision and commitment to truly revolutionary customer service.

The team members of Metric Property Management who developed a unique revolutionary model for tenant retention in the Metric CARES Commitment.

Paul R. Timm, Ph.D., who recognized the need to motivate customer loyalty and developed the "E-Plus" strategy to do just that.

CEL & Associates, Inc., of Los Angeles, who developed methodologies for benchmarking real estate management performance.

The more than 50 revolutionaries identified in the Bibliography whose writings have inspired both this work and the revolution we see becoming the vision for an industry previously devoid of a passion for customer service.

Towne Realty Inc. in Milwaukee and The Ryan Companies in Minneapolis whose policies and practices directed to their "internal customers" (employees) help them retain their "external customers" (tenants).

The Allen Morris Real Estate Services Company in West Palm Beach, Florida; Carter-Crowley Properties in Dallas; CIP Property Management Services, Inc., in Austin, Texas; COMPASS Management and Leasing, Inc., in Atlanta; DIHC Management Corporation in Atlanta; Hiffman Shaffer Anderson Inc. in Chicago; Koll Management Services, Inc., in San Diego; Newmark Realty, Inc., in New York City; Northco in Minneapolis; PREMISYS Real Estate Services, Inc., in Houston; Stein & Company of Chicago; SunLife of Canada in British Columbia; Trammell Crow Company in Dallas; Transamerica Corporation in Miami; Transwestern Property Company in Houston; Westcor Partners in Phoenix; and WilsonSchanzer Real Estate Services in San Antonio who shared with us their revolutionary strategies for "wowing" their tenants. They are setting a new standard of customer service for commercial real estate managers to benchmark.

At Miller Commercial, we acknowledge the help and assistance of Mitzi Pangman who, in addition to her real job as administrative assistant, typed the manuscript and its numerous revisions. Her suggestions were invaluable to this completed work.

Thanks also go to the four editorial consultants who reviewed the manuscript to assure its accuracy, readability, and appropriateness for our audience. Thomas W. Gille, CPM®, President, Real Estate Analysis and Learning Systems in San Francisco; Joseph W. Karp, CPM®, SCSM, Vice President and Director of Operating Properties, Weingarten Realty Investors in Houston; Robert D. Oliver, CPM®, Executive Vice President, Urban Retail Properties Co. in Boston; and R. Bruce Smith, CPM®, Second Vice President and Manager of Corporate Real Estate Administration, The Chase Manhattan Bank, N.A., in Rochester, New York, also contributed examples from their experiences to enrich this book.

We wish to recognize our friends and associates on the professional staff of the Institute of Real Estate Management, including Joseph T. Lannon, Publishing and Curriculum Development Manager, and Joyce Travis Copess, Staff Vice President, Communications and Education. A special thanks to Caroline Scoulas, Senior Editor, who consistently kept us focused and provided the publishing and editing expertise to turn our manuscript into *THE Tenant Retention Solution*.

Finally, we extend our thanks to the publishers and authors who granted permission to reprint excerpts from their books and articles. Specific acknowledgments are cited in the Bibliography and/or Endnotes and incorporated in exhibits as appropriate.

Howard K. Lundeen, CPM®
Laurence C. Harmon, CPM®
Kathleen M. McKenna-Harmon, CPM®

About the Authors

Howard K. Lundeen, CPM®, is President of Miller Commercial Management Company, a full service commercial real estate firm with offices in Dallas and Arlington, Texas. The company's portfolio consists of office buildings, office/warehouse facilities, and shopping centers (4.7 million square feet total) managed for major institutional clients. Previously, Mr. Lundeen was a principal in and Chief Operating Officer of Kelley, Lundeen & Crawford Company and President of Kelley, Lundeen & Crawford Management Company, which merged with Miller Commercial in 1994. He has been actively engaged in commercial real estate for more than 22 years.

Mr. Lundeen achieved the CPM designation in 1982. He has an MBA degree from Brigham Young University and, in addition to being on the National Faculty of the Institute of Real Estate Management (IREM), he was instrumental in developing—and he also teaches—the popular IREM/CIREI course, "Managing and Marketing Troubled Assets." He also serves on the Real Estate Advisory Board of North Lake College in Irving, Texas, and on the Marriott School of Management Alumni Board at Brigham Young University in Provo, Utah.

In addition to speaking engagements and seminars, Mr. Lundeen facilitates strategic planning for several large real estate companies, and he utilizes his operational experience to develop customer-focused operating manuals for clients. His company won an IREM award in 1992 for its Property Management Operations Manual. He is a past-President of the Dallas IREM Chapter, and he has been named "CPM of the Year" by the chapter.

Mr. Lundeen has taught extensively at local real estate schools in Dallas and is a guest lecturer at North Lake College in Dallas. He also developed the Professional Property Manager Training Program for the Commercial Institute of Coldwell Banker University. This is a certification program taught across the United States by Mr. Lundeen for Coldwell Banker, to certify their commercial property management affiliates.

Mr. Lundeen is a member of the Building Owners and Managers Association (BOMA) and on the faculty of its educational arm, the Building Owners and Managers Institute (BOMI), where he teaches a course in asset management. He is active locally in the North Texas Association of Realtors (NTAR) and nationally in the Commercial Investment Division and the Property Management Council of the National Association of Realtors (NAR).

Howard Lundeen is a Senior Vice President of IREM, Education Division, where he previously served as a Course Board Director. He is a popular speaker, seminar leader, and in-house company consultant with a national reputation as an effective communicator and trainer. A contributor to the *Journal of Property Management (JPM), THE Tenant Retention Solution* is his first book project.

Laurence C. Harmon, CPM®, is Chief Executive Officer of McKenna Management Associates, Inc., AMO®, and President and founder of GreaterData, Inc., both in Minneapolis. His real estate experience includes nine years at McKenna Management, initially as a property manager and marketing director. His current responsibilities include business acquisition, teaching and consulting, and property management for institutional investors. GreaterData conducts marketing research and market research related to residential property management. In addition to his marketing experience and expertise, Mr. Harmon has a law degree from Stanford University and is admitted to practice law in California, Oregon, and Minnesota.

Mr. Harmon achieved the CPM designation in 1990 and is an active member of the Institute of Real Estate Management, where he serves on the Publishing, Membership Development, Management Plan, and Ethics Committees at the national level. He is currently chairman of the Ethics Appeal Board and vice-chairman of the Publishing Committee. He has served as Executive Councillor and Chairman of the Candidate Guidance Committee of the Minnesota Chapter of IREM; he founded the Minnesota "Buddy-Up!" system that links CPM members and Candidates for the purpose of helping Candidates with the preparation of their management plans. "Buddy-Up!" and similar programs have been widely adopted in several states.

As a member of the Minnesota MultiHousing Association, Mr. Harmon has chaired its Legislative Committee. He also teaches apartment marketing courses at Hennepin Technical College in Minneapolis.

Kathleen M. McKenna-Harmon, CPM®, is President of McKenna Management Associates, Inc., AMO®, and the Towle McKenna Company also in Minneapolis. These management firms have a combined portfolio of approximately 3,500 apartment, condominium, and townhouse residential units in 20 properties, as well as some 500,000 square feet of commercial space in the Twin Cities Metropolitan Area and Baltimore. McKenna Management has developed and restored the historic Downtown Minneapolis YMCA building as an apartment property, and other developments and acquisitions in the Twin Cities and on the West Coast are actively under way.

Ms. McKenna-Harmon has more than 23 years' experience in managing and marketing real estate. She has also taught real estate courses at Saint Cloud State University (Minnesota), University of Wisconsin (Stout), and the University of Minnesota.

Ms. McKenna-Harmon achieved the CPM designation in 1980 and is an active member of the Institute of Real Estate Management at both the chapter and national levels. Currently, she is a member of IREM's Executive Committee and serves on the IREM National Faculty. She has served on the Membership Standards Committee and the Advanced Membership Standards Committee for six years; she chaired these two committees in 1989–1990 and again in 1990–1991. A former IREM Regional Vice President, Ms. McKenna-Harmon is a Senior Vice President of IREM, ARM® Division.

She was president of the Minnesota chapter of IREM in 1984 and its CPM of the Year in 1992. She has chaired every chapter committee and served in all councillor and officer positions in that organization. In addition, Ms. McKenna-Harmon is an active member of the Minnesota MultiHousing Association. She has held each executive office and served as MHA president in 1990–1991.

The Harmons are co-authors of *The Resident Retention Revolution* and *Contemporary Apartment Marketing: Strategies and Applications,* also published by IREM, and they lecture and consult extensively on the subjects of market research, real estate management and marketing, and tenant retention.

About the Institute
of Real Estate Management

The Institute of Real Estate Management (IREM) was founded in 1933 with the goals of establishing a Code of Ethics and standards of practice in real estate management as well as fostering knowledge, integrity, and efficiency among its practitioners. The Institute confers the CERTIFIED PROPERTY MANAGER® (CPM®) designation on individuals who meet specified criteria of education and experience in real estate management and subscribe to an established Code of Ethics. Real estate management firms that meet specific organizational and professional criteria are granted the status of ACCRED-ITED MANAGEMENT ORGANIZATION® (AMO®). Individuals who meet specified educational and professional requirements in residential site man-agement and subscribe to a Code of Ethics are granted the status of ACCRED-ITED RESIDENTIAL MANAGER (ARM®).

The Institute's membership includes nearly 9,500 CPM members, ap-proximately 3,600 ARM participants, and more than 660 AMO firms. CPM members manage more than 7.6 billion square feet of nonresidential real es-tate representing nearly 52% of the office, shopping center and retail space in the United States. More than half of its members manage office buildings; more than a third manage shopping centers and other retail properties, and one quarter manage industrial parks and warehouse space. CPM members also manage more than 9.6 million residential units.

For more than sixty years, IREM has been enhancing the prestige of prop-erty management through its activities and publications. The Institute offers a wide selection of courses, seminars, periodicals, books, and educational materials about real estate management and related topics.

To obtain a current catalog, write to:
    Institute of Real Estate Management
    430 North Michigan Avenue
    P.O. Box 109025
    Chicago, Illinois 60610-9025
or telephone (312) 661-1953.

Contents

THE
Tenant Retention
Solution

Prologue

Psychologists say that any one or a combination of three things is needed to overcome resistance to change: (1) a cataclysmic event, (2) a clear vision of where the change will lead, and (3) the experience of taking the first step in a new direction.

For many American businesses, the first condition—a cataclysmic event—is already a reality or is lurking just beneath the surface, like an incipient earthquake. . . . Whatever the case, the cataclysm will either force the company to change for the better or will drive it out of business.

The second condition for change—a clear vision of where you want to go—is one that tests the leadership qualities of any management group. . . . [That] vision is indelibly clear. American companies *must* set their sights on improving service delivery, product quality, and customer satisfaction.

As for the third condition, taking those first steps can be scary, but you'll never get anywhere if you don't start. Some companies have already started, and we can learn from them.

—LAURA A. LISWOOD, *Serving Them Right*

Beginning in 1985 with the publication of *Service America!* (Ron Zemke and Karl Albrecht's manifesto to American businesses on behalf of American consumers), there has been a cascade of self-help books—and a host of reform movements—designed to improve the quality of sellers' economic relationships with buyers. The stimuli have been numerous, organic, and complementary: The upsurge in competition from Japan and other Pacific Rim countries; consumers' heightened awareness of value and its relationship to price, and their jealousy of their dwindling leisure time; and the disturbing tailspin in the quality of customer service are only three among those most obvious and notable.

Two years after the publication of *Service America,* the godfather of the service-regeneration movement—Jan Carlzon, the president of Scandinavian Airlines System (SAS)—added his articulate voice to the reform effort. In his semi-autobiographical treatise, *Moments of Truth,* Carlzon recorded his experiences in revitalizing SAS, which he accomplished in a remarkably short time: In 1981, the year he was appointed president, SAS lost $8 million; two years later, while the airline industry overall was losing $2 billion annually, SAS posted a hefty $71 million profit.

Carlzon and those who came later have much to teach American companies about improving the way they do business. For example, Carlzon was one of the first to recognize the singular importance of frontline employees to business success and, along with it, the need to revamp the corporate hierarchy in order to enable the front line to flourish. Indeed, the definition of the roles, rights, and responsibilities of company leadership and frontline servers can be traced directly to Carlzon and his contemporaries. Such potent concepts as "partnering"—that is, nontraditional yet powerful alliances between a firm and its own staff and customers—and "benchmarking"—identification and importation of the "best practice" of industry leaders into a company's own operations—are two recent outgrowths of Carlzon's insights into enhancing a firm's operations.

Running parallel to the self-help concepts pioneered by Carlzon and his followers—"customer service," "satisfaction," "value"—is the "quality" movement launched by Joseph Juran and W. Edwards Deming. Deming, a statistician, was one of the founders of quality control in the United States and is considered the catalyst behind the success of Japanese industry.

Change agents in a particular business may consider themselves to be proponents of one or more of the "customer service," "satisfaction," or "total quality management" philosophies. Fortunately, there is a rich and varied literature to guide the journey to service excellence. Many of the publications are cited at length in this book (see also the Bibliography).

The Incipient Tenant Retention Revolution

Whether the goal is described as cementing relations between a company and its customers, improving the volume and quality of repeat business the firm does with its customers, or helping to deliver better value to clients, the overriding purpose of any company's self-help efforts is to enable it to stay in business and, perhaps, also to prosper. For a company to become customer-focused, which is an essential prerequisite to achieving this purpose, it must undergo a radical transformation—from compulsively inward-looking to resolutely outward-looking. The companies of the future will increasingly and aggressively strategize ways to prune the bureaucratic shrubbery that interferes with providing intensive kid-glove treatment for their customers.

Unfortunately, most businesses need substantial prodding to be roused from their self-satisfied, bureaucracy-buttressing slumber. The quote at the beginning of this prologue sets out the three prerequisites, any one (or a combination) of which can trigger awakening: First, a cataclysmic event; second, a good idea of what the post-revolution finished product will look like; and third, taking the first step along the revolutionary freeway.

There have been several national-scope cataclysmic events in the real estate industry that have affected the economic viability of commercial properties during the past decade. Arguably, the most ruinous are the drastic tax reforms of 1986, which gutted most of the after-tax yields to real estate investors and owners, and the consequent collapse of the savings and loan industry a few years later. A variety of other national calamities—overbuilding, declining rental rates, eroding property values, lending institution failures, and environmental concerns—have contributed their share to the decline of the real estate industry. At the local level, other debacles may actually overwhelm the national issues. In any event, there has been a surfeit of situations and circumstances that can be accurately characterized as "cataclysmic" for commercial real estate—the downsizing of corporate America is a prime example. Clearly, Liswood's first requisite to overcoming resistance to change has been met.

The second stage—the image of the eventual, post-enhancement condition—is difficult to visualize. Indeed, the transformation of a real estate management company from tenant-tolerant to tenant-focused, from self-centered to client-centered, and from conquest marketer to aftermarketer, is probably the most profound metamorphosis a firm can experience. A central purpose of this book is to provide a guideline—a roadmap, if you will—for the journey.

The final condition, of course, is taking the first step in the direction of the finish line. As the Chinese proverb instructs us: "A journey of a thousand miles begins with but a single step." This statement is, of course, beyond dispute; what is less clear in the business context is *who* is responsible for taking it. We would argue that company leadership needs to initiate the expedition, and we suggest an itinerary in this book. Equally important, we recommend that the trip be undertaken in a spirit of *KAIZEN*—that is, one step at a time, bit-by-bit, rather than in the tumultuous way that typifies most revolutions.

The Customer Service Revolution ·

People can have the Model T in any color—so long as it's black.

—HENRY FORD

Everybody in the company has to understand that the total existence of a company depends upon the customer, so if the customer is not satisfied, he is not going to be a customer tomorrow, and if he is not a customer tomorrow, we don't have a business tomorrow.

—HARVEY LAMM, president of Subaru of America

When you hear hoofbeats, expect horses.

—DONALD R. LIBEY, *Libey on Customers*

Henry Ford never heard the "hoofbeats" that are ringing in the ears of Harvey Lamm—and of everyone who markets goods and services to the finicky, value-conscious consumers of the 1990s. In 1910, Ford produced and sold 19,000 "Tin Lizzies," enjoying a virtual monopoly in the new car business; by 1990, however, while annual production had reached 1,380,000—a nearly 75-fold increase over 1910 figures—the Ford Motor Company's market share of new car and truck sales in the United States had dropped to less than 15 percent. (Its market share continued to slide, falling nearly one percent in 1991.)

Those "hoofbeats," after all, are the sounds of the competition, thundering after capricious consumers. Whether you are selling thoroughbreds, Thunderbirds, or office space, your potential customers can select from a marvelous cornucopia of options undreamed-of in Ford's day. It is not enough to capture your customer once. The challenge is in making that customer loyal because your customers are, as Richard Schonberger vividly remarked, "poised to fly, like a nervous flock of geese in a grain field."

Faced with the test of trying to compete with one of the Big Three automakers, what options are available to a Harvey Lamm whose market share for the sporty Justy, the Imprezza, and the rest of the Subaru models is less than one percent of the U.S. car market? If Lamm is anything like other Davids who grapple with such Goliaths as Nordstrom, Federal Express, L. L. Bean, Domino's Pizza, Marriott, SAS, Xerox, IBM, and Disney World, his challenge is especially daunting. Each of these institutions has spent tens of millions— and sometimes *billions*—of dollars in an effort to transform their companies into customer-aware, customer-attentive, customer-focused, or *customer-driven* firms. Based on the quotation that opened this chapter, it is reasonable to assume that Lamm opted for a customer-centered orientation. In doing so, however, he was committing himself, his company, his employees, and Subaru stockholders to a lengthy, dreary, and generally thankless process that was very likely to fail. As Karl Albrecht and Ron Zemke have described the transformation required, Subaru's task is akin to "trying to teach an elephant to dance."

The Revolution in Retailing

The commercial revolution that burst forth in the mid-1980s, spearheaded by a marketing wizard who had recently been promoted to head a sinking Swedish airline, is fundamentally about customers—current customers, former customers, potential customers. The foundation of this revolution is that producers of goods and services must ascertain what people want to buy before trying to sell to them; thereafter, the bundle of characteristics and components of the purchase—all of its nonphysical attributes—are designed according to consumer preferences as well. Taken to its extreme, this focus on—even obsession with—customers absolutely transforms the corporation: For example, customers of the so-called 360-degree company decide who is hired, promoted, bonused, and fired. In these and other firms, owners and managers abandon their corner offices to work on the front lines where they can listen to and talk with their customers directly. A variety of approaches have sprung up in an effort to win customer allegiance—the "total quality management," "continuous quality improvement," "customer service," "total customer satisfaction," "value-added," "customer-driven/learning organization" and "defection management" movements, as well as a host of others. This retailing revolution involves a paradigm shift about the way companies do business—a movement from one way of seeing the world to another—and has the potential to transform the very *nature* of retailers' businesses.

Implications of the Revolution for Commercial Property Management

What are the implications of this retailing revolution for the real estate industry and, in particular, for the commercial property management business?

First, the underlying principles of *conquest marketing* predominant in the retail trades in the 1970s and early 1980s—that prospective customers are readily accessible in unending supply; that the essence of marketing is to attract new customers; that retention of loyal customers is irrelevant—were equally prevalent in the commercial real estate industry. Likewise, the flip side of conquest marketing, so-called *retention marketing* in which customers are considered to be *stakeholders* in the enterprise, is equally applicable to real estate managers. (Retention marketing will be considered in chapter 4.)

Second, commercial properties traditionally have been operated in much the same manner as the businesses they seek as tenants—the longer a company is in business, the less attention it tends to pay to its customers. The natural propensity of any company engaged in any enterprise is to turn inward and, in its introspection, to isolate itself from its clients. Imperceptibly, its operations are arranged to cater to the owners, managers, and employees—its so-called *internal customers*—at the expense of its *external customers,* the people who buy the products and thereby pay the staff's salaries and keep the companies afloat. As a result, the customer relations process becomes impersonal, aloof, and mechanized. Rules and regulations, policies and procedures, standards and forms are prepared, interpreted, and revised so that the company comes first, the customer last. From signs in convenience stores blaring "No Shoes, No Shirt, No Service!" to lease provisions that proscribe, prohibit, and punish, companies establish—and then nourish—adversarial, potentially confrontational, and probably unpleasant relationships with their customers. Fortunately, as is the case with conquest marketing, retailers have developed a collection of customer-friendly approaches that can be productively transported to the commercial property management business—where the array of external customers includes not only tenants but their employees, suppliers, and patrons as well.

Third, the stimulus to emigrate from an inward to an outward focus—that is, from serving themselves to delighting their customers—is almost invariably the result of some calamity. For American retailers, the crisis has grown out of market conditions that force them to devise a means of differentiating their products from those of their competitors. Often the competition includes foreign firms that turn out mass-produced goods of comparable quality at substantially lower prices.

As a flood of lower-priced, look-alike products saturates U.S. markets, the quality of customer service in that competitive environment has likewise deteriorated. There is a crisis in selling that mirrors the downturn in sales.

Shoddy selling practices have fueled customer cynicism to the point that consumers have become conditioned to negative outcomes from the products they buy and the services they receive, both at the point of sale and thereafter. Customer service is appallingly bad at the front lines and no better at the middle or the rear, where the managers and owners can be found.

Recognizing that there are only two primary ways to attain competitive advantage—either by doing things better than others, or by doing them differently—retailers have overwhelmingly opted for the former. Market leaders are breaking away from the pack by bundling one or more "intangible perquisites" together with their goods, thereby leaping ahead of their rivals. The adjunct may consist of various service elements (implementing complaint practices or offering guarantees), satisfaction gauges (testing to ensure that customers are happy postpurchase), or quality measures (instituting "total quality management" or aiming for "zero defects")—all designed to provide greater (perceived) value for the price paid.

This newfound devotion to customers is based on a blinding flash of the obvious: *Satisfied customers are a company's most precious resource.* Retailers have discovered, albeit belatedly, that the essence of their business—whatever their business—is to "manufacture" satisfied customers, and then to look for ways to improve their customers' satisfaction. Satisfied customers are the source of the company's profits and referrals to potential customers. They are, in fact, *partners* of the firm whose repeat purchases will help grow the business in the future and serve as a barricade against the insidious infiltration of competition. The myriad techniques that retailers have discovered, then tested and refined, are illustrative for managers of office buildings, shopping centers, and other commercial properties; and we will consider them in detail in subsequent chapters.

As you can see, two complementary calamities—increasing competition and decreasing quality of customer service—spurred a commercial revolution that has resulted in the evolution and appreciation of the art of creating and retaining retail customers. Two parallel predicaments of equal seriousness have been transforming the commercial real estate industry.

First, the explosive growth in the number of commercial properties brought to market during the 1980s outstripped business growth and space demand. Office vacancy rates nationwide nearly quadrupled between 1980 (when the total was 4.6 percent) and 1990 (when it reached 20.0 percent). Several major metropolitan areas reported even higher vacancy rates—Dallas at 25.8 percent and Houston at 24.9 percent were coming down from respective highs of 30.9 percent in 1986 and 31.8 percent in 1987. (Improvement has been slow indeed; both Dallas and Houston still had vacancy rates greater than 20 percent as of September 1994. The picture is not much brighter for other types of commercial space: At the beginning of 1994, regional shopping centers seemed to be faring much better than smaller centers in some markets, but mall vacancy overall is expected to remain high for

---

The Value-Price Relationship

In the 5,000 or so years it has taken human beings to evolve from cave-dwellers to farmers who bartered for their needs in the town square to urbanites and suburbanites who transact their business in office buildings and shopping centers, what might be called their "customer quotient" has changed radically. Whereas survival once required people to devote no less than 80 percent of their time to production (participating as consumers perhaps 20 percent of the time), they now devote nearly full time—and at least as much effort and attention—to being customers.

In a pure purchase environment constructed on a multilayered, multinational, competitive infrastructure, individuals develop a singular skill and talent for consumption. Americans are especially sophisticated and masterful customers because of the extent, variety, and intensity of their experiences. If there is any one characteristic that can be used to describe consumers in the waning moments of the twentieth century, it is their single-minded devotion to consumption.

It has become commonplace for retailers to include "value" and other attributes—"quality" and "service" are noteworthy examples—together with their basic product offering. This technique, known as "bundling," enables sellers to compete on a basis other than, or in addition to, mere price. Product attributes such as value, quality, and service, which have nothing to do with price competition and little to do with the underlying product, are calculated to *overwhelm* price as a purchase motivator. Consequently, in almost every type of marketplace, price as the sole determining sales message no longer has anything like its previous vitality.

---

some time to come (1995 and beyond). Industrial vacancies, on the other hand, appear to be declining (below four percent in the tightest markets as 1994 was winding down, with the highest rates in the low teens). There is, in short, too much vacant space searching frantically for commercial tenants.

A complicating factor is that much of this product was designed without adequate consideration being given to the needs or preferences of potential end users—i.e., different kinds of businesses. As a result, vacancy rates have escalated, and property owners and managers have resorted to widespread price-cutting in an effort to reduce their losses. This approach invariably leads to a diminution in the *value* of commercial properties, as well as a camouflaging of their actual economic occupancy beneath physical occupancy figures and an undercutting of the *pro forma* rent projections for future years' operations. The result is that the properties do not deliver economic performance consistent with the estimates made at the time they were financed initially.

The Value-Price Relationship *(continued)*

People in the business of managing commercial properties are in a unique position: Many of the marketing concepts that have revolutionized retailing, "bundling" among them, have yet to impact the real estate industry greatly. It is striking to note, however, that the people who work (and/or live) in properties owned or managed by others—the industry's customers—are themselves pioneers and practitioners of these very concepts.

American consumers recognize that the *value-to-price relationship* determines their satisfaction with their purchases. Whether the price is low or high, if the value of the product exceeds its price, customers are satisfied. Indeed, customers will *always* be willing to pay for what they get. The most savvy customers inevirtably are willing to pay a high price to obtain high value: This is how they define a "bargain."

From a seller's point of view, a price supported by a high margin of profit is always the most satisfactory price. From a customer's perspective, high value is the prerequisite to satisfaction. The most mutually satisfying consumer relationships combine high value and high price. Thus, the "win-win" situation for both customer and vendor is *always value and never price.*

In the commercial real estate industry, value will be sought—regardless of price—because where people conduct their business to some extent involves a continuing "purchase" in the form of rent or mortgage payments year after year after year. Regardless of the dollar amount, commercial tenants are likely to perceive their particular rent as "high"—most are locked in for multiple years with rates subject to periodic escalations—and because of this perception, their expectations of value will be high as well. It is expectations, perceptions, and actual experiences with the product that define value in the retail trades. The same applies to the rental of office, store, or warehouse space. What tenants receive for their rent dollars—in addition to and apart from the use of the leased space—will determine whether they will want to remain your tenants when their lease terms end.

The disparity between supply and demand may have resulted from overbuilding during the 1980s, when loans for commercial development were easily obtained, but the problem has been exacerbated by other factors. Radical downsizing of businesses, often due to technological advances, is a major consideration. Computers make some types of office tasks more efficient (e.g., accounting, record keeping, generation of reports) and the people who perform them more productive, while voice mail and answering machines are replacing receptionists and customer service personnel. Just-in-time inventory programs mean less warehouse space is needed by retailers, distributors, and manufacturers. On the horizon are interactive shopping programs (a combination of computer and television technologies) that mean retailers

Changing Demand for Commercial Space

Business decisions about office or store space—where to locate, how much rent to pay, etc.—are usually based on extensive research of a geographic area, including availability of space and competitive lease terms. Because a multiple-year lease for thousands of square feet of space at rates in excess of ten dollars per square foot per year ($10/sq ft/yr) translates into hundreds of thousands of dollars in rent—in addition to the costs of an address change (stationery, telephone installation, office furniture, among a host of details), lost employee productivity, and the move itself—setting up a new commercial venture or relocating an existing one represents a major long-term business decision.

Once established or relocated, there is usually very little reason for a business to move. In an overbuilt market, however, opportunities to relocate to a newer, more prestigious office building (from class B or C to class A) are likely to abound. Large space users may be wooed with periods of free rent, discounted rates, landlord-paid interior finishes, paid moving expenses, buyout of an existing lease, or even a reduced pass-through proration. Any or all of these same kinds of inducements might be offered to a retail tenant.

Even in markets that are not overbuilt, demand for office space is lessening as major corporations downsize their businesses. Those that occupy most of a building they own may simply make more space available for lease to others as tenants. Some may move out and build or lease elsewhere. The departure of Sears, Roebuck and Company's headquarters from Sears Tower in downtown Chicago for a suburban location is an example that impacted an already overbuilt office market.

The trend toward downsizing has not only meant reductions in staff and consolidation of operations at fewer (or more central) locations. Companies are also looking at what their people do—and *how* they use their office space—and modifying their space needs accordingly. Sales personnel often need office support services rather than a specific office space because they call at

will be thinking hard about all the space they devote to displaying merchandise for sale. These and other emerging technologies only add to the challenges facing managers of commercial properties.

The second calamity to befall the real estate industry is the failure of the thrifts at the end of the 1980s, which resulted in the sale of securities, properties, and loans worth more than $330 billion with another estimated $100 billion yet to come.

In this disheartening environment characterized by too much product, much of which is inadequate or inappropriate and has failed or is failing in the market, resourceful real estate managers and leasing agents have begun to experiment with techniques to differentiate their commercial properties

---

Changing Demand *(continued)*

their customers' places of business. Professional service firms (consultants, auditors, accountants), which typically provide their services at the customers' office, operate similarly. An office that was maintained for a regional or national manager who visits a company's branch locations every few weeks may become temporary office space for any employee who visits that remote site. This phenomenon has become known as "hoteling."

New technologies in "officing" are also affecting how many office tenants conduct their day-to-day business, lessening the need to provide offices for staff members who are only on site occasionally and reducing the amount of space allocated to individual employees or their functions. Computers, modems, facsimile machines, cellular phones, and voice mail are making it possible for employees to work at home or just about anywhere else. While the amount of space required to operate a business was traditionally based on an average of 250 square feet per office worker, some companies are using half of that area or less. A tenant may lower its rent expense as a result of such downsizing, but this change also means office buildings will require more tenants to achieve the same levels of occupancy.

Nor are offices alone in the trend toward downsizing their leased space. Discount merchandisers (so-called category killers), manufacturers' outlets, direct mail catalog houses, and home shopping networks on cable television are all competing with retailers for the same customers. In recent years, some of the same technologies (computers, faxes) as well as the burgeoning air shipment business have also impacted the space needs of retail operations. Where it was once necessary to maintain a certain level of inventory to fulfill sales expectations, stores can now keep less merchandise on hand and have replacement stock dropshipped from manufacturers or distributors in two days or overnight. This has also impacted some manufacturers. Rather than produce large quantities of some items and hold this inventory for orders, they are prepared to manufacture to the distributor's or merchandiser's quality and quantity requirements and ship their products on short notice.

---

from others in their markets. They know that the financial fortunes of investment properties depend to a great extent on marketing skills—tactics that will attract prospective tenants to a particular property instead of its competition. Many of them, either out of desperation or following the example of successful retail marketers, have seized on various "intangible perquisites"— especially those having a service component—as means of positioning their properties ahead of their competition.

At about the time that the faint outlines of the looming savings and loan (S&L) disaster could be discerned, the Institute of Real Estate Management (IREM) Foundation commissioned Arthur Andersen and Company to con-

Changing Demand *(concluded)*

It is to everyone's advantage if a business can remain in place because part of the success of any commercial enterprise is its location. This may mean allowances for additional improvements or decorating—possibly as a landlord expense. Offers to reconfigure a tenant's current space or facilitate relocation within the building may have to be among the ideas that are brought to the negotiating table to retain current commercial tenants.

To retain those large space users that are downsizing, as well as attract office tenants whose space and operational needs are similar, office buildings in the future will have to be more flexible in their space configurations so they can be tailored to tenants' needs. Inclusion of many of the high-tech communications facilities in newer buildings—the so-called smart building—and addition of these capabilities in existing ones (retrofitting) will help attract and keep good tenants.

There is another view, however. Because part of the office environment is the ability to observe work being done and interact with supervisors and co-workers face-to-face, "home officing" and "telecommuting" may be on the horizon but are not likely to happen everywhere overnight. Working at home means working independently; and while some employees can work alone effectively, supervisors may have difficulty keeping track of workers' hours and productivity, which could blur the definitions of employment status. However, as technology expands the options and capabilities, including such things as "videoconferencing," these can become cost-effective alternatives for more and more businesses.

[NOTE: Distinctions between hourly and salaried employees and other issues that may affect an employer's ability to embrace the new technologies are defined in the Fair Labor Standards Act. This is an issue for office tenants as employers and is beyond the scope of a book on tenant retention.]

duct a survey of the real estate industry. The results were published in 1991 as *Managing the Future: Real Estate in the 1990s.* In addition to cataloging the nation's real estate and identifying its owners, the goals of the survey were to discover what major players in the investment real estate field considered to be the most critical issues facing the industry, as well as significant short-term trends and important factors in managing their inventory.

According to *Managing the Future,* the value of all U.S. real estate (including single-family homes) was estimated to be nearly $9 trillion, and the nearly one third of the total identified as commercial property (31 percent) was valued at $2.655 trillion (these are 1990 figures). Not surprisingly, the authors of this report discovered that the chief concern of major owners is "the space glut and what it means for the future." The owners consider the most likely solution to this immense problem to be tenant retention:

The Importance of Tenant Mix

Real estate investors and managers seek to maximize the mix of tenants at a commercial property. Tenant mix is important for many reasons. Part of the mix is who the tenants are. An office building tenanted by lawyers or accountants will attract tenants from among similar professionals and related services because proximity facilitates the conduct of their business. Major national (and international) companies add prestige to an office building by virtue of their size, credit rating, and type of business or clientele; they have a presence and a financial base that is different from businesses whose customers and transactions are strictly local and add to the attraction of a particular property as a business location.

Older office buildings in established central business districts (CBDs) typically included some ground-level retail tenants whose businesses were directly accessible from the street. This attracted shoppers and passersby to the building whether they had other business there or not. Office buildings developed more recently have excluded this retail component from the tenant mix or brought it into the recesses of the ground floor or lobby area as a building amenity. Where there is a retail component, it is sometimes configured as a shopping "arcade" or a "food court," although neither individual tenants nor the arcade or food court itself may have direct access from the street. This factor limits the customers they can attract, and visibility and accessibility are critical to generating retail sales. While few may argue about the merits of leasing space in an office building to office users exclusively, the absence or inaccessibility of convenience retailers—drug-sundry stores, newsstands, coffee shops, etc.—can diminish the value of an otherwise prime office location. Recruiting and retaining employees is made more difficult for tenants if their personnel have to walk or drive a distance to eat lunch, buy a newspaper or a candy bar or a greeting card, or cash a check. Vending machines and automatic teller machines fill some of these personal needs, but only part of the time. For many years, the presence and diversity of the retail businesses in CBDs helped them maintain a competitive edge over suburban office locations. Today, however, suburban office parks are often located near or adjacent to retail centers, and such access to shopping and restaurants is an added feature they can promote to prospective tenants.

Where tenants are located in relation to other tenants is, perhaps, a more pointed consideration in shopping centers. Department stores located at opposite ends of an enclosed mall will attract large numbers of shoppers who must traverse long distances to go from one of these anchor tenants to another and thus are likely to be attracted to the ancillary or specialty shops in between—the amount and regularity of traffic is critical to generating sales for such nondestination retailers.

> **Tenant Mix** *(continued)*
>
> Getting the tenant mix right is an important consideration. Property owners and developers want to lease to tenants who will pay premium rents and attract other tenants who will do the same. Prospective tenants want to locate where they can maximize the benefits to their business. A prestigious location and the caliber of the tenants already in place are among the factors prospects will weigh along with the rent and other costs. At shopping centers, prospective and actual tenants are also concerned about synergy and traffic flow. Shopping center developers and managers who are responsible for leasing consider other factors as well, such as merchandise quality and pricing—Bonwit Teller and Nieman Marcus have different price levels and clienteles than do Montgomery Ward or J. C. Penney or Woolworth. An upscale jewelry store or furrier is less likely to locate in an area whose demographic profile is dominated by low to mid-level incomes and two-worker families because the customer base will not be adequate for its type of business. At shopping centers and enclosed malls that have anchor tenants, the type of anchor tenants (e.g., department store, supermarket, discounter) will determine the types of ancillary or specialty shop tenants that can be attracted to lease there—the smaller tenants' merchandise must be a good match with that of the anchors, so that all the tenants can benefit from the traffic they generate individually. A good tenant mix at a shopping center represents a good match of products and services, to each other and to the customer base the center serves—i.e., the trade area.

▶ Almost every interviewee said the most important tasks involve serving tenants. . . . Retaining tenants is more important than obtaining them. . . . They regard retention as more efficient and less disruptive than continual, successful re-leasing. . . . In the interviews, it was heard repeatedly that real estate is revenue-driven, and that without good tenant retention there are no other problems to solve.

This report constitutes an especially thorough job description for the property manager of the future. In ranking the importance of property management tasks, tenant retention, lease negotiation, obtaining tenants, and handling tenant relations are at the very top of the list. The findings in the 1991 IREM Foundation report are echoed in more recent publications, including *Emerging Trends in Real Estate: 1994* and *BUILDINGS* magazine. The following is from Forecast 1994 compiled by the editorial staff of *BUILDINGS*:

▶ Tenant retention is the most fundamental operations concern of the '90s, and one that happens, quite literally, every day.

A Basis for Revolution.   How do you go about launching a campaign to actively retain tenants (rather than perpetuating tenant turnover at your properties)? When the history of the commercial real estate business has been conquest marketing—treating tenants as though they are just rent checks—is there a good starting point for instituting retention marketing?

It may be best to turn for guidance to the godfather of relationship selling—Jan Carlzon, the president of Scandinavian Airlines System (SAS). Carlzon realized that the future of his company was being decided in the routine contacts between his customers and his frontline employees. Whether SAS succeeded or failed, then, depended more on people than on airplanes. He described the situation in this way:

▶ Last year, each of our 10 million customers came in contact with approximately five SAS employees, and this contact lasted an average of 15 seconds each time. Thus, SAS is "created" in the minds of our customers 50 million times a year, 15 seconds at a time. These 50 million "moments of truth" are the moments that ultimately determine whether SAS will succeed or fail as a company. They are the moments when we must prove to our customers that SAS is their best alternative.

Moments of Truth.   This sensational thought—that the fortune of any company is being decided, right now, on the spot, out on the front lines where the least-experienced, presumably lowest-paid, and least-motivated employees are deciding the fate of the company—is the foundation for the drastic changes in customer relations that followed. The revolution in service, satisfaction, quality, and value is founded on Carlzon's "moments of truth."

Because moments of truth provide the vibrant intellectual foundation for the customer service revolution, it is important to understand what they are and why they are central to the success of every business. Karl Albrecht defined the moment of truth as "any episode in which the customer comes into contact with any aspect of the organization and gets an impression of the quality of its service." A moment of truth, then, is the basic atom of a firm's service orientation, the indivisible building-block upon which its wares—goods, services, whatever—are presented to the public. The totality of a company's moments of truth constitute its image, its reputation, its good name.

Moments of truth in the management of commercial real estate come in endless variety. Many of them involve direct interaction between management employees and tenants' employees, suppliers, and clients. Others, the ones that might be characterized as "impersonal" moments of truth, nonetheless create impressions. Advertising, for example, is a moment of truth. Another is the "curb appeal" of your property. Entering a parking lot, walking through an elevator lobby, being greeted by a leasing agent or a property manager are all powerful, indelible moments of truth that occur within a span of minutes. A conversation with the accounts receivable clerk in a management company's main office, calling in a service request, picking up a package in the office of the building—the bouillabaisse of potential moments of truth is boundless.

Carlzon's genius lay not only in recognizing (and christening) moments of truth, but also in conceding that he was powerless to supervise their transmission—by his own estimate, 50 million of them, every year! Instead, he realized that the only way to improve his company's chances of delivering quality moments was to transform SAS into a truly customer-focused company. This required, in his view, several basic, yet drastic, steps. The first was to refashion the airline:

> ▶ In a customer-driven company, the distribution of roles is radically different. The organization is decentralized, with responsibility delegated to those who until now have comprised the order-obeying bottom of the pyramid. The traditional, hierarchical corporate structure, in other words, is beginning to give way to a flattened, more horizontal, structure. This is particularly true in service businesses that begin not with the product but with the customer.

The frontline employee, according to the Carlzon model, became the nucleus of the company:

> ▶ [Their] efforts were suddenly imbued with greater value within the company. All the employees received special training on providing service and, to many of them, the content of these courses was secondary to the fact that the company was investing time and resources in them. They had frequently gone unappreciated. Now they were in the limelight.

The stimulus for this transformation was, of course, the company leadership, the people who, ironically, stood to lose the most because of the change, at least in terms of traditional measures of status:

> ▶ The initiative for [change] must originate in the executive suite. It is up to the top executive to become a true leader, devoted to creating an environment in which employees can accept and execute their responsibilities with confidence and finesse. . . . To succeed he can no longer be an isolated and autocratic decision-maker. Instead, he must be a visionary, a strategist, an informer, a teacher, and an inspirer.

According to Carlzon, being customer-focused requires vigilant attention to the interests of a company's clients, beginning with a redefining of the nature of the business from the customer's perspective:

> ▶ Given today's increased competitiveness and emphasis on service, the first step must be to acquire a customer orientation. To a certain extent, this means looking at your company and deciding, from the

customer's point of view, what business you're really in. For example, is SAS in the airline business? Or is it really in the business of transporting people from one place to another in the safest and most efficient way possible? I think it's obvious that the answer is the latter.

The next step is to isolate, and then eradicate, potential impediments to a customer's access to the company's services. As Carlzon soon realized, many of these obstacles—what might be called "negative" moments of truth— have been erected over time by the company itself:

▶ As I learned more about SAS, I was amazed at how many of its policies and procedures catered to the equipment or the employees, even if they inconvenienced the passengers. Equally amazing was how easy these practices were to spot—and to rectify—by looking at them from the point of view of our target customer, the frequent business traveler.

As you can see, the notion of "moments of truth" and the implications of this illuminating concept suggest that traditional ways of organizing and operating corporations are fundamentally flawed. Indeed, the numerous Fortune 500 companies and others who took Carlzon's message to heart followed his lead and "flattened" the organization of their companies. This model literally places frontline employees toward the top of the organization chart; middle managers, "bosses," and all other employees are clearly subordinate. The message? *"If you're not serving the customer, you'd better be serving someone who is."* This principle, in turn, became the foundation for what has come to be known as *empowerment*. As Carlzon explained it:

▶ If we are truly dedicated to orienting our company toward each customer's individual needs, then we cannot rely on rule books and instructions from distant corporate offices. We have to place responsibility for ideas, decisions, and actions with the people who *are* SAS during those 15 seconds: ticket agents, flight attendants, baggage handlers, and all the other frontline employees. If they have to go up the organizational chain of command for a decision on an individual problem, then those 15 golden seconds will elapse without a response, and we will have lost an opportunity to earn a loyal customer.

Customers' needs—real and perceived—are often difficult to define. In the management of commercial properties, this can be especially vexing. However, real estate managers can apply the methodologies of market research to collect information about tenants' expectations. (Use of these market research tools will be addressed later in this book, beginning with a discussion in chapter 2.)

Customer Focus.   Becoming customer-focused means regenerating the corporation, redefining its leadership, empowering its employees. Heady thoughts, and ones that are only beginning to be embraced in real estate management. The potential for improving operations at commercial properties is huge, and potentially overwhelming. Before we begin to consider the implications of Carlzon's thinking for real estate management, we need to regain our perspective:

▶   The story is told of the sultan who awoke in the middle of the night and summoned his wizard. "Wizard," he said, "my sleep is troubled. Tell me: What is holding up the earth?"

"Majesty," replied the wizard, "the earth rests on the back of a giant elephant."

The sultan was satisfied and went back to sleep. He then awoke in a cold sweat and summoned the wizard. "Wizard," he said, "what's holding up the elephant?"

The wizard looked at him and said, "The elephant stands on the back of a giant turtle. And you can stop right there, Majesty. *It's turtles all the way down.*"

This story is included as an admonition. While it is absolutely essential to begin restructuring your companies with a view to improving service to your tenants, the restructuring process is potentially overwhelming. You need to remember that you can institute this process by adopting a rather minimalist approach: It is possible to begin the task by making small improvements in the daily delivery of value to your customers; managers of commercial properties can, as Jan Carlzon himself suggests, decide to be "one percent better at 100 things instead of being 100 percent better at one thing." These are the turtles that support the elephant.

It is well to remember that the Japanese, who have perfected in practice the abstruse theories of total quality management, zero defects, and all the rest, have a word— *KAIZEN*—that means ongoing, daily enhancement in the performance of a company, undertaken by everyone in the organization. In contrast to the Western style, which tends to adopt drastic overhauls—usually fueled by huge infusions of capital—as a means to achieving its goals, KAIZEN would have managers realize small improvements in the status quo as a result of ongoing efforts. The Japanese can appreciate the simplicity of turtles.

The Roads to Revolution

If you don't know where you are going, THE SCARECROW SAID TO DOROTHY, it
doesn't matter which road you take.

— *The Wizard of Oz*

When the goal is to develop a service orientation, there are three roads real
estate managers may choose. One road leads to control of your customers'
experiences. Another road guides the hiring of service personnel. The third
leads to a pot of gold—word-of-mouth advertising.

Road One: Managing Your Customers' Experiences

Real estate managers know from their own backgrounds as consumers that
customers decide whether to be patrons of a company—or to continue their
patronage—primarily on the basis of their contacts with its frontline employees. Whether these episodes are characterized as "moments of truth" (per Jan
Carlzon), or as "guest contact points," "critical incidents," or "points of encounter" (according to later commentators), the quality of customers' interactions with a company's frontline servers—its clerks, receptionists, waiters,
etc.—are instrumental in its success.

Carlzon teaches that these interactions between customer and company
are inherently random, subjective, and unpredictable. Moments of truth are
frequently unsupervised as well—because of their nature, *they are not sus-
ceptible to being supervised*. While moments of truth may or may not involve
direct human contact, those incidents of human association—the so-called
high-touch connections that occur in such places as building corridors and
leasing offices—are especially vivid and memorable to the customer. These
contacts might be characterized as customer-initiated interviews with the

products and services the company offers to the market. Such interviews are a test of the value of the goods; the results provide a perception of the quality of the company's customer service. Only if they are satisfied with how the company defines the service component of the product will prospects become customers and current customers be transformed into long-term clients.

Once commercial real estate managers understand the fluky nature of moments of truth and recognize their significance in initiating and maintaining long-lasting customer relationships with the organization, they can manage these moments in two complementary ways: first, by trying to control moments of truth whenever possible and, second, by attempting to influence moments when they cannot be controlled.

Retailing versus Commercial Property "Moments of Truth." The challenge of managing moments of truth in real estate management is probably more demanding than it is elsewhere. The difficulty is that the most significant moments of truth in commercial property management—the interactions between staff members and customers and potential customers— are *continuous*. Unlike the situation in the retail trades, where the workday ends when the store closes, real estate managers and their staffs are *never* off duty, and many of the encounters with their customers are inescapable. Working in commercial property management is akin to working at a hospital or hotel—businesses in which the moments of truth are high touch, occasionally unpleasant, and perpetual. Added to this is the fact that lease terms of five or ten years—or longer—are not uncommon, so the relationship created by a lease will not go away. Thus, while for some retail salespeople every single customer may be a unique encounter, at commercial properties, the same management team members encounter the same tenant personnel day after day and year after year.

Although moments of truth in the management of commercial real estate are potentially incessant, it is prudent to attempt to catalog and control them. Managing customers' experiences—the *outcomes* that your clients have with your company—is the goal. If you assume that your customers are continually assessing and then banking the positive and negative outcomes they have with you, then their decisions whether to continue doing business with you are always at risk. If you inventory the most likely interactions your tenants and their employees and customers can have with your properties and your personnel, and if you strategize ways to improve the quality of those interactions, then you can boost the number of *beneficial outcomes* your customers experience.

Cataloging "Moments of Truth."   It is possible to chart the most prevalent moments of truth that tenants and prospective tenants have with commercial properties and their staffs. This process, called *critical incident* *analysis* or service *blueprinting,* is the first step in building a service-oriented culture in your company. Blueprinting maps the critical contacts between your customers and your products to help you devise ways to add value to these contacts. Here's an example.

Because office buildings, shopping centers, and industrial properties are "wasting" assets—i.e., they break down, gradually deteriorate, and become obsolete over time—preventive maintenance and repair are exceedingly important. They delay the aging process and preserve value for the owners. Consequently, repair and maintenance is a significant part of the management staff's responsibility and comprises a major portion of the property's annual budget. It is also a critical incident in the relationship between the property and individual tenants. Although the paperwork is typically called a *work order* as directed to your internal customers (i.e., staff), it is actually a *service request* from an external customer (i.e., a tenant).

When you endeavor to map this particular critical incident, you might find that its component elements are the following:

1. A maintenance need is discovered by a tenant's employee;

2. The maintenance request is transmitted to a member of the management staff, who prepares a written order that describes the problem;

3. The written request is directed to a maintenance employee;

4. The employee proceeds to the tenant's leased space and effects the repair; and

5. Some follow-up is done to ensure the tenant's satisfaction.

This sounds simple and fairly routine. Yet if managers wish to *add value* to the service-delivery process at commercial properties, there are several ways to do so. One is to institute a program of direct follow-up with tenants to determine whether the maintenance request was completed satisfactorily and assure that there are no unresolved problems. This follow-up can be done in person or by telephone—a particularly *service-focused* team member might be assigned to do this exclusively. (Some management companies use work order forms that require the tenant's signature as an indication that the work was completed to the tenant's satisfaction.)

You might also consider encouraging tenants to contact a particular maintenance person *directly* by circulating the worker's digital or voice pager number to them. Before implementing this innovative method of processing service requests, you would, of course, need to do some fairly extensive advance planning. This might include developing relevant hiring and training procedures for maintenance workers, providing appropriate supervision and feedback, and establishing rewards for successful performance. Once in place, however, this enhancement to traditional practice has the potential to

Service Visibility
and "Getting Your Hands Dirty"

Although value and its allied attributes—service and quality—are intangible and invisible, they are nonetheless measurable. Consumers routinely focus their five senses, along with intuition, judgment, and other skills to decide, for example, whether goods appear to be worth their selling price, whether a store employee has served them capably, or whether to return unsatisfactory purchases for a refund—and, indeed, whether they wish to continue patronizing the particular store at all.

People's talent for gauging the merit of goods and services is probably a consequence of living in a pure, multilayered, global consumer environment. By habit, inclination, and education, consumers make these determinations almost instinctively. However, as impersonal as much of consumers' behavior is, they are regularly and rudely made aware of the deplorable state of customer service—despite its scarcity, consumers nonetheless value the human touch. As Zemke and Schaaf have observed:

▶ Service in America today is terrible. Everybody says so, right? If true, that's ironic, because today's consumers are willing to pay a premium to have their basic needs met in a timely and efficient manner, and they'll be pleasantly surprised if they're treated with a little dignity and respect in the bargain. In principle they're not asking for much. In practice it seems that today's consumers—be they wholesale, retail, commercial, or trade—might as well ask for the moon as for a modicum of responsive, respectful treatment.

reduce, and perhaps even eliminate, the paper-processing and possible misinterpretation or mishandling of service requests that can occur when someone who answers a call is unfamiliar with maintenance problems—or, just as likely, busy with other responsibilities.

Whether or not you adopt such a revolutionary way of handling service requests, you might consider revamping your maintenance schedule—in particular, the hours that maintenance personnel are on duty. Service delivery generally conforms to a certain *demand rhythm*. For example, because patrons of fast-food establishments and banks tend to frequent those establishments at certain hours, line personnel are scheduled to accommodate the periods of greatest demand, and additional resources are made available when they are required. We believe that service rhythms can be detected in the property management business as well, and that it is worthwhile to make plans to accommodate them.

Most commercial tenants are typically "at work" at the property during most of the hours when maintenance people are normally on duty, and therefore are likely to discover most of their maintenance or repair needs when

---

Service Visibility *(continued)*

In this environment in which customers yearn for personal attention, care, and concern, yet almost invariably expect and receive the opposite, savvy marketers can deliver products "bundled" with additional desirable characteristics—intangible perquisites, if you will—and make their customers aware that the "bundle" contains these additional features. Ron McCann made this recommendation:

▶ Let people know what they are receiving. This can be done in many ways. You will find ways to suit your situation. Banks could advertise their commitment to get statements out on time. Repair companies could inform customers of special warranties. How can *you* let people know they just received extraordinary service? Answer that question and you'll fulfill the last of the three steps to becoming extraordinary.

Michael LeBoeuf admonished businesses to keep in touch with their customers:

▶ If you fail to stay in touch with your customers, they won't be aware of the good service you're giving them until something goes wrong and they don't get it. But by staying in touch after the sale or between sales, you can remind them of the fine service you give, make them aware of new products and services, and offer information to help them get more for their money. Periodic telephone calls, personal letters, newsletters, and occasional social calls are all good vehicles for staying in touch. But by all means, stay in touch and let them know that their satisfaction is priority number 1 with both word and deed.

---

help is readily available. Exceptions to this would be businesses that stagger their employees' work hours—many offices effectively extend their business day by two hours or longer, from the once typical eight hours between 9:00 A.M. and 5:00 P.M., by allowing their workers to arrive as early as 7:00 A.M. and stay as late as 6:30 P.M. Retailers may have store hours from 9:30 or 10:00 A.M. to 8:30 or 9:00 P.M. (in some areas, even as late as 9:30 or 10:00 P.M.); some drugstore and grocery chains have stores open around the clock. Where tenants' business hours are at variance with the management company's "normal" work day, there is greater likelihood that tenants will discover maintenance or other service needs when help is *not* immediately available. If you were to schedule maintenance personnel in shifts corresponding to tenants' business hours, some might start to work before tenants and their employees and customers arrive and others would still be working when tenants' employees are leaving. In this way, maintenance and janitorial work could be done while tenants were present to watch its progress—and to ask personally for additional service if they needed it. The fact that work is *visible*—i.e., that the consumers of the service are allowed to see

---

Service Visibility *(continued)*

Making service *visible* is nearly as important as providing it at all. Consider the array of ethnic restaurants that perform the entire food preparation and cooking procedure at the diner's table—and then charge a premium price for the experience—or expensive car wash operations that allow the patron to see the entire process, from high-powered washing through sudsing and, finally, waxing. How about bakeries that publicly feature their employees' cake-decorating skills? The examples are numerous, and the lesson is clear: Visible service is valuable service. Visibility becomes part of the product "bundle" and thereby is entitled to pricing consideration in addition to—and separate from—the goods themselves.

Managers of commercial real estate have a host of opportunities to let their tenants know they are being served. For instance, landscaping, lawn mowing, and window washing can be scheduled at times when tenants' personnel are arriving for work or leaving for home. Straightening runners or door mats or vacuuming area rugs also makes it apparent that this work is being done. Even though these are ordinary tasks of building upkeep, people generally are not aware that they are being handled until, for some reason, they are not done. The wise commercial real estate manager will strategize ways to make even routine tasks visible to tenants. It is also important to "tell" tenants—e.g., via notes or newsletters—that specific work has been done or changes have been made.

Alternatively, service can be made visible after the fact. For example, in the parking garages of office buildings managed by Urban Retail Properties Co., staff members wash the windshields of all vehicles parked there during the day. A small card (business card size) inserted under the windshield wiper lets the car owner know this was done and includes the message: "Have a nice day!" This service is performed once or twice a week, at no charge to the car owners.

---

the work being done, as well as its results—tends to make the work *more valuable* to the customer as well.

We would offer this caution, however: These innovative approaches to provision of maintenance services require careful planning and much forethought because of the potential for loss of control, especially at large properties.

Visibility Adds Value.   Have you ever gone to a restaurant where a salad, the main course, or dessert was prepared by the chef right at your table? It is certainly a unique experience because you can judge first-hand the excellence of the food, appreciate the skills—and personality—of the chef, and savor the sights and smells while the food is being prepared. Perhaps best of

---

Service Visibility *(continued)*

A related service principle—and of equal importance—is the admonition to "get your hands dirty!" This means that service is more meaningful if the service provider becomes *personally involved* in its delivery. Commercial property managers can follow the lead of the apartment manager in the following example:

> The site manager at Martinique Apartments scheduled parking lot maintenance and sweeping of the underground garage. She provided notice to her residents in advance of the work telling them that their cars should be moved and that these areas would not be available again for parking until the jobs were completed.
>
> Despite this notice, a few residents either failed to move their vehicles or returned them to the lot before the work was done. As a result, four cars were splattered with mud and covered with dirt.
>
> Although these residents technically were at fault, the manager decided to have their cars washed and waxed. Instead of delivering coupons to the residents or arranging to have the work done by professionals either on or off the site, the manager and her staff held an impromptu car wash in the parking lot. Because they volunteered to do the work themselves—even though it would have been much easier to hire professionals—the surprised residents showered the staff with praise. One of the delighted residents reciprocated by baking a cake and serving it at the monthly staff meeting. Thereafter, the "Great Annual Martinique Car Wash and Barbecue," in which the staff washed residents' cars, sponsored a picnic for residents, and played volleyball and softball with them, became the centerpiece of the property's resident retention program.

---

all, the experience can be quite entertaining. Restaurants that do this have made the visibility of work-in-progress their distinguishing feature.

Traditionally, janitorial work in offices and stores has been done at night, after employees and customers have departed. When they return the next day, everything is in its proper place and sparkling. Service at commercial properties is *invisible* by design. It is taken for granted. However, real estate managers can follow the restaurants' lead by letting tenants see what is being done for them. For example, you can schedule people to empty trash cans or police retail centers during busy shopping periods, or you can assign someone to clean the entrance doors of office buildings while the majority of tenants' employees are arriving for work. Polishing brass, changing lightbulbs, and any number of other common area maintenance tasks can be made visible without being intrusive or disruptive.

Even if you do not put any of the suggested work order refinements in

Service Visibility *(concluded)*

The lessons commercial property managers can draw from this are clear:

1. If your parking lot or garage requires work, you may not be able to schedule it when there will be no cars present.
2. Tenants should be advised well in advance so their personnel can move—or remove—their cars. Written notices or announcements may not be enough; follow-up telephone calls will ensure compliance. Also, it may be necessary or appropriate to arrange an alternative parking location, which should be indicated in the notice. (Rehabilitation or other construction that encroaches on tenants' employee parking areas is a similar opportunity.)
3. If any cars belonging to tenants (i.e., company cars) or their employees are soiled in the process, make it up to the car owners.
4. A "car wash" staffed by management team members can be a great way for people to get to know one another. It can also be a special "thank you" to tenants and their personnel.
5. Imagination is all that is needed to expand such a people-oriented "service" activity into a picnic or a party.

Even if such a "car wash" would be unworkable at a commercial property you manage, the idea of management team members and tenants' employees getting together should not be overlooked. You might consider holding volleyball or softball games—or even a tournament—with a team from the management company playing against tenant personnel or the management company team being one of several teams, each of the others representing one or more tenants. The competition could be held in a nearby park or fieldhouse if they cannot play at the property. Another possibility is for the building to sponsor a food drive to benefit a needy family or a local charitable organization and solicit support from tenants and their personnel.

Davidow and Uttal believe leaders should take an active role in service-delivery:

► Getting their hands dirty keeps top managers in touch with the problems of customers and the experience of the front line, and it shows everybody that serving customers is important. Never getting down into the trenches is dangerous.

Finally, Soichiro Honda, the founder of one of the most successful multinational companies (Honda Motors), recounted his personal, "hands-dirty" formula for success as follows:

► The man at the top of an organization must personally do things that others would hate to do most.

place, you might consider a variety of ways to follow up with your tenants to ensure their satisfaction with work that has been done for them. Typically, someone acting on behalf of the management office—the property manager or another staff member—telephones a tenant after the work has been completed to determine whether it was acceptable. Another way to measure satisfaction with the results of a service request is to invite tenants to complete a simple questionnaire that asks whether the maintenance personnel were pleasant, whether the response was timely and the work was performed properly, and whether there is additional work that could be done. While a questionnaire is less personal than face-to-face contact, it is more likely to elicit a candid response.

A basic characteristic of service-oriented organizations is that customers are encouraged to complain and to register needs for additional service. When these needs are discovered and met, customer loyalty usually follows. The problem, of course, is that real estate managers have to know about a deficiency before they can remedy it. The example follow-up form in exhibit 2.1 represents a straightforward approach to accomplishing this purpose. Equally important, it provides a nominal paper backup that can be used for record-keeping purposes in the management office. Such a questionnaire can become a self-perpetuating opportunity to provide service to your tenants upon their continuing request.

We also recognize that this approach may be at variance with most management company's standard operating procedures for commercial properties. Because maintenance services may be charged back to the tenant, formal acknowledgment or approval of the work may be required—i.e., an authorizing signature on the work order or other documentation. If that is the case, you might incorporate follow-up questions into your work order authorization or use a separate questionnaire as the official sign-off by the tenant or merely as a follow-up mechanism. The objective is to solicit requests for additional service; the methodology can be whatever works for you.

Blueprinting and Mapping Critical Incidents.   These suggested refinements to traditional work order systems and procedures used to administer maintenance requests illustrate how "blueprinting"—the process of identifying and characterizing customer-contact opportunities—can improve service delivery processes. The key to these improvements is mapping the contacts between your tenants, your property, and your management team in order to see how these contacts occur; writing them down in sequential order; and then deciding how you can intervene to improve their quality for your tenants.

The blueprinting process is vastly improved when as many participants as possible are involved, either formally or informally. Seen in this way, the methodology is akin to brainstorming sessions where people spontaneously contribute all kinds of ideas, primarily solutions to particular problems. The

---

Exhibit 2.1
Example Service Follow-Up Questionnaire

PLEASE LET US KNOW HOW WE HANDLED YOUR SERVICE REQUEST.
(RETURN QUESTIONNAIRE TO THE MANAGEMENT COMPANY OFFICE.)

SUITE/STORE NUMBER/ADDRESS _____

DESCRIPTION OF WORK DONE _____ (Date)

_____

_____

_____

_____

Management Staff Name/Signature

	YES	NO
WERE WE PROMPT?	☐	☐
WERE WE FRIENDLY?	☐	☐
WAS THE REPAIR ADEQUATE?	☐	☐
IS THERE ANYTHING ELSE WE CAN DO?	☐	☐

COMMENTS: _____

_____

_____

_____

Tenant Signature   Date

This type of follow-up questionnaire can be printed on brightly colored card stock (about 5″ wide x 8″ deep) or made part of a work order/authorization form for tenant sign-off. Any requests for additional work produce more work orders which, in turn, yield more completed questionnaires.

---

management team—most especially including representatives from management, marketing, maintenance, and accounting—play a part, as do central office personnel and the tenants themselves. (This approach has been implemented successfully by Marathon Realty Company, Limited, at the IBM Marathon Building in Montreal.)

The involvement of the tenants may range from their personnel sitting in during your staff meetings to one-on-one interviews where you ask them such questions as, "What would you think if we did . . . this way?" or "We've been thinking of trying something a different way. How would you like it if we did . . . ?" These types of questions ask for a reaction or response to your proposals. If you want the tenants' people to make suggestions, you might ask, "How do you think we should do . . . ?" or "How can we make . . . better for you?"

Brainstorming "Failpoints" in Service Delivery.   What are some other productive subjects for blueprinting? Remember, the goal is to improve the so-called critical incidents that contribute to customers' and potential customers' satisfaction—i.e., to tenant satisfaction and retention. In addition to work order processing, critical incidents that spring to mind include curb appeal, billing and collections procedures, staff appearance (a dress code), advertising and marketing enhancements, techniques for dealing with overly demanding tenants, handling after-hours emergencies, tenant communications, "social" events involving tenants and management personnel, and a host of others.

We recommend that you focus on a single critical incident in each staff meeting. In considering what items to include for discussion, try to determine those areas in your customer relations program where you are most likely to disappoint your tenants or their employees. Some examples might be:

Tardy or incomplete maintenance
Inadequate janitorial work
Inaccurate billing notices

Whatever the particulars, the purpose is to identify all of the failpoints that make your tenant retention efforts chancy. *Failpoints* are critical incidents that demand the immediate and close attention of your entire management team.

Whether you call it blueprinting, mapping, critical incident analysis, or something else, this type of strategizing can be extraordinarily productive, not only because collaborative thinking tends to bring particularly valuable insights to the surface, but also because the results are collectively "owned" by all of the participants—those whose enthusiasm to implement their solutions is correspondingly higher. ("Outer-circle" thinking, an elegant form of brainstorming, will be discussed later in this chapter.)

Employee Failpoints and Burnout.   Thus far we have considered planning for predictable moments of truth from the perspective of your customers. It is also worthwhile to consider the benefits that blueprinting can provide to your management team.

We believe that one of the negatives of commercial property management is that frontline employees are inordinately subject to burnout. The intense, nonstop, and sometimes negative moments of truth that occur between management team members and tenants are emotionally laborious and result in employee dissatisfaction and turnover. This is particularly true

---

Positive and Negative Moments of Truth

It is imperative to acknowledge—and accept—that there are two possible outcomes from every incident. *Positive* moments of truth—those contacts that have been handled successfully—prove that a strategy works. *Negative* moments of truth, on the other hand, are particular failpoints. While they do not necessarily disprove a strategy, they do indicate that the frontline server involved in the interaction somehow did not connect with the tenant (or the tenant's employee).

While it is possible to establish strategies for the ordinary moments of truth (the routine service request, for example), it is even more important to have procedures in place for handling the *extra*ordinary contacts—the so-called failpoints (e.g., emergencies or personal crises).

---

for management and maintenance employees who are at their worksite 8 to 10 hours per day. As Petra Marquart, a former property manager who teaches customer service techniques, put it, our business is "hard on the spirit." We agree.

For employees, strategizing moments of truth is also a means of combatting the draining effects of the emotional labor that characterizes many aspects of commercial property management. Blueprinting, as we have described it in this chapter, enables them to plan in advance how to handle a variety of critical incidents, some of which involve high-touch contacts with tenants' personnel. Having collectively considered alternative possibilities and arrived at a preferred approach, frontline personnel will comprehend both that there is a satisfactory way to respond to these situations—they have, in a sense, been *empowered to act*—and that other members of the management team (including their supervisors and the company executives) understand the realities of the intensely human interactions that occur at the front line.

Jeffrey Disend described the importance of support for frontline personnel this way:

▶ Frontline people need to know that the rest of the organization is there to support and assist them in serving customers. When people know they can depend on the systems, equipment, procedures, and people behind the scenes to deliver, keep commitments, and handle problems, they can act more confidently and with less stress.

Employee satisfaction will be revisited in chapter 3, where we will consider empowerment and its benefits in greater detail. To continue this discussion, we need to look more closely at the importance of frontline servers and the difficulty of their task. Rick Johnson, manager of business seminars for Walt

Disney World, one of the premier customer-driven companies, had this to say on the subject:

▶ How many times will your people on the front lines be tested today? And how many times will they succeed in earning or renewing the respect and loyalty of another customer or client? Your organization's reputation, its investment in facilities, products, services, and staff, even its prospects for the future, are all on the line every time your people deal with your customers.

Obviously people are the key to enriching customer contacts with your company. According to Donald Porter, director of customer service quality assurance for British Airways, the server *is* the company for the customer:

▶ If you're a service person, and you get it wrong at your point in the customer's chain of experience, you are very likely erasing from the customer's mind all the memories of the good treatment he or she may have had up until you. But if you get it right, you have a chance to undo all the wrongs that may have happened before the customer got to you. *You* really are the moment of truth.

Road Two: Hiring Nice People
to Serve Your Customers

Hal Rosenbluth is the owner of Rosenbluth Travel, a Philadelphia-based travel agency that experienced a 7,500 percent growth in revenue—from $20 million to $1.5 billion—in about twenty years. His strategy for success—which is embodied in the title of the book he co-wrote with Diane McFerrin Peters, *The Customer Comes Second: And Other Secrets of Exceptional Service*—is that employee quality is *the* single most significant "moment of truth" for his firm's customers.

▶ At its most basic common denominator, the formula for our company's success is that we have more nice people than [our competitors] do. Niceness is among our highest priorities because nice people do better work.

Rosenbluth reasoned that if he had nice people serving clients, and if he took personal responsibility for ensuring his employees' own on-the-job satisfaction, his customers would be the beneficiaries:

▶ Companies are only fooling themselves when they believe that "The Customer Comes First." People do not inherently put the customer first, and they certainly don't do it because their employer expects it. Only when people know what it feels like to be first in someone else's eyes can they sincerely share that feeling with others.

Hiring As an Exercise in KAIZEN.   The example from Hal Rosenbluth can be used to recall one important point and make another. First, as we noted in chapter 1, the Japanese theory of steady, gradual, continuous progress as a means to excellence—called KAIZEN—is a revolutionary departure from the American approach which assumes that improvement is accomplished only by means of fundamental, thorough, radical change. KAIZEN enables you to seek ways to leverage the greatest possible benefits for your company and yourself by looking for incremental improvements achieved daily over the life of your business. These points of leverage can become what some commentators term "lighthouses for change"—that is, specific initiatives undertaken companywide for the customer's benefit that will have the greatest positive and visible impact in focusing attention on the company's capacity to deliver quality at the lowest feasible cost. We think managers of commercial properties can follow the Japanese example and begin to reinvent their companies by taking the first step outlined here—i.e., concentrating on the quality of the company's employees and their job satisfaction.

Benchmarking Rosenbluth Travel.   Second, Rosenbluth's teachings can be coupled with another approach called *benchmarking*. This approach is based on the theory that the best practices in place at one company or in an industry may be imported by another business, even if the two firms are not engaged in the same enterprise. For example, in an effort to improve relations with their tenants, managers of commercial properties might seek guidance from certain retailers in the areas of signage, customer newsletters, or collections practices. Although benchmarking has evolved into a rather sophisticated technique for effecting improvements in business practices, at its heart lies the old admonition to avoid reinventing the wheel wherever possible. (Benchmarking is the subject of chapter 8.) A closer examination of the experiences of Rosenbluth Travel reveals some benchmarks that can be helpful to managers of commercial real estate.

First, you need to keep constantly in mind the importance and the contentment of your employees as the foundation for improving the performance of your business. As Rosenbluth put it:

▶   Every company operates on a hierarchy of concerns. Ours is: people, service, profits. In that order. The company's focus is on its people. Our people then focus on serving our clients. Profits are the end result.

Hal Rosenbluth believes that the successful economic performance of a company is driven by the happiness of its employees, rather than the reverse, and that contented employees are less likely to seek out other employment in an attempt to find satisfaction.

Second, as property managers direct attention to their "internal" customers—that is, their employees—they need to begin by hiring nice people, as Hal Rosenbluth did:

▶ Tenet number one is, *look for nice people*. The rest will fall into place. Too often, a person's job history carries more weight than his or her human values. What's in someone's heart can't be discovered in a resume.

The truth is, in real estate management, energy, enthusiasm, and attitude are often more important than specific experience.

Employees as Business Partners.   "Hiring nice" requires both common sense and a willingness to change the way you do business. No longer can you hire only on the basis of a prospective employee's prior job experience and skills: You are looking for "people" people—those who derive their satisfaction mostly from interacting with others. When you adopt as a company credo "people, service, profits," you redirect—and sharpen—your focus. If colleagues come first, customers second, and profits third, your employees become your business partners—i.e., your associates, colleagues, and friends. When managers of commercial properties hire service personnel, they are not only hiring for their customers, they are implicitly asking the question, "Is this prospect a person I want to trust with the future of my company?"

One way to "hire nice" is to go about the process as Rosenbluth Travel does—by seeking the participation of other nice people (i.e., current employees) in your hiring and promoting decisions:

▶ It's important to get as many people as possible involved in the selection process, because we need to bring into the company only those who can work well with the team we have in place. For that reason, candidates for senior leadership positions spend time with our current senior leaders, and their input is crucial. To round out the process, prospective leaders are often interviewed by those they will lead as well. We're seeking people who will inspire their teams. Who better to make that judgment than the team itself?

"Shared Fate."   Rosenbluth's skepticism of resumes and his firm's reliance on its employees (its internal customers) in arriving at hiring and promoting decisions is an extension of another Japanese concept—shared fate. "Mike" Morita, head of Sony Corporation's Rancho Bernardo manufacturing facility in California, described it this way:

▶ In the Japanese business culture, we think of our jobs in terms of *shared fate*. That means that all employees in the company share the same fate. The success—or failure—of the company affects all of us the same. The only way we can make our lives secure as individuals is to make sure the company remains competitive. We have to work together to make the best products we possibly can. So it is extremely important that each person understands the needs of the company, and each is willing to contribute his or her best efforts to make it successful. . . . Each person's contribution goes together with the contribution of every other person for the best result.

Once the principle of shared fate is understood, digested, and practiced in the company, the ability of the firm to focus its attention on achieving good results for its external client—the customer—is enhanced. William Ouchi, author of *Theory Z: How American Business Can Meet the Japanese Challenge,* had this to say:

▶ The successful delivery of service requires people to perform an unnatural act: to work at an extraordinarily high level of interdependence, working not only for their own ends but toward a successful outcome for the customer.

The subject of hiring will be augmented in the next chapter with a discussion of empowering and compensating employees. The road to a service orientation turns now to customer referrals.

Road Three: Compelling Customers to Tell Others About You

A look at another company provides an opportunity to benchmark techniques for "wowing" your customers. T. Scott Gross has brought a unique brand of showmanship and salesmanship to an otherwise ordinary business—a drive-through fried chicken restaurant in San Antonio, Texas. He has been so successful that he has written a book, *Positively Outrageous Service: New and Easy Ways to Win Customers for Life,* and constructed a successful consulting practice based on his experiences. According to Gross, "Positively Outrageous Service is the story you can't wait to tell."

The idea that it makes sense to try to "WOW!" a customer is probably based on the common-sense notion that much of what one vendor is trying to sell—or rent—is pretty much the same as what is generally available in the market, and sometimes the competition is even priced lower. In a competitive environment filled with products that are essentially equivalent, attempting to *delight* potential customers, as well as current customers, makes good marketing sense. If you are successful, you set your product ahead of the competition and add lasting value to it.

"Positively Outrageous Service"—Gross uses the acronym POS—has five elements.

1. It is *random and unexpected*—that is, it contains an element of surprise and novelty that jolts the customer because it is so unexpected.

2. It is *out of proportion to the circumstance.* This characteristic solidifies the unexpected nature of the service activity—because it is disproportionate, it is also extraordinary.

3. It invites the customer *to play, or be highly involved* in the activity. This quality requires that the service incident be fun for the customer—if it is, it solidifies the impression that the company itself is user-friendly.

4. It generates *compelling word of mouth.* The "WOW!" experience is so stunning that the customer simply cannot wait to tell others about it.

5. It creates *lifetime buying decisions* and fosters customer retention.

When the service encounter is unexpected, disproportionate, fun, and compelling, customers are disinclined to shop elsewhere because they are convinced they will be disappointed if they do.

One of the reasons managers of commercial properties should strive to provide their tenants with an unexpected service experience is precisely because so much of the service people receive is so shoddy. Indeed, as Davidow and Uttal have described the situation:

▶ "Crisis" is a strong word but no exaggeration. Most customer service is poor, much of it is awful, and service quality generally appears to be falling. At the same time, the penalty is growing for companies that render inferior service. Customers . . . are getting smarter about the value of service. They're increasingly frustrated and more willing than ever to take their business elsewhere.

The other reason commercial property managers should strive to improve their level of service delivery is that it pays to do so. Good service organizations strive to meet their customers' expectations; outstanding service companies endeavor to dazzle their customers in unforgettable ways. If they are successful, these firms achieve a marketing advantage that can be detected at the bottom line. In the words of Dunckel and Taylor:

▶ If you are selling the same product as your competitor, the difference in success will be measured by how the customer is treated, both during and after the sale. Initially, you and your competitor start evenly matched. But it is the intangible cosseting and concern, the customer service, that adds value and makes the buyer return again and again. Then you have a very measurable assessment of service: the bottom line—the repeat customer—money—greater profits.

What Is Service?

Karl Albrecht and Ron Zemke are the pioneers who first identified the importance of service and attempted to characterize it. Their books have been widely read for almost a decade, and they have had tremendous influence on American and international businesses, especially those whose operations include a specific service component (e.g., retail sales) or consist primarily of a rendered service (e.g., a beauty salon). In *Service America! Doing Business in the New Economy,* they defined ten characteristics of service. We think these can be expressed as seven general attributes of service that are directly applicable to commercial real estate management and tenant retention.

1. Unlike manufacturing, which requires a defined location, service is *decentralized*—it is rendered where the customer receives it—commercial tenants and their personnel receive your services in their workplaces.
2. Service is *time-bounded;* it is created at the instant of delivery. In commercial property management, the instants of delivery are not only the fulfillment of specific service requests, but also the points of contact when requests or complaints are received—e.g., the moment the telephone is answered.
3. While the experience of a rendered service is *personal,* someone has to deliver it. This is the defining role for your management personnel.
4. The service experience is unique to the recipient, but the requirement for delivery makes it *interactive.* It is important for the customer to connect with the right person to solve a problem quickly.
5. Service is *nonreproducible;* proper delivery of service the first time is critical because opportunities to do it again are rare. If service cannot be delivered properly, the only recourse is to make reparations or apologize. Because of this, you must have in place strategies for service recovery.
6. Because service is *experience-specific,* customer satisfaction is usually greatest when service can be rendered one-on-one. Having to deal with many different people to make a purchase or file a complaint—to get any kind of action—reduces customer satisfaction.
7. The quality of a service is *expectation-related.* Customer satisfaction depends on the recipient's subjective perception of the service, which is based on his or her expectations.

In an attempt to create a "WOW!" experience for your customers, whether it is designed to meet Scott Gross's requirements or to pass other tests that are more or less rigorous, you need to keep two disclaimers in mind: First, it is fruitless to capture the attention of your customers in order to direct it to an inferior product. To make this point more colloquially, if you put lipstick on

---

What Is Service? *(continued)*

A commitment to service delivery is critical to assuring the quality or value of a service. Planning and training—and staff buy-in to your service program—are key steps along the path to success. Ron Zemke and Dick Schaaf distinguished between products and services this way:

▶ To begin with, a product is a tangible, a service an intangible. A product takes up shelf space, has a shelf life, can be inventoried, depreciated, and taxed. A service doesn't exist until it is called for by the recipient. It needs no shelf space, has no shelf life, and most certainly is not an asset that can be easily inventoried.

Because service is intangible, it does not exist until it is requested. Its existence depends on the recipient not only wanting and needing it, but also taking an active role in its production as well as its consumption. Involving tenants' personnel in the service process will add to tenant satisfaction overall. Even more important, it will reduce the cost to the provider. Heskett et al. elaborated on this point:

▶ Self-service concepts employ customers as part of the service delivery system. The most effective insure that customers are trained, through clear instructions, in how to be good "helpers." The range of activities in which customers are willing to engage is rather remarkable. Whether they pump their own gas, as a majority of U.S. consumers do; bus their own dishes; or haul their own furniture purchases, customers enable service providers to reduce demand on the delivery system during peak periods, thereby providing incentives in the form of lower prices to encourage customers to increase their participation further.

---

a pig, what you have is a pig with red lips. Second, as soon as customers begin to anticipate the little extras you provide, those extras become part of the "bundle," the package of value that you are selling. That is why it is vital to keep in mind Gross's admonition that the "WOW!" experience must be *random and unexpected.*

How do you go about creating "WOW!" experiences for your tenants? One place to start is to find out how "WOW!" differs from merely "okay" or "pretty good." Fortunately, Theodore Levitt, a professor of marketing at Harvard (and a true marketing genius) has provided a model. In *The Marketing Imagination,* Levitt describes four levels of attributes that customers expect every product or service to have: generic, expected, augmented, and potential. (These are often represented as a series of concentric circles.)

The *generic* product, according to Levitt, is the package containing the fundamental attributes of the goods—the rudimentary, substantive "thing" that people require the product to have. For the steel producer, as Levitt says, the generic product is the steel itself; for a bank, it would be money to loan. The generic product, then, is the "table stakes" necessary to be minimally in business. In the business of commercial property management, the generic product would be the physical building or office suite or store space that the prospect rents—i.e., the "vanilla box" together with exterior signage, loading docks, and a contact person who is the landlord or acts on the landlord's behalf.

As businesses move outward beyond the so-called generic product, they bundle additional levels of support and service with their goods, thereby increasing the customer's perception of their value. This naturally results in a higher price for the improved goods, as well as greater customer satisfaction, product loyalty, and splendid word-of-mouth. The *expected* product might be termed support because it includes whatever the organization does to make the basic product more reliable, accessible, useable, enjoyable, convenient, dependable, accurate, or useful. In the management of commercial properties, the expected product, in addition to the "vanilla box," might be contemporary amenities that are characteristic of other comparable properties in its market. Depending on the market and the tenant profile, these might range from covered parking to an in-building sandwich shop or full-service restaurant. The expected product (property) most likely would also have friendly, helpful personnel available on site to handle tenants' requests—i.e., management team members who are readily available at all times to assist with maintenance and other service needs—and service is prompt, competent, and friendly.

The *augmented* product goes beyond what customers expect, by bundling additional benefits with the expected product, offering more than customers believe they need or have come to expect. The augmented product becomes "aspirational"—what buyers would really prefer among the competition, assuming that real or anticipated impediments (for example, high price or limited availability) could be overcome. Certain automobiles, vacation locales, and brands of jewelry—how about Lexus, Gstaad, Rolex?—are readily identifiable as leaders among augmented products. They are presumed to be peerless, supreme, incomparable. Whether or not they are the most expensive—and some augmented products are not—prospective customers consider them to be the *ultimate* acquisition of their type; their proud owners believe that they enjoy a *relationship* with such products and the people who sold them.

In the management of office buildings and shopping malls, the augmented product—in addition to offering the qualities and characteristics of expected offices or stores—probably has some traits of the finest hotels and resorts. Their leased space and common-area amenities would be unique in their markets—e.g., richly appointed building features and fixtures, a wide range of food service and entertainment options, extensive interior and/or exterior landscaping with seasonal color splashes, and high-profile security services. Other possibilities include a well-equipped fitness center (including a personal trainer) for tenants' employees or daycare facilities for their children. An office building might include a newsstand that sells candies, cigarettes, and magazines; a concierge, or so-called valet services (dry cleaning, laundry, shoeshining). More important, their in-building support staffs would be matchless in their responsiveness, friendliness, and helpfulness. It is significant to note that the *augmented services tend to be more people-intensive*. Every feasible means would be employed to determine tenant satisfaction. No tenant need or preference that surfaced would go unmet. Tenants and their employees would describe their experiences working in the building as delightful or perfect, and they would boast to others about their pleasure.

Interestingly, the enhancements to expected products that result in augmented goods usually entail small dollar investments that yield enormous payoffs. Typically, enrichment by means of meaningful human touches is involved—warmth, attention, intuitive gestures that make having the item absolutely exceptional in every respect. Of course, the challenge to those who wish to distinguish their products from others—i.e., to market augmented goods—is to motivate the frontline performers in their companies to deliver moments of truth that are consistent with this enhanced concept of the product. As Jan Carlzon knew, employees at the front lines of companies—often the most junior, lowest paid, and presumably least motivated—do business in the third ring (the outer circle of the defined components of a product). That is where they get their job satisfaction. The third ring is their territory.

Too often, however, the augmented product becomes the expected product, and customers can easily be seduced by a competitor offering a lower price or a new or different service. The *potential* product, then, relates to customer satisfaction based on perceptions—service is perceived as "good" when expectations are exceeded and "poor" when expectations are not met. According to Levitt:

▶ "Augmented" is everything that has been done or is being done to attract or keep the customer, while "potential" is anything that could be done but isn't being done yet.

Exhibit 2.2 is a representation of the Levitt paradigm as it might be applied to commercial properties. (Meeting customers' expectations will be addressed specifically in chapter 6; finding out what customers expect requires market research.)

Outer-Circle Thinking.   Using the Levitt paradigm, the goal should be to market an augmented commercial property to your customers, current and future. You need to plan a strategy for reaching—and surpassing—that goal, a methodology for defining the potential product. One way to achieve this is to use a form of old-fashioned brainstorming—called outer-circle thinking—

Exhibit 2.2

The Levitt Paradigm Applied to Commercial Properties

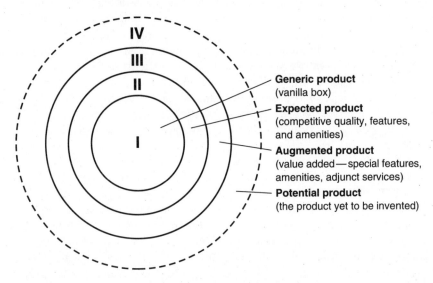

Generic product
(vanilla box)

Expected product
(competitive quality, features,
and amenities)

Augmented product
(value added—special features,
amenities, adjunct services)

Potential product
(the product yet to be invented)

In the marketplace, the *generic product* (I) is what it is; in general it is sold on the basis of price. The *expected product* (II) includes features and amenities equivalent to comparable properties; it is sold on the basis of quality. The *augmented product* (III), on the other hand, encompasses features and amenities that exceed the competition; because a major component is personal service, its selling point is a relationship. The *potential product* (IV) requires constantly changing definition.

---

among the site staff. While brainstorming is often used to focus on solutions to a single problem, the goal here is to explore possibilities without limitations.

Outer-circle thinking is a creative, unrestrained process for bringing ideas and suggestions, especially nontraditional ones, to the surface among members of a group. The first rule is that the participants cannot be judgmental about any thought that surfaces. Indeed, group members should be encouraged by the leader to propose, at least initially, the most unlikely and even outlandish and extravagant ideas.

The leader begins the session by summarizing the purpose of the meeting. The statement might be something like this: "We need to think about improving the services and amenities offered at our properties. We'd like our customers—our tenants and prospective tenants and their personnel—to have a once-in-a-lifetime experience, one they can't wait to tell their friends and clients about. What could we do—or what could we provide them—that

Business Intelligence—
Finding Out What Customers Expect

Most of the self-help business books exhort practitioners to "get close" to their customers. It is only through frequent, personal interactions with a company's clients that a firm can gain an understanding of their perceptions and expectations. Relationship-nurturing, then, as a complement to relationship-initiating, is the *sine qua non* of customer-driven companies.

Continuous and careful listening to customers is the indispensable prerequisite to serving them. The smallest companies inherently listen best. The street-corner hotdog vendor or the proprietors of a "mom and pop" dry cleaners are continually in contact with their clients. They cannot help but listen to their customers; face-to-face customer connections are inevitable.

The trick for a company that is organized hierarchically—with servers at the front line and bosses in the corner office—is to ensure that customers' voices are clearly heard in the executive suite. Tom Peters challenged owners and managers to come out from behind their desks so that they can watch and listen to what is going on at the "line of scrimmage" where the fate of their companies is continually being decided. "Management by Walking Around" (MBWA) is perhaps Peters' most evocative contribution to the business literature.

There are frontline servers at the line of scrimmage in every company, whether the business is a kiosk in a shopping mall or IBM. If the feedback loop—the communications link between the front line and management—is a clear channel, the company can make the necessary mid-course corrections to guarantee that service-delivery problems are solved and customer complaints are addressed expeditiously.

The transmission devices that can be employed range from MBWA to more sophisticated market research techniques. Because frontline servers are in the best position to gather on-the-spot business intelligence from customers, some firms have devised formalized techniques for debriefing their own employees. As Sam Walton, the founder of Wal-Mart, said, "Our best ideas come from delivery and stock boys." Other companies rely on questionnaires and focus groups as preferred methods of capturing and forwarding customer input.

they would consider absolutely incredible? Don't worry about what it might cost: Let's talk about what it would take to make them say 'WOW!' "

Each member of the group is asked to contribute one idea which the leader records on a flip chart. If the group is large, perhaps it can be divided into sections, with each section reporting a thought until every contribution has been listed. The results of such a session might look something like this:

Business Intelligence *(continued)*

The simplest and least-expensive way to listen is across a table or a desk. When a customer's voice is conveyed via some substitute medium (e.g., a questionnaire), the sound is altered or muted, either because the vehicle itself lacks spontaneity or because it injects the inquirer's own subjectivity into the feedback loop, or both. Questionnaires tend to be designed for universal applicability—one size fits all—and they may limit the potential responses by providing an array of specific answer-choices. While the results can be counted, totaled, and averaged, they may not yield any specific recommendation. Focus groups, on the other hand, are typically composed of ten or a dozen participants who are demographically similar to the company's own customer base. Focus sessions facilitate the kind of in-depth exploration of a subject that is beyond the reach of a questionnaire. Because they can be videotaped or otherwise monitored by company leadership, the filtration problems that compromise other market research tools are minimized.

In the management of commercial real estate, it is useful to convene focus groups from among your tenants periodically. Because their management and professional personnel are likely to have different opinions than subordinate (support) staff and what these groups consider important may differ substantially from the expectations of the decision-makers who signed the leases, you should strive to collect information from a cross-section of your tenants' personnel, but not necessarily in the same focus group.

Focus groups need some structure—a time frame, a topic for discussion—but specific questions should be open-ended to elicit thoughtful responses. Results will not be quantifiable; the entire process is subjective. However, a focus session can be a wonderful source of ideas for new services or facilities to add to a property and suggestions for improving what you already do well. This type of forum invites discussion and elaboration of ideas as participants raise questions and build on each other's contributions. Such focus groups are brainstorming sessions with a defined goal whose participants have a vested interest in the outcome.

We would add a caution, however: It may be desirable occasionally (or always) to take a more formal approach, which has the advantage of impartiality. Market researchers who conduct focus sessions typically employ a trained facilitator who can channel the discussion and keep to an established agenda. Although a do-it-yourself approach may be more economical in terms of out-of-pocket costs, a professional facilitator has the ability—and the authority—to prevent a focus group from becoming a mere gripe session. (If that happens, you will find that few of your tenants will be willing participants in future focus sessions.) A professional facilitator can also overcome participants' reluctance to comment about "sensitive" issues (e.g., management personnel or specific incidents) and elicit complaints that might not otherwise be brought to the surface.

As new tenants are moving in, have "lunch" delivered to their stores or offices—e.g., pizza and root beer.

Place a large jar of wrapped candy at the reception desk of each office or industrial tenant in the evening. The jar should have the logo or name of the building and include the building ownership or the name of the management company.

Print and distribute a property newsletter for tenants of office buildings, shopping centers, or industrial sites. Highlight a specific tenant each month—describe their product or service, a company history, and names of their employees.

Send the tenants "anytime" cards—not only on holidays—thanking them for their business.

During the summer, serve tenants' employees a hotdog and ice cream lunch on the grounds, in the parking lot, or in the main lobby of the building; serve hot chocolate to welcome the first snow of winter.

Have a monthly party for tenants' employees whose birthdays fall during that month. Provide cake, ice cream, and soda. Include balloons and the singing of "Happy Birthday," if possible.

Buy ice chests imprinted with the building logo. Fill them with soft drinks and sandwiches. Have someone from maintenance deliver them to new tenants' leased space on move-in day. See if there are any problems that maintenance can fix *right away!*

Schedule an Easter egg hunt inside the office building or on the lawn area of an industrial park during the lunch hour.

After testing the emergency evacuation system of a commercial building, hand out a small first aid kit to each tenant.

The possibilities are almost endless. What is surprising is that many of the ideas involve very little or no expense. (Many of the activities listed here involve food, the costs of which can be minimized, and games need only require people to bring their imaginations.) Almost all of them require the sort of high-touch, personal contact between frontline staff member and tenant employee that has the potential to *delight*.

The following comment from David Freemantle, an English expert on the subject of customer service, effectively summarizes the purpose of outer-circle thinking:

▶ One of the most exciting aspects of customer service . . . is to discover innovative little ways of pleasing the customer even more. This can be a real test for any progressive customer caring company.

The provision of unsolicited little extras is a creative and challenging opportunity all staff can enthusiastically respond to. It enables people to be themselves, to give of themselves, to express themselves in a way that is pleasing to the customer. It enables staff to put themselves out for the customer.

Revolutionary Hiring
and "Zapping"

Managers have to select their people well, provide them with a strong foundational culture in which to work, offer them strategic direction, and equip them with the company-specific skills and knowledge they need to perform their roles. *And then the managers need to get out of the way, so the people can get the job done.*
——Valarie A. Zeithaml, A. Parasuraman, and Leonard L. Berry
Delivering Quality Service

In truly customer-driven companies, the aim is to *delight* customers, to serve them in increasingly imaginative and memorable ways, to forge ongoing bonds with them, and to smash barriers that impede these relationships with customers or make them unpleasant in any way. These are *the firms of the future*—successful companies that are already in control of their business and will remain so.

The firms of the future are beginning to acknowledge that their customers include not only those who purchase their goods and services (external customers), but also the people who work within the organization (internal customers—their employees), and even suppliers whose products are transformed by the company for sale. Cultivating affiliations between these various customers and the company is the essence of what is known as "relationship marketing," or "partnering," where buyer and seller acknowledge their common interests and consider themselves to be invested in each other's continued success. Terry Vavra put it this way:

▶ Marketing has, over the years, shifted in its orientation from *tricking* customers to *blaming* customers to *satisfying* customers. Its future success depends upon its skill to integrate customers systematically into the conduct of business. Whether this is an accurate characterization or not, marketing's posture to date has caused an escalating confidence gap between marketers and consumers. Today, consumers cynically anticipate marketers making a profit by exploiting them rather than by satisfying their wants and needs.

The goal of having satisfied customers is a revolutionary—and highly pleasurable—concept, and one we believe is at least as achievable in the management of commercial real estate as in retailing. Our goal as real estate managers should be to create contented tenants who believe they are partners in their landlords' success. Realizing this ideal begins with attending to our employees. That is the approach advocated by James C. Whiteley in *The Customer-Driven Company: Moving from Talk to Action*:

▶ You create service quality by hiring externally focused people— people who like people—then giving them a vision of service, a knowledge of what the customer needs, and support that lets them do their job.

Strategizing Ways to Hire Customer Service Superstars

First you will need a carefully designed composite *abilities and attitudes profile* of the employee you are seeking. A review of the job description for the position will tell you what technical skills are required. That is the easy part. The challenge is to include in the list the *personality traits* that would make a candidate a winner in your organization. To get started, ask yourself: "Who among my current employees has a history of *delighting* the people who represent our tenants and supporting his or her fellow employees?" Try to isolate the characteristics of these people; write them down—and then aggressively pursue them as you interview applicants. Zemke and Bell offered this additional counsel on the process:

▶ The quest for the potential service star begins with a clear view of the service role you are seeking to fill. Treat the vacancy as an opening in a play. If you select an ideal (the applicant who comes closest to embodying the qualities best suited for the service role) rather than choosing someone "just like me," you may skirt the lure of choice that results in an unfair personnel practice.

Some companies, recognizing that their own best employees may be an excellent source for finding others, initiate the employment process internally. That is what T. Scott Gross has advocated:

▶ Find one knock-down, drag-out winner and you're hot on the trail of a whole flock of them! Start with your own employees. Which one is a [winner]? Next ask her [or him] to help you recruit a friend. Don't worry. They won't just drag in a warm body. Winners like to work with other winners, and that's exactly whom a winner will recommend.

Carl Sewell, a Dallas automobile dealer who now owns ten Cadillac dealerships—having expanded his business from $10 million in the late 1960s to $250 million in 1990—uses this technique as the centerpiece of an aggressive hiring program.

▶ We almost never advertise. The people we really want—the best people—already have jobs. They're not searching the help wanted ads or updating their resumes. In fact, most of the successful people we've hired have never had a resume. We sought *them* out, because we had heard about the job they were doing somewhere else, or, as happens most often, they were referred by a friend. *As a rule, people who are exceptional performers are friends with people who are exceptional performers, so we pay a lot of attention when one of our people recommends a friend.*

Other firms, recognizing that service winners are in short supply, hire such people even when they have no jobs available. As Scott Gross has said:

▶ The problem with winners is that, like cops, they never seem to be around when you need one. If you are serious about hiring winners, you must be prepared to hire one anytime you find one.

Marketing for Human Resources.   One reason why customer service is so poor is that companies recruit job candidates based on their technical skills, rather than their history of delivering service at the front lines. We believe that the hiring decision should be based in part on an assessment of the candidate's ability to relate to customers, to respond appropriately to their needs, to take initiatives on their behalf, to be an advocate for their interests (to the company). Recruiters fail to look for these qualities because customer service is not a priority within the company, because they do not aim high enough when they set minimum qualifications for new hires, and because they are not very creative in their recruiting efforts. Berry and Parasuraman addressed these same issues:

▶ Why do so many executives permit the wrong people to carry the company flag in front of customers? Part of the answer is the failure to think and act like a marketer when it comes to human resource issues. Marketing is used by most firms to compete for *sales* market share but not *talent* market share. Read the look-alike employment ads in the fine print in a local newspaper. Is this an effective way to compete for talent? The same firms that compete intensely and imaginatively for customers compete meekly and mundanely for employees.

Jim Clemmer, an advocate of service quality, decried the shortsightedness that he found in both hiring and training:

▶ Take a look at your *internal* education and awareness. It is amazing how many organizations will spend megabucks and megahours planning and executing powerful, slick campaigns aimed at their external customers. Many will then turn around and spend 10 bucks and two hours bringing the people on board who ultimately decide whether those external advertising messages are fact or fiction.

In other words, employees are an investment, and recruiting and hiring should be considered in those terms. The need to fill a vacant position—and the effort to do so quickly—can lead to hiring the wrong candidate. Ultimately, the time and cost to correct the error—i.e., to terminate and replace the inappropriate (ineffectual) employee—will exceed the expense of hiring the right person in the first place.

Searching for Company Ambassadors and Business Partners.   You know from your own experiences that some people prefer to work with things—they are project-driven—while others truly gravitate to situations in which human contacts, and sometimes unpleasant or challenging ones, predominate. Because your objective should be to employ people who will be ambassadors for your company as well your own professional colleagues—i.e., your *business partners*—the first hiring rule for the firm of the future is: *Look for nice people.* Real estate management companies need to employ people who naturally care about others, who *thrive* on personal (customer) contact and believe it to be a vital component of their business lives. Isolating people-oriented applicants from others is a difficult task—because job applicants so often claim that they "love people," resumes and past job references are unreliable predictors of this skill. As Rosenbluth and Peters have warned, "Too often, a person's job history carries more weight than his or her human values. What's in someone's heart can't be discovered in a resume."

In the management of commercial real estate, hiring is complicated by an increasing emphasis on computerized reporting. The real estate management business naturally lends itself to computer applications—rent rolls, pass-through expense prorations, financial analyses, and year-to-date comparisons of a host of subjects are all number-based—and that tends to attract people who are good at working with machines and thus prefer programs over people. While there is nothing wrong with this preference, such people should not be at or near the front line where customer contact is inescapable. The reason, as you will see later in this chapter, is that the firms of the future will be horizontally structured rather than hierarchically organized. Thus, *all* employees—not just those who answer telephones, respond to service requests, or staff the building management office—will be customer service personnel who work at the front line.

As real estate managers, when you go about the hiring process, you are really performing two complementary—and momentous—tasks: First, you are recruiting for your tenants; and by doing so, you are in fact searching for that unique person in whom you are willing to entrust the future of your company. You should begin by looking for *customer-friendly* employees who have outgoing personalities, enthusiasm, and an honest desire to serve. The firms of the future—companies that succeed in creating superior value for their customers—are, as William Band observed, "nearly fanatical in their desire to recruit good 'human raw material' into their organizations. They spend inordinate amounts of time and energy getting it right the first time in their hiring decisions." Part of "getting it right" means searching until you find a candidate who *thrives* on customer contact.

We recommend that interviews for commercial property management jobs include an opportunity for applicants to recount stories that reveal their attitudes toward tenants and their employees. For example, you might say, "Tell me about a time when you encountered a particularly irate individual who worked for a tenant and how you resolved the problem." A variation on this approach goes like this: "It's understandable that sometimes we get really upset with our tenants' people. Everybody does once in a while, but there's a big difference between an angry confrontation and reminding someone about the requirements under a tenant's lease. Tell me about one time during the last six months when you had to get tough with someone and how you handled it."

Although they may be somewhat less effective overall than the "story-telling" technique suggested in the preceding paragraph, so-called open-ended questions are another way to reveal a candidate's attitudes. Examples of questions designed to display a candidate's service values are: "What does customer service mean to you?" Or, "Have you ever encountered what you would consider to be *world-class* customer service? Describe the situation for me."

Role-play is yet another strategy that can be used to reveal a candidate's attitudes toward customer service. For example, the interviewer might play the part of an irate store owner who has waited an inordinate amount of time to have a signage design approved, while the candidate acts as the recipient of the telephone call.

In all of these types of situations, the quality of the process the candidate uses to answer your questions is far more important than whether his or her answers are "correct." Remember, interviews are inherently artificial and false. Freemantle has characterized them as "a process of mutual seduction . . . based on illusion, pose, facade and front." Accepting this reality as a caution, we would commend the group interview as a potential way to expose deception and phoniness in a candidate's responses.

Team Interviewing.   One way to set about the hiring task is to involve as many people as possible, not only in job interviews, but also in the eventual hiring decision. After all, part of the "fit" you should be looking for is between the new employee and your current team. For this reason, the entire organization should be given the opportunity to evaluate the candidate's suitability for the job, as well as explore his or her match with the company culture. Tom Peters gave similar advice:

▶ The task of transforming raw recruits into committed stars, able to cope with the pace of change that is becoming normal, begins with the recruiting process per se. The best [companies] follow three tenets, unfortunately ignored by most: (1) spend time, lots of it; (2) insist that line people dominate the process; and (3) don't waffle about the qualities you are looking for in candidates.

Here's an example of what we mean: The personnel department at Disney—known as "central casting"—places the ability to get along with others at the top of the list of job specifications for new "cast members" (prospective Disney employees). On the theory that the personal dynamics occurring during the interview process can provide useful clues about candidates' friendliness and attentiveness to others, Disney relies on group interviews of job candidates.

Intensive group interviewing gives the team the opportunity to gauge an applicant's "fit" with the company culture. Equally important, because group interviewing communicates the firm's mission to all participants, this type of employee selection process allows an applicant to evaluate whether he or she shares the firm's values. The procedure is thus a *dual-purpose* selection strategy: In effect, you are *selecting-in* employees who meet your exacting employment standards and, in addition, helping candidates *select-out* for themselves if they feel this "fit" is missing for them. Part of the interview process should therefore be devoted to letting candidates know the team's expectations and vision for their performance, as well as what they should anticipate—good and bad—in their daily work. (Having your superstars participate in or even lead the team interview is one way to assure that these messages are delivered.) Most important, prospective employees need to understand that serving tenants is what keeps the company in business. Considered in this way, the interview process is a *training opportunity* that should not be missed.

Now, assume that you have completed the interviews, and that several of your employees have been involved in the screening effort. How should you proceed? One way is to ask the participants the "feel good" questions:

How did you feel when you were talking with this person?

After you filter-out the applicant's natural nervousness in the interview situation, do you feel good about the applicant?

Do you think this person will help or hurt the performance of your team?

Is this a person who will fit in?

Scott Gross has recommended the following approach:

▶ Spend a few minutes in casual conversation. If you wind up feeling good (and you don't have to quantify this scientifically), chances are you've got a winner on your hands. It shouldn't take you long to decide. In fact, if after more than a minute or two you don't have a strong, positive intuitive message, call in the next applicant. *After all, most service jobs—and nearly every job is a service job—rely heavily on first impressions.*

Intuition-Based Selection. Although you will need to evaluate candidates based on objective criteria that can be documented, the use of intuition to *assist* in making a hiring decision seems entirely appropriate. Assessing a candidate's communication skills, friendliness, compatibility, and service orientation, among other qualities, is inherently subjective. Part of what you will be looking for in the new hire is itself intuitive and instinctive—how well will the candidate respond under pressure when there are no guidelines and no supervisors around to help? The following example from a residential property has implications for managers of commercial real estate, too.

Halloween 1992, more than three feet of snow fell in the Twin Cities area—the earliest and heaviest snowfall in history. Apartment managers and owners, unprepared for a storm of such magnitude, scrambled to find individuals and companies who could plow-out their sites. At one sprawling suburban townhouse property, however, the best efforts of the owner couldn't accomplish snow removal. Several days dragged by. Residents attempted to dig their cars out of the parking lots, producing banged fenders and fiery tempers, the latter vented upon the innocent staff, one of whom was an unfortunate part-time leasing agent named Sharon. Bombarded by angry residents, yet unable on her own to get the plowing done, Sharon decided to try to make amends. Donning boots, goose-down coat, and mittens, she slogged off for downtown.

Nearly an hour later, she entered a flower shop and purchased every single red rose in its stock. Sharon returned to her property and delivered one rose to each apartment, apologizing to the residents for their inconvenience. The response was instantaneous: Their venom immediately disappeared, and the irate telephone calls evaporated.

We include this story of "The Rose in the Snow" to illustrate an important point: The hiring process should be designed so that the participants in the job interview can evaluate candidates' ability to be resourceful, to "think on their feet." Intuition is a trait that is, unfortunately, in short supply—in commercial property management as in other types of business. When real estate managers hire on the basis of technical skills alone, they risk screening-out people like Sharon, and that is a mistake.

It is one thing for people to be "trapped" in their homes, quite another to be stranded at work or elsewhere. Inclement weather poses different challenges for managers of commercial properties because it may create a genuine emergency situation—one in which intuition and resourcefulness are required to save the day. On a busy day, a large office building or shopping center is likely to have dozens or even hundreds of its tenants' customers on site in addition to the regular population of tenant employees. While formal emergency procedures provide specific guidelines and typically include the admonition, "Don't panic!" they are often noticeably silent on ways to achieve calm amid chaos. Is it logical, therefore, to expect a number-cruncher to deal effectively with emergencies like the one recounted in the story of "The Rose in the Snow?"

Shannon Johnston of Kaset, Inc., a customer consulting company in Tampa, Florida, said the same thing:

▶ There are two parts to every customer interaction—the business side and the human side. Both are there, and they exert themselves more or less at the same time. Most people want to—at least try to—ignore the human side. My rule of thumb is that if you teach people to handle the human side first, the business side goes much quicker.

One way to ascertain a candidate's potential resourcefulness is to ask, "What would you change—what innovations would you implement—in your current job to become more people-responsive?"

Company Acculturation and Skills Training

A major part of the training task is successfully completed when the recruiting and hiring processes have been handled competently. We believe that service winners need less training, at least at the outset of their employment, than do nonservice winners who may have abundant technical skills but lack a ser-

---

Pre-Employment Psychological Testing

Yet another potentially fruitful employee screening technique, though also a legal minefield, is pre-employment psychological testing. The use of certain types of aptitude, intelligence, and personality tests is designed to assist employers in determining the fit between a candidate's attitudes and personality and an available job. These tests can be used to measure specific personality traits in order to avoid hiring individuals who are likely to commit illegal acts for which an owner or manager may be liable, as well as to help in the determination of an employee's aptitude for assignments requiring certain personality traits.

While the use of these types of tests generally appears to be allowed by the law, there are significant legal risks for the employer who implements such testing indiscriminately as an employment screening device. One potential restriction on the use of psychological testing for this purpose is the Americans with Disabilities Act (ADA). In addition, a case decided by the California First District Court of Appeal in 1991 *(Soroka v. Dayton Hudson Corporation),* has sharply limited the use of pre-employment psychological testing in California. The ADA and *Soroka* may be construed in the future to preclude employers from asking questions in pre-employment psychological tests which probe into areas now covered by civil rights laws. Nonetheless, it appears that current law in most states allows an employer to use a standardized psychological test so long as it has been screened by an expert in the field to remove questions that carry a potential of revealing the prospective employee's religion, gender preference, mental disability, or other factors identifiable as relating to classes protected by federal or state civil rights law.

[NOTE: It is imperative for the employer who wishes to utilize psychological techniques for screening prospective or current employees to *seek advice of legal counsel before proceeding, minimally to avoid claims of discriminatory practices.*

The value of psychological testing, based on some managers' experiences, is that it can be helpful in selecting-in candidates who are people-oriented (and selecting-out those who are not); some companies do this to create a "team profile" that helps determine candidates' "fit" with an existing group. By itself, such testing is less helpful in distinguishing potential superstars from average performers.]

---

vice orientation. Davidow and Uttal drew the distinction between these abilities as follows:

► Service leaders seem to have found a working balance between technical training, which covers the details of performing a job correctly, and social training, which focuses on the interpersonal values, attitudes, and techniques needed to render good service. And they understand that customer service training fails unless it includes lessons in how to treat internal customers, the people inside the company whose ability to serve outside customers depends on their getting service from colleagues.

The goal of the hiring process, then, is to employ people who will bring to the job those innate interpersonal traits that the organization believes to be essential. Social skills are therefore a hiring issue rather than a subject for training. We believe that training programs designed to improve employees' attitudes—whether the employees are new hires or already in place—are inappropriate and ineffective. Even monetary incentives fail in this regard. Moreover, they indicate a sense of desperation that the company's own employees are quick to detect. People do not respond to lectures that teach such platitudes as "the customer is always right." Indeed, although the bulk of in-service instruction is devoted either to improving skills or improving attitudes, most of the latter is really so-called smile training. Karl Albrecht, who coined the phrase "smile training," characterized it this way:

▶ Smile training is another popular fix with executives who want to do something quick and noticeable [to improve employee performance]. I use the term *smile training* to denote the style and intent of such training, not to disparage the general idea of training front-line people in service skills. Effective training almost always has a useful place in a major service initiative, but the key word is *effective*.

In effect, frontline employees *are* the company. Meaningful investments in their learning and development are really product development. Attention to employees' information needs, therefore, assures that the company is marketing the best product it is capable of producing. Smile training, by contrast, is condescending—it insults employees' intelligence by implying that smiles (or other "cosmetic" approaches) are an acceptable substitute for sincere attention and caring.

Having distinguished social instruction and so-called smile training from skills education, we turn to what we believe is an appropriate curriculum for new hires in commercial property management positions. First, new employees need to know how they fit with the organization. They also need to understand the company's goals, strategies, objectives, and philosophy—the corporate vision. (These are addressed in chapter 7.) We call this phase of learning "acculturation." Jeffrey Disend, author of *How to Provide Excellent Service in Any Organization,* described it this way:

▶ The first phase [of employee training] is a general orientation to the organization. This orientation covers who you are and what you do; your history, traditions, and values; how you're organized and where you're located; who your customers are; how you do business; your goals and mission; your products and services; and your industry and your competition.

In addition, the new employee needs basic administrative facts about the new company that will allow him or her to function properly—work schedules, pay dates, insurance information, etc.

We mentioned so-called smile training earlier and cautioned against its use, mostly because it is trivial: It frequently degenerates into attempts to teach employees literally how to smile at customers. While the goal of such training—helping frontline employees deal effectively with customers—is laudable, the methodology is demeaning. What is really needed is an ability to solve problems and delight the customer in the process.

On the other hand, no matter how personable new employees are, we believe that some instruction in how to achieve good tenant relations is imperative, even if it is refresher work and even though the content may be "soft." In this phase of employee indoctrination, the new hire not only learns the skills that will facilitate productive relations with tenants and their personnel, but also—and perhaps more important—discovers that the company places a premium on positive dealings with its clients. Here are some subjects we recommend be included:

- Telephone techniques

- Listening and responsive communications skills

- Handling people who are upset (i.e., tenants' personnel)

- Ways to establish credibility and trust in interactions

- Determining the expectations of tenants and their employees

Notice that nowhere in this curriculum for the first stage of employee training is job-specific instruction mentioned. We believe that skills training should be reserved for a later phase. At the beginning, the organization needs to concentrate on impressing upon the new hire the fundamental importance of the customer to the business. According to Donald Libey:

▶ [The new employee needs to learn] the company's culture about customers and the importance of thinking of them as the [company's] primary asset . . . . Your objective for this portion of the training process should be the creation of a fully furnished customer advocate and customer ambassador for your company.

Libey has also admonished companies to:

▶ Begin looking at your training program from The Customer's point of view. Focus all of your training from the outside in, not from the inside out. And, most important, make sure that the people who are responsible for training at your company are the people who have spent the most time in direct customer contact.

At Urban Retail Properties Co., for example, management trainees are required to spend some time doing all jobs—clean restrooms, pull a security patrol, supervise snow removal through the night, perform maintenance tasks—so they understand what is expected of each employee in order to maintain service performance standards *above* the expectations of their tenants.

The next phase of new-hire training orients the employee to a specific work unit, which may be the management office at the property (or the management company's central office). This instruction includes how communications flow within the work unit and between that unit and the central office (or vice versa), how problems are resolved, how decisions are made, what behavior will be rewarded, and what behavior will be unacceptable.

Finally, in the last phase of employee training, job-specific instruction is highlighted. The new employee receives instruction in his or her position, including a review of job descriptions, standards, and responsibilities. The employee is taught how the job meshes with the mission of the organization, why it is important, and how its outputs (and errors) affect others. It is only during this phase that specific job skill training begins. This is also an opportunity for cross-training so staff members can effectively fill in as needed. For example, in many hotels when the registration desk is very busy, bellmen will check in guests so they do not have to wait.

Empowering Your Company's "Quality Strategists" to Let the Tenant Win

Quality hiring and training is designed to prepare new employees to represent you to the market, in effect to *be* your company for your tenants and their people. You want new employees to be effective in their work, but what does it mean to "be effective?" We believe that, for the firms of the future, employees' effectiveness will increasingly be measured by whether they serve as "quality strategists" for the companies that hire them. All of the hands-on attention during the hiring and training process—as we have described it here—creates employees who are *empowered* to devise ways of delighting your internal and external clients, to take risks on behalf of your customers—the tenants of your properties. In short, the future rallying cry in commercial real estate management will be, "Let the Tenant Win!"

"Let the Tenant Win!" is the contemporary version of "user-friendly," a term used extensively to gauge the ease of using computers and other consumer products. (The discipline of *ergonomics* was an outgrowth of that concept; we will discuss "customer ergonomics" in chapter 9.) What we are talking about is devising strategies to make real estate management companies and their commercial properties user-friendly. One such strategy is to empower frontline personnel to act independently as all-around, autonomous, customer-pleasing company ambassadors.

Empowering Employees to Be "Boss Surrogates."   What does it mean to say that an employee is "empowered?" Why should you go through an exhaustive recruiting and training process for the purpose of producing "empowered" employees? Employees are "empowered" when they are boss-surrogates—people who act as though they own the business—they take responsibility; they have the authority to make on-the-spot decisions. The empowerment process visibly removes any shackles, real or imagined, that an employee might have felt impeded the fulfillment of a customer's needs or wishes. In *Delivering Quality Service: Balancing Customer Perceptions and Expectations,* Zeithaml and co-workers described the hiring-training-empowerment loop this way:

▶ Managers have to give back to service providers the freedom to serve that they have unnecessarily and unproductively taken away from them. Managers have to select their people well, provide them with a strong foundational culture in which to work, offer them strategic direction, and equip them with the company-specific skills and knowledge they need to perform their roles. *And then the managers need to get out of the way, so the people can get the job done.* Managers cannot make the transition to leadership as long as employees are so bundled in red tape that they cannot follow the lead.

According to Disend, the message from managers to employees who have been empowered is essentially this:

▶ You can only control what *you* do, so you must act at all times as if you are the *only one* in the organization who can help customers. In everything you do, especially when dealing with customers, assume that no one else in the organization is available at that moment to help the customer. You have to do what is right for the customer and what is best for the company. You're *it*. It's your responsibility.

Empowering Employees to Deliver Matchless "Moments of Truth."   Companies empower employees for several reasons. The main reason is that *empowerment is unavoidable:* The owner cannot be everywhere at once. In the real estate management business, it is physically impossible for an owner—or a management company, for that matter—to be present simultaneously at all of the points of contact between tenants and their personnel and the property and the management staff. A porter busily vacuuming hallways and chatting with someone about plans to remodel the elevator cabs; a maintenance technician adjusting thermostats to resolve an

HVAC problem or helping a new office tenant with a move-in detail (e.g., hanging pictures in the tenant's conference room); a marketing director talking on the telephone about an upcoming shopping center sidewalk sale; a leasing agent showing an industrial building to a prospect—all of these, in a thousand variations and permutations, are part of the everyday, day-after-day management and maintenance of commercial properties. The common characteristics of property management tasks are that they are conducted simultaneously; they require some degree of personal (tenant) contact; and, while they can be supervised, all of the activities at a property cannot be supervised on-the-spot by a single person.

Jan Carlzon recognized the challenges and importance of these customer-contact interludes. In his opinion, moments of truth determine whether a company will succeed or fail. Moments of truth between employees and customers are the line of scrimmage for amusement parks as well as airlines—and for office buildings, shopping centers, and industrial sites. Rick Johnson, manager of business seminars for Walt Disney World, believes that every aspect of an organization is on the line whenever frontline people deal with customers. However, it was Carlzon who proposed the solution to the puzzle of how to ensure that SAS' "moments of truth" could be instilled with quality, even though he could not be physically present at each point of delivery. His approach? Place responsibility for ideas, decisions, and actions with the frontline employees.

"Zapping" Your Employees.   Jan Carlzon's legacy to business management is enormous. The core of it, in addition to the "moments of truth" nomenclature already noted, is that the inspiration for empowering employees—which, as we have noted, is inescapable—lies in the leadership of the company, specifically leadership that is ready to embrace change and take risks. As Carlzon described the situation:

▶   The top executive . . . must communicate with his employees, imparting the company's vision and listening to what they need to make that vision a reality.

Empowerment, then, is born of necessity and imparted by visionaries. Yet, while delegation of authority is fated, it is also desirable. The second reason for empowering employees is that their job satisfaction and productivity soar, and the company reaps the benefits, not just in improved employee morale and performance, but in reduced tenant defections caused by poor service and mechanical reliance on company policies and procedures (i.e., rulebooks) for decisions. (Rules are the focus of a later discussion in this chapter.)

One of the most popular, albeit improbable, nonfiction best-sellers in recent years is a slim paperback book titled, *Zapp!® The Lightning of Empowerment: How to Improve Quality, Productivity, and Employee Satisfaction.* Written in the form of a fable, *Zapp!* recounts the adventures of one Joe

Mode, a supervisor in a fictional business whose department is beset by escalating demands on the part of his boss, his owners, and his customers, while the company itself is trying to fend off increasingly effective competition. The solution to all of these problems—not surprisingly, in light of the book's title—is employee empowerment, the state of being *Zapped.*

Prior to initiating the empowerment effort, Joe Mode's company had experimented with pep talks, quality circles, higher pay, participative management, job enrichment, quality of work life, work teams, suggestion systems, and a host of other approaches, all to little effect. In the notebook he kept, Joe listed what was wrong with his company:

▶ • Hardly anybody gets excited about anything that has to do with work.

- The things [employees] do get excited about are outside of work.

- My people care about their paychecks, their vacations, and their pensions. Beyond that, forget it.

- The general attitude is: Don't do anything you don't have to do. Then do as little as possible.

- All day, it's like everybody is in slow motion—until it's time to go home. Then it's like watching a videotape in fast forward.

- I talk about doing a better job and what happens? Lots of blank looks.

- Nobody takes any more responsibility than they have to. If the jobs don't get done, it's my problem, not theirs.

- Everybody just does enough to get by so they won't get yelled at or get fired.

- Nobody cares about improvements; they're all afraid of change. (Me, too, if I'm honest about it.)

- I say, "If you don't shape up you won't have jobs." But all that does is demoralize them, which makes it worse.

- Whenever I try to motivate people, the results (if any) are short-lived.

We have described Joe Mode's predicament in such detail, not only because it typifies the state of much of real estate management—and American business generally—but also because the post-empowerment situation is such an improvement. (The importance of leadership will be elaborated in chapter 7.)

Job Satisfaction and Reducing Employee—and Tenant—Turnover. The satisfaction of frontline employees is at least as important in the management of commercial real estate as in traditional retailing. We believe that "burnout"—the state of emotional fatigue caused by repetitive job tasks and incessant customer contact—leads to dissatisfaction and resignations and is a direct cause of employee (internal customer) turnover.

The latter component of burnout—what psychologists have identified as the "contact-overload syndrome" and what service commentators describe as "emotional labor"—can contaminate the quality of the moments of truth that employees have with tenants and their personnel. Employees who are angry, apathetic, or withdrawn transfer these feelings to tenants and create a negative impression of themselves, their properties, and their companies—a direct and avoidable cause of tenant (external customer) turnover.

Dealing with "Contact Overload."   What are the antidotes, if any, to contact overload? We believe there are several. One, of course, is initial instruction in such "soft" subjects as listening (skill development), telephone techniques, handling upset customers, and the like. Zeithaml et al. described the significance of this component of training this way:

▶ Companies can engender confidence in employees by training them in the skills needed to satisfy customers. Training that relates to the specific services offered by the firm helps the contact person be and feel capable when dealing with customers. Training in communication skills, especially in listening to customers and understanding what customers expect, gives employees a sense of mastery over the inevitable problems that arise in service encounters.

Another technique, which we discussed in chapter 2, is to ensure that frontline employees have the resources of the company, whether financial, personnel, or administrative, available when needed. We might describe these as internal employee support systems. As Jeffrey Disend has characterized the situation, when frontline people know they have support within the organization, they can act with confidence and will be less stressed. Clearly, the essential vaccine against contact overload is employee empowerment. According to Disend:

▶ Employees are superstars whose talent is waiting to be unleashed. They can do anything and everything—set standards, check quality, manage budgets, train. Employees can be trusted if they feel important and responsible. The people closest to the customer—the front line—can and should have the freedom to make decisions on the spot about how to satisfy customers. Their decisions are supported by management. Rules and practices that demean people or hinder their ability to serve the customer are eliminated.

Employee Empowerment in the Management of Commercial Real Estate.   How do real estate managers go about the process of empowering

"Firing" Customers: The Pareto Principle

An early twentieth-century Italian economist, one Vilfredo Pareto, formulated what is known as the "80–20 rule" or the "law of mal-distribution." The Pareto Principle hypothesizes that as much as 80 percent of the effort expended in a process is caused by as little as 20 percent of the input. Pareto's insight has led others to extrapolate from the principle, concluding, for instance, that 80 percent of a result—a firm's sales, for example—are produced by 20 percent of another driving force—in this situation, a particular segment of the company's product line.

The Pareto Principle has significant potential for American businesses in general. An analyst might observe that a particular one-fifth of a firm's goods draws four-fifths of company resources, and this knowledge leads the business to revamp its product line. Marketing personnel might note that approximately 80 percent of purchases in any one year are made by fewer than 20 percent of customers. As a consequence, they could recommend that the bulk of the firm's customer relations campaign be redirected to those few clients who are vital to success, with less attention paid to their many other clients, each of whom has only a modest impact on the company's profitability.

The extent to which this principle can be seen in the management of commercial real estate will vary. At the very least, it may be apparent at large office buildings, shopping centers, or industrial sites, where there are large numbers—perhaps hundreds—of tenants, and wide ranges of space needs and business uses are represented. In such situations, it is possible that only 20 percent of the tenants may be the source of 80 percent of the property's rental revenues. Certainly in researching the target market of prospective tenants for these properties, leasing agents will try to find the best match between a tenant use and a particular space, or they will look for a business use that compliments an existing tenant mix in order to optimize the established ratio and maintain the income stream.

Apart from the revenue aspect, we believe that a slightly modified Pareto Principle is operative in commercial real estate management as well. Stated succinctly, we believe that a very few tenants—probably no more than 3 percent—are likely to consume perhaps as much as 95 percent of the "emotional labor" a property management team has available. By emotional labor, we

---

their employees? One starting point is to consider techniques for empowering both "internal" customers and "external" customers simultaneously. As we noted earlier in this chapter, "Let the Tenant Win!" will increasingly be the motto of the real estate management firms of the future. One purpose of empowerment, therefore, should be to enable your internal customers to use their imaginations to solve the problems brought to them by your external customers. Here is an example: One constant in real estate management is

"Firing" Customers *(continued)*

mean the effort expended by frontline personnel to meet the service expectations of tenants and their personnel. Because this work has a significant emotional—as well as physical—component, those who perform it are subject to a substantial amount of stress. Berry and Parasuraman have described the problem very succinctly:

▶ The morale, job satisfaction, and job commitment of front-line service employees are inversely related to the frustration levels of customers they deal with day after day. Interacting with frustrated customers demanding explanations and restitution for defective services can demoralize employees, deflate their enthusiasm for their jobs, and decrease their commitment to their companies.

Psychologists have characterized this reaction as the "contact-overload syndrome"—akin to job "burnout"—which, in turn, is responsible for so much obnoxious behavior that frontline personnel display to their customers. As Karl Albrecht put it:

▶ The person we're tempted to describe as lazy, indifferent, uncaring, and not qualified for a service job may actually be in the advanced stages of burnout because of contact overload. In other words, a great deal of negative behavior on the part of frontline service people is *normal behavior.* That doesn't mean we have to approve of it or consider it acceptable, but it does mean we need to understand it and deal with it in human and humane terms.

Company management's ability to recognize this syndrome, together with its willingness to take effective action to remedy the problem, demonstrates the firm's support for its own internal customers. In their book, Berry and Parasuraman observed that:

▶ Companies should make a concerted effort to explore ways for assisting their service-recovery staff to relieve tension. Courses on coping with stress, group meeting with peers to discuss job-related pressures, and facilities for physical exercise are some of the possibilities. Providing customer service personnel with a pleasant and soothing work environment also will be helpful.

We believe that frontline management personnel at commercial properties are especially prone to contact overload. Their work day, unlike those of retailers and other service providers, does not necessarily end at 5:00 P.M. Indeed, the work "day" for the on-site management team may be only *starting—precisely because* their tenants' business day has ended. The ordinary custodial maintenance—the work done by the janitorial crew—typically requires only minimal personal contact with tenants' employees who may view janitorial workers, and their work, as intrusive. However, work-

"Firing" Customers *(continued)*

load demands with budget preparation, escalation billings and emergency service calls contribute to this contact overload. Other management team members' contacts with tenants' personnel— explaining property operating expense pass-throughs and escalation billings, handling emergencies—are potentially infinite in number and indefinite in duration.

Because contact overload is commonplace in commercial real estate management, and because we agree with Albrecht that it is appropriate for owners and managers to take action to reduce its impact on their personnel, we recommend that an owner or property manager consider "firing" those few tenants whose demands are so overwhelming and unreasonable as to cause burnout among the members of the on-site management team. "Firing" in this instance, of course, involves notifying the tenant of the decision not to renew its lease, in accordance with the notice provisions of the lease document (and applicable law).

This is a risky concept, yet one that, in our opinion, deserves consideration. We have found that when the demands of one tenant—or a few tenants—are overwhelming and unreasonable, it can be exceedingly difficult, not only to satisfy their needs, but also to provide an acceptable level of service to the other tenants. In effect, the toxins that accumulate when servers try unsuccessfully to meet the exorbitant requirements of a handful of demanding individuals spill over and contaminate their dealings with the vast majority of reasonable ones. This is, perhaps, the clearest application of the Pareto Principle in the management of commercial real estate.

The following are some hypothetical examples of what we mean. They represent the kinds of tenant expectations that are impossible in a practical sense to satisfy.

A telephone call to the building management office—after midnight—demanding that someone rush to a tenant's office to fix an HVAC problem that is hindering a major, round-the-clock project in progress.

A maintenance technician who is working on an emergency involving the fire alarm system being approached by a tenant who insists that the technician install some long-awaited door signage immediately.

A tenant's chief accountant who, without notice, demands immediate access to the management company's accounting records so she can audit the CAM billing her employer just received.

Each of these kinds of situations is typical of a tenant-imposed requirement of immediacy, based on a presumptive emergency occurring at a time when there is no one available to respond to it or when the management employee's other duties justifiably deserve

"Firing" Customers *(concluded)*

priority. Because they are usually the culminating event in a sequence of similar episodes, they cause an inordinate amount of stress. As Albrecht noted in *At America's Service*:

▶ A person can handle just so many of these miniature emotional events in a given period before he or she begins to feel tense, overloaded, tired, and jaded. . . . [The contact-overload syndrome] is unhealthy for the person having it. It can induce psychological stress that can carry over into his or her personal life as well as make work life unpleasant and unrewarding.

Although "firing" a tenant should be an absolute last resort, it should not be ignored as an option. Because of the very real costs (dollar losses) that can result—especially if you are competing for tenants in an overbuilt market—you should explore every avenue for overcoming the situation. While it may not seem so, a particular business can be very important to the overall tenant mix at a property. Only when other (less extreme) measures, such as telephone calls and meetings with the tenant's people, have failed to produce results should a tenant be fired.

The fact is, the personnel who represent certain tenants may have service requirements that are so outlandish and unreasonable that reasonable people, even people accustomed to working in labor-intensive, high-stress environments, cannot satisfy them. In these circumstances, we believe property owners and real estate managers should consider the needs of their other customers—internal and external—and elect to discontinue those unfortunate business relationships that are continually problematic.

[NOTE: The decision to "fire" a tenant should not be taken lightly. You must be certain that the problem originated with the tenant's people—i.e., that you are not being given a wrong impression by your team members in order to cover up poor performance by the management staff. Given that commercial tenants are represented in varying degrees by their employees, from hourly wage-earners to salaried executives, it is incumbent on the real estate manager to explore every avenue to resolving the problem of a particularly demanding tenant.

Unlike a similar situation with a residential tenant, where there is a potential for a claim of personal discrimination, the long duration of commercial leases, considerations of tenant mix, and potential economic impact on the property as a whole weigh heavily in favor of a cautious approach. Careful review of the particulars of the tenant's lease is imperative, and advice of legal counsel should be sought. Of particular concern is the potential for the manager's actions to be interpreted as discriminatory (e.g., if the tenant is a minority-owned business) or as a violation of the tenant's rights under applicable landlord-tenant law.]

the inevitable breakdown or malfunctioning of equipment. Coin-operated vending machines are a particular source of frustration, and property managers typically learn about such equipment failures only when some person (a tenant's employee or customer) lets them know about the problem. We will return to the subject of *planning* for the inevitable equipment breakdown in chapter 6. (Service "recovery" is a way of providing structure to employee empowerment.) For now, we will consider some alternatives that are available to the manager confronted by a frustrated individual—call him Sam—who has fed a fistful of coins into a vending machine without success. Consider these responses:

> "I'm sorry. I know how you feel, but I'm afraid I can't help you. We've been having a lot of problems with that machine. You see, it's serviced by a vending company. It's their company policy to have you fill out this claim form and they'll reimburse you directly."

> "I'm really sorry; I hate it when that happens to me. And it always seems to happen when you really want a snack or a cold drink, doesn't it? Let me try to make it up to you," as she hands Sam two dollars. "Why don't you sit down for a few minutes while I call the vending company? I need to get this problem taken care of right away."

> "I feel really badly that you lost your money; I'll give the vending company a call immediately. But what can I do to make up for your inconvenience?"

Note that in all of these vignettes, the manager was sincerely apologetic about Sam's frustration and wanted to do something to compensate for it. In the first instance, "vending company policy" prevented the manager from providing immediate satisfaction; and the "solution" that was offered instead—completing a claim form and trusting the vending company to provide compensation—would undoubtedly be unsatisfactory to Sam, escalating his dissatisfaction and possibly resulting in a truly unpleasant experience for both of them. This would constitute both a negative "moment of truth" for Sam and an instance of "contact overload" for the manager. Both could easily have been circumvented by empowering the manager to act independently of the rulebook.

In the second situation, the manager has the freedom to settle the problem on the spot. The disparity between the amount of the loss and the amount offered—probably at least a dollar—is an effort to account for the so-called "hassle factor" related to Sam's experience.

In the third situation, the manager is not only empowered to solve the problem immediately, but also to *involve Sam in the solution*. Hervey Feldman, president of Embassy Suites hotels, prefers resolutions of customer problems that involve the guests themselves:

▶ We let customers adjust their own grievances. We ask for their opinion of what it will take to make things right, and if they can't think of anything, we often refund the room charge. . . . Employees and hotel managers learn about the adjustments we've made after the fact, and that may irritate them, but I really don't care about who's right. The customer is *always* right. Explanations, excuses, and alibis don't cut it.

In an article in the *Harvard Business Review,* Christopher Hart, James Heskett, and W. Earl Sasser, Jr., reported the following from their own studies:

▶ More than half of all efforts to respond to customer complaints actually reinforce negative reactions to service. The surest way to recover from service mishaps is for workers on the front line to identify and solve the customer's problem. Doing so requires decision making and rule breaking—exactly what employees have been conditioned against . . . even if they'd like to help the customer, they are frustrated by the fact that they are not allowed to do it.

Most often, the company is the source of this frustration. Karl Albrecht has said as much:

▶ Employees, for the most part, want to a do a good job; they want to give good service to their customers. If they're not doing it, more than likely something is standing in their way, and more than likely it's the organization. It's up to management to create the conditions that make service excellence possible and worthwhile. Employees will come through.

The Illusory Risk of Oversatisfying Customers.   The notion that employees should be empowered to use their imaginations rather than company guidelines to solve customers' problems, to make instantaneous decisions at the front lines without the benefit of supervision, is unsettling to some. One concern is that employees will go overboard on behalf of customers. However, Jan Carlzon has provided a common-sense answer to this:

▶ What's the danger of [employees'] giving away too much? Are you worried about having an oversatisfied customer? That's not much of a worry. You can forget about an oversatisfied customer, but an unsatisfied customer is one of the most expensive problems you can have. [The] danger is not that employees will give away too much. It's that they won't give away anything—because they don't dare.

Colorful Rules and Regulations.   Empowering employees to satisfy customers requires a company to be a "learning organization" in order to adjust to changing circumstances. Michael Beer, Russell Eisenstat, and Bert

Spector, a group of organizational behavior and management professors, put it this way:

▶ Create an asset that did not exist before—a learning organization capable of adapting to a changing competitive environment. The organization has to know how to continually monitor its behavior—in effect, to learn how to learn.

This means the firms of the future will have to "get out of the way" and allow customers—both internal and external—to work cooperatively to resolve problems. These companies will have to strive as well to liberate their customers from unnecessary regimentation. Here's an example: Commercial leases, in addition to listing the names of the landlord and the tenant(s) and specifying the lease terms, typically contain rules and regulations which are intended to protect the property and the rights of other tenants. The need for these protections—for both parties—is real. Commercial leases represent major dollars to both sides, and the omission of specific safeguards creates potential liabilities (and opportunities for lawsuits). We wonder, however, if it is always necessary to express the requirements in such harsh terms. The language of some commercial lease provisions is often brief, blunt, and somewhat brutal. The following are examples of what we mean:

ALTERATIONS OF LEASED PREMISES: Tenant shall not be allowed to make alterations to the demised premises without Landlord's express written permission. At the discretion of the Landlord, any additional improvements approved by Landlord must be removed by tenant prior to lease termination.

ASSIGNMENT AND SUBLETTING. Tenant shall not sublet or otherwise assign the demised premises without Landlord's written permission. If Tenant requests Landlord approval of a sublease or assignment agreement, the documentation shall be prepared according to such terms as Landlord determines.

These types of clauses are fairly typical. The first is designed to allow the landlord to control any additional improvements to the leased space and protect the integrity of the building. The second restricts a tenant's ability to assign or sublet the leased space independently and thereby leave the owner with a potentially unsatisfactory successor. In effect, by stating these lease provisions in such an emphatic, negative way, real estate managers are treating the overwhelming majority of tenants like potential offenders in order to catch the very small number who really *are* offenders. Worse, the impression conveyed to your customers by including this sort of language in your leases is unnecessarily harsh. In effect, you are telling your tenants at the outset of your business relationship that you predict they will not comply with their leases. On the other hand, addition to the alterations and assignment clauses of a balancing statement—e.g.: Landlord shall not unreasonably withhold or delay approval—would, in our opinion, "soften" the language somewhat by simply stating that the tenant is entitled to timely notification of the landlord's decision.

In fact, service commentators condemn such negative language. For example, Peter Glen is striving to create a generation of service "guerrillas" who will demand to be served in accordance with their own unique preferences. (His motto is: Tell 'em what you want, and how you want it, and make 'em do it, just that way!) As he put it:

▶ Doesn't it lift your heart when you show up at the front door of the store and signs greet you saying, NO FOOD, NO DRINKS, NO TANK TOPS, NO EXCHANGES, NO RETURNS, NO STROLLERS, NO BARE FEET, NO SMOKING or NO SHIRT, NO SHOES, NO SERVICE? *Welcome to the store!*

Also according to Glen, "Bad signs are any signs that depress the customer. Bad signs are bad service."

Everyone would agree that some rules and regulations are essential tools for real estate managers. The rent-payment requirement, for example, is absolutely necessary—if managers fail to enforce it, the property will be bankrupted. There are some other "requirements" as well:

- Rules regulating the storage and handling of flammable materials in stores (or offices) are necessary to ensure the safety of workers and customers alike.

- Regulations that deter office tenants from installing their own locks are indispensable because law enforcement and emergency services personnel may need access to their leased premises.

- Regulations regarding the reporting of accidents and/or defects in equipment are needed to minimize liability as well as prevent damage to the equipment, the demised premises, and the building.

These examples are representative of the relatively few rules and regulations that are in place to prevent injury to people or damage to the landlord's or the tenant's property—most of them are prescribed by local fire codes or other laws. Such rules cannot be broken, and real estate managers would be considered negligent if they failed to enforce them. These types of rules might be referred to as "red" rules. Conversely, there are other rules that exist for the convenience of the landlord, the site employees, or the management company; these can be called "blue" rules.

The lease clause regarding store "signage" is another example. Typically, the lease sets limits on the dimensions, content, and artistic presentation as well as the placement of signs identifying the store. Landlords establish these kinds of limitations within the lease because they represent a desirable means of controlling the overall appearance of the property. However, apart from structural considerations (the ability of a wall to support signage, potential damage to an exterior finish) and the need to comply with local ordinances that regulate signage size and placement, which most people will understand, the issues of graphic display and size are likely to be considered restrictive by a prospective retail tenant. Also from the tenant's perspective, such a signage clause may seem to limit the store's ability to compete. In this case, the landlord's concern would seem to be a matter of taste, the tenant's one of visibility—and the question remains: How can signage criteria (specifications) be worded effectively without creating (or implying) restrictions on the tenant's ability to compete in the marketplace? To paraphrase Peter Glen, in this instance, "bad lease clauses are bad service."

The question for the real estate manager is identical to the one to be considered by the retailer: Which rules are clearly "red" ones, and which are "blue?" Then, are the blue rules really necessary, or do they exist "because we've always done it this way?" Alternatively, can the same goals be achieved in ways that are more customer-friendly?

We recommend that you keep in mind certain complementary guidelines propounded by the service gurus as you cull the red rules from the blue and decide whether to keep the blue ones in place. Anderson and Zemke have cautioned against thoughtlessly discarding rules:

▶ Without formal and informal rules, service would become chaotic— and customers would never know what to expect. Just because you think that breaking or bending a rule won't cause the ceiling to fall down doesn't mean you should take it lightly. Know the nature of the rule in question, the reason for the rule, the consequences of not following it, then help your customer make the system work.

On the other hand, A. S. Neill has recommended activism in making these decisions:

▶ Think of your role as that of a release valve, not that of a restraining force. We need more green flags and less yellow; more rivers and less dams.

The goal of real estate managers, then, should not be to discard the rulebook or eliminate all policies and procedures but, rather, to thin the rulebook to its bare essentials in order to eliminate as much as possible the barriers between themselves and their customers. (This includes working with legal counsel to develop a more user-friendly, customer service-oriented—yet legally enforceable—lease that complies with all applicable laws.) *Empowering your people makes the necessary rules work for a company's external customers as well as its internal ones.*

The Retention Revolution

Customer Type	Marketing Effort	Value to Marketers	Cost of Programs
New customers (acquisition programs)	High	Low	High
Current customers (retention programs)	Moderate	High	Moderate
Current customers (expansion programs)	Low	Moderate	Low

—KEVIN J. CLANCY and ROBERT S. SHULMAN, *The Marketing Revolution*

Clancy and Shulman, former principals of Yankelovich Clancy Shulman (an international marketing research and consulting firm), call these marketing alternatives the "Death Wish Paradox." It illustrates the point that the relentless pursuit of new customers is the most expensive and labor-intensive, yet least cost-effective, strategy a company can pursue. Conversely, the practice of marketing to a company's current customers, either in an effort to retain them or to induce them to expand the business they are currently doing, results in the greatest yield.

The Fallacy of Conquest Marketing

"Conquest" or "acquisition" marketing has been and continues to be a centerpiece of American business. Expansion of a company's client base by luring first-time customers or a competitor's clientele is both a staple of retailing and the overriding goal of traditional advertising and marketing. Consider these facts:

- During the period 1960 to 1990, U.S. advertising expenditures increased more than tenfold, from slightly less than $12 billion annually to nearly $130 billion.

- Between 1965 and 1991, the cost of a 30-second television spot rose from $19,700 to $106,400.

- In 1989, the top 100 advertisers spent a combined $34 billion on advertising—an average of $340 million each.

- From 1984 to 1991, the number of television advertising vehicles increased to an annual volume of more than 300,000 commercials.

There has been an explosion in the number and types of advertising media. During the last decade or so, consumers have witnessed the debut of cable TV and the proprietary television program (the "infomercial"); videocassette sponsorships; specialized television networks in schools, airports, restaurants, supermarkets and the like; sponsored sporting events and even sports arenas; as well as targeted direct mail, outward and inward telemarketing, and a swarm of others.

The temptations of this cornucopia of seductive media are almost irresistible, no less so for those who market office or store space than for those who deal directly with consumers. Their applications for the commercial real estate environment are apparent and alluring. Managers of commercial properties are constrained only by their budgets and their imaginations—and, hopefully, common sense.

The commercial real estate environment—its ethos, its very *culture*—validates conquest marketing and all it entails. Marketing is one of the few discretionary expenditures that even the spendthrift property owner or real estate manager strives to protect or perhaps augment. When occupancies lag, real estate managers are pressured to root out new tenants and to free up whatever funds are deemed necessary to launch new advertising adventures to entice them. Bonus structures and commission schedules are crafted specifically and exclusively to reward leasing velocity. Disagreements, disputes, and confrontations among leasing personnel over entitlements to bonuses are commonplace. Reporting formats that display closing ratios or conversion rates—relating marketing efforts (and dollars spent) to numbers of prospects and signed leases—distract attention from other, more valid, gauges of a property's success. Especially disturbing is the tendency to offer the best deals to prospects: New office tenants, for example, may reap the benefit of a totally renovated leased space with a custom interior finish and new carpeting, while current tenants are expected to pay top rates and swallow hefty rent escalations with little or no improvement to their existing space being offered during a multiple-year lease term. At a shopping center, prospects might be offered landlord-paid build-out of their leased space while established tenants will have paid for their own. At an industrial property, the negotiated rent and improvement allowances might be similarly varied. Differing definitions of net leases, and varied approaches to common area maintenance pass-throughs and rent escalations—in shopping centers, there are also percentage rent and merchants' association or marketing fund payments to consider—complicate the marketing and leasing of commercial space in the first place and retention of individual commercial tenants later on. Indeed, the main business of a large real estate firm with a varied portfolio of commercial properties—sometimes even its *exclusive* business—seems to be to snare new customers. Clancy and Shulman put it this way:

▶ Surprisingly, there seems to be a sense in marketing that finding and closing new customers (acquisition programs) are more exciting than holding on to current customers (retention programs) or increasing business volume among current customers (expansion programs).

In this chapter, we will examine the conquest marketing mentality—to see how it holds up under scrutiny—and suggest some alternatives that might supplant it. Exhibit 4.1 presents a straightforward comparison of turnover costs versus retention costs for a hypothetical office tenant.

The Costs of Tenant Turnover

One of the principal challenges to real estate managers is to find opportunities to control the financial performance of the properties in their portfolios. So many of the major expenses—utilities, for instance, as well as property taxes, insurance, and repair and replacement costs—continue to increase year after year, surging upward to engulf whatever modest gains may have been realized by instituting rent increases or reining in maintenance costs or capital expenditures. The business of real estate management in these circumstances is mostly *reactive*—comparing the performances of buildings to budgetary forecasts, responding to tenants' complaints, repairing outdated capital equipment. Property management can be a lifeless business indeed when the imaginations of its practitioners are so confined.

Nonetheless, there are significant opportunities for a commercial property manager to be *proactive*. An accurate Tenant Turnover Analysis (exhibit 4.1) will quantify a number of costs whose magnitude you may not be aware of, yet ones that a skillful manager *can* affect. The data needed to construct such an analysis—tenant finish allowances, rent concessions, rental rates and lease terms—are easily captured from individual leases or lease summaries or from various financial reports. A thorough analysis will illustrate, first, the cost in dollars of losing a particular tenant and, second, a close estimate of the cost of incentives that could be offered in an effective tenant retention program.

Exhibit 4.1
The Cost of Tenant Turnover

Consider a tenant who occupies 8,000 useable square feet of office space at $15.50 per square foot per year (based on 9,200 rentable square feet) and whose lease expires in nine (9) months. Because problems with the HVAC system have contributed to poor relations with this tenant's personnel, it is questionable whether the tenant will renew the lease. Current market conditions have stabilized under the following terms:

Lease Term:	36 months
Rental Rate:	$17.00/sq ft (rentable)
Common Area Factor:	15%
Finish Allowance:	$12.00/sq ft for a total remodel; $3.00/sq ft for a renewal—based on useable square feet
Moving Allowance:	$2.00/sq ft (useable)
Time to Re-Lease:	6 months
Leasing Commission:	$1.15/sq ft for new leases and $0.38/sq ft for renewals—based on rentable square feet and the full term of the lease

Using these data, the following comparison can be made:

	Cost to Keep Tenant	Cost of New Tenant
Lost Rent @ 6 Months	—	78,200
Finish Allowance	24,000	96,000
Moving Allowance	—	16,000
Leasing Commission	10,488	31,740
Total Cost	$34,488	$221,940

Incremental Cost of Losing this Tenant $187,452

It would cost nearly *six and one-half times as much* to acquire a new tenant as it would to retain the current one ($221,940 ÷ $34,488 = 6.44).

The distinction between rentable and useable square feet is an important one because of its impact on the dollars involved. In this example, the area on which the rent and the leasing commission are calculated (rentable area) is 1,200 square feet larger than the basis for calculating finish and moving allowances. The difference is the 15% common area (or load) factor.

There are likely to be some surprises in store when your analysis is completed. First, you will have a heightened appreciation of the economic value each of your tenants adds to the properties you manage. Sharing this information with your management team may prompt all of you to be more attentive to your tenants, more responsive to their people's concerns, and even more creative in dreaming up imaginative ways to delight them. Second, you will be able to quantify—and properly categorize—the costs to the property of lost business with current tenants. This latter aspect may persuade you to create an aggressive tenant retention program and then allocate to it the financial resources that your analysis has demonstrated it deserves.

What are the lessons to be learned from this type of analysis? First of all, the incremental cost of losing and replacing a tenant is significant when consideration is given to the many costs associated with tenant turnover. While these costs are readily identifiable, their magnitude may be camouflaged because they are likely to be spread innocuously among various income and expense categories. In exhibit 4.1, the $187,452 incremental cost of losing one tenant is based on a fairly typical office size. This detailed analysis emphasizes the significance of the loss incurred as a result of poor tenant relations associated with ineffective maintenance.

Second, the analysis reveals how important tenant retention is compared to the tremendous costs of tenant turnover. Out of a total of 100 office tenants, only a handful might move out in a given year, but the loss of only three tenants who occupied comparable square footages would cost more than half a million dollars ($187,452 × 3 = $562,356); loss of any tenants who occupy larger spaces would add more than $23,000 per 1,000 useable square feet to the cost of losing a particular tenant ($187,452 ÷ 8 = $23,431.50/1,000 sq ft). If rents or other leasing parameters are higher in your area, the cost will be proportionately larger.

A landlord is much better off spending the resources to adequately service an existing tenant's occupancy needs and thereby minimize the costs associated with tenant turnover. Such expenditures may include tenant premises remodeling, carpet replacement, additional signage, and resolution of service problems. Incentives should also be evaluated: You might consider allowing a period of free rent at lease renewal to offset some of the tenant's remodeling costs, adjusting the base year to the current year for escalation purposes, and/or lowering the rent (to bring the rental rate in line with market rates) if that is necessary to retain the tenant.

The "Unavoidability" of Tenant Turnover.   Some would argue that tenant turnover is generally unavoidable: Temptingly low rental rates in an overbuilt market, often sweetened with generous tenant improvement allowances and a period of free rent, can be a strong lure, especially for businesses that need to accommodate corporate growth or company downsizing. Even though retail and office service tenants have a strong incentive to stay put—apart from the expense involved, they risk losing customers when they change locations, and long-distance moves add to employee turnover—such businesses are represented by people who can and do react personally to their encounters with building management and maintenance personnel. The underlying reason for tenants' leaving may well be dissatisfaction with the *quality* (or quantity) of the service they have been receiving.

As a point of comparison, it is interesting to look at statistics on the reasons why customers stop doing business with retailers. One survey concluded that customers stop buying because:

1% *die*

3% move away

5% form other relationships

9% leave for "competitive" reasons (e.g., price)

14% leave due to dissatisfaction with product [and]

68% leave *because someone—some representative of the seller— was rude, indifferent, or discourteous to them.*

These statistics underscore one striking fact that is fundamental to understanding why some companies—and not others—are successful: Price, whether high, low, or middling, is *not* a pivotal ingredient in most business relationships, although it may have been instrumental in their formation. Instead, the critical factor is the way sellers treat their customers. This *attitudinal* component of commercial affiliations—the seller's friendliness, reliability, and honesty, among a host of companionable traits—drives commercial prosperity. Sellers' attitudes, then, clearly influence customers' assessments of whether they have received *value* from the product they purchased commensurate with the *price* they paid for it. Indeed, when a customer feels that a vendor—or more likely, an agent of the vendor, such as a salesclerk—has been "rude, indifferent, or discourteous" at some point, the buyer feels *poorly served*. Rudeness, indifference, and discourtesy are characteristic of the negative "moments of truth" that poison commercial dealings. In our opinion, attitude is one of the ways that buyers measure the quality of the service they receive, and it is a determinant of the value of the product itself. The same can be said of management team interactions with the decision-makers who represent commercial tenants.

The Costs of Poor Service

Service researchers have discovered additional disturbing data that illustrate the instability of most buyer-seller relationships. Kristin Anderson and Ron Zemke described the phenomenon this way:

▶ As many as *one customer in four* is dissatisfied enough to start doing business with someone else—if he or she can find someone else who promises to do the same thing that you do but in a slightly more satisfying way.

In short, at any point along the consumption continuum, twenty-five percent of any business is undependable.

As if *that* bit of news is not frightening enough, pollsters have discovered

---

Exhibit 4.2
The Costs of Poor Service

Gross potential rent	$ _____		Line A
Total number of tenants	_____		Line B
Percentage of dissatisfied tenants	× _____	.25	Line C
Number of dissatisfied tenants (C × B)	= _____		Line D
Percentage of dissatisfied tenants apt to switch	× _____	.70	Line E
Number of dissatisfied tenants who are apt to switch	= _____		Line F
Average annual revenue per tenant (A ÷ B)	$ _____		Line G
Annual revenue at risk because of poor service (F × G)	$ _____		Line H

Adapted from *How to Provide Excellent Service in Any Organization: A Blueprint for Making All the Theories Work* by Jeffrey E. Disend (Radnor, Pennsylvania: Chilton Book Company, 1991), p. 74. Copyright 1991 by the author. Used with the permission of the publisher.

NOTE: Percentages are from the TARP report cited in the text (from Disend). This calculation, based on tenants, assumes comparability of leased areas and rental rates. In a commercial property where there are wide variations in office or store sizes and rental rates, the revenue at risk is likely to be understated by a substantial amount.

---

that perhaps as few as *four percent* of those disenchanted customers bother to communicate their discontent to their business partners. Instead, most of them—seventy percent is a conservative estimate—simply pack up their checkbooks and credit cards and take their business elsewhere. (Because these dealings are potentially fragile, chapter 5 will address techniques for smoking out customer complaints and converting them into ties that will bind buyers and sellers.)

Calculating the Costs of Poor Service in Commercial Real Estate Management. Assuming the same considerations that clinch success in other commercial enterprises operate in the real estate business, the same percentages can be used to calculate a property's revenue lost because of poor service to tenants using the formula shown in exhibit 4.2. The results of applying this formula to a hypothetical example—Sterling Tower—are shown in exhibit 4.3. These figures demonstrate the disastrous impact that an ineffective tenant retention program or a mistaken hiring decision—particularly one at the front line—can have on a property's bottom line. In a six-month period, for example, a surly property manager at Sterling Tower could cost the property nearly a quarter of a million dollars ($475,200 annual loss ÷ 2 = $237,600)—or more.

The Costs of Negative "Word-of-Mouth"

Additional data—what might be termed the "word-of-mouth" numbers—illustrate the power of negative personal recommendations and suggest how

Exhibit 4.3
Example of The Costs of Poor Service

Property Name: **Sterling Tower**
Size: **225,000 sq. ft.**

Total number of tenants in the property	34
Percentage of dissatisfied tenants	.25
Number of dissatisfied tenants	9
Percentage of dissatisfied tenants apt to switch	.70
Number of dissatisfied tenants who are apt to switch	6
Average annual revenue per tenant @ 6,600 sq ft × $12.00/sq ft	$79,200.00
Annual revenue at risk because of poor service	$475,200.00

NOTE: This calculation is based on comparable leased areas (225,000 sq ft ÷ 34 tenants = 6,617 sq ft). In most situations, leased premises are not equal in size, and rental rates may differ substantially based on tenants' individually negotiated leases. However, this does not alter the fact that *the loss of six tenants* at Sterling Tower represents nearly half a million dollars in lost rent ($79,200 annual rent × 6 tenants = $475,200)—almost one-fifth of the total annual gross potential rental income for the property is at risk ($79,200 × 34 tenants = $2,692,800; $475,200 ÷ $2,692,800 = 17.6%).

reputations are made—and lost. In a landmark study, the Technical Assistance Research Project (TARP) reported that, after retail customers stop doing business with a particular vendor—and as we have already shown, most do so because of one or more negative "moments of truth" that they have experienced—they eagerly share these episodes with others. According to the TARP report, the average dissatisfied customer tells eight to ten other people about his or her ordeal; fully *thirteen percent* of unhappy customers tell *twenty or more* people! Furthermore, even if they complain, and their complaint is resolved satisfactorily, it takes twelve *positive experiences* to correct for each bad one.

By applying the lessons from the TARP study, it is possible to measure the amount of revenue that is lost because of negative word of mouth. Exhibit 4.4 constitutes an extension of the calculation in exhibit 4.2, applying this same methodology to real estate. Exhibit 4.5 shows the number of potential tenants whose impressions of Sterling Tower are apt to be impacted by the negative word of mouth from representatives of former tenants who may have been disenchanted with the property, as well as the *potential lost revenue opportunity*—the dollars at risk—because of the same phenomenon. What is most frightening about the negative-word-of-mouth numbers is that you will never have an opportunity to do business with these potential tenants—they will have rejected you outright *before* you could invite them to see your property for themselves.

At a retail property, tenants' dissatisfaction with management or the services it provides is more likely to strain the landlord-tenant relationship, rather than result in wholesale tenant defections. In retailing, sales produc-

---

Exhibit 4.4
Costs of Negative Word of Mouth

Number of dissatisfied tenants who will switch (Line F)	_____	Line I
Number of potential tenants who rent elsewhere due to negative word of mouth, assuming the dissatisfaction of one tenant is imparted, on average, to eight others (Line I × 8)	_____	Line J
Potential lost revenue opportunity to the property caused by negative word of mouth (Line J × Line G)	_____	Line K

References are to exhibit 4.2.
Line F is the number of dissatisfied tenants apt to switch.
Line G is the average annual revenue per tenant.

NOTE: This calculation is an extension of the example in exhibit 4.2 and is similarly based on assumptions of equivalent leased areas and rental rates.

---

tivity is the prime motivator—if a store generates maximum sales volume and the location cannot be duplicated, the tenant will not close the store because of poor service or negative word of mouth. However, this does not mean dissatisfied tenants would not tell others—companies they do business with, including clients, competitors, and others who might be interested in leasing space at the property—about their unhappiness. The impact of negative word of mouth on prospective tenants is potentially devastating.

The Importance of Reducing Tenant Turnover.   Evidence that owners of investment real estate are becoming aware of the exorbitant costs of tenant turnover at their properties can be found in *Managing the Future: Real Estate in the 1990s,* a study commissioned by the Institute of Real Estate Management Foundation and conducted by the Arthur Andersen Real Estate Services Group. The study found that the chief concern of the major owners of U.S. real estate—among both interviewees and survey respondents—is "the space glut and what it means for the future. On a scale of one (high significance) to three (low significance), survey respondents scored vacancy at 1.24. . . . Tenant procurement, and especially tenant retention, are major concerns." The IREM Foundation report concluded that owners expect that the property manager of the future will have demonstrated skills in controlling tenant turnover:

▶ The dominant theme is tenant relations. Almost every interviewee said the most important tasks involve serving tenants. Most interviewees said retaining tenants is more important than obtaining them. While emphasizing that the entire real estate business is

Exhibit 4.5

Example of the Costs of Negative Word of Mouth

Number of dissatisfied tenants who will switch	6
Number of potential tenants who rent elsewhere due to negative word of mouth	48
Potential lost revenue opportunity to Sterling Tower—the dollars at risk because of negative word of mouth	$3,801,600.00

NOTE: This calculation assumes each of the six (6) tenants who would move out of Sterling Tower would influence the rental decisions of eight (8) other commercial entities (6 × 8), yielding a potential lost revenue opportunity of $3,801,600 (48 prospective tenants × $79,200 average annual revenue per tenant).

revenue-driven, [owners] regard retention as more efficient and less disruptive than continual, successful re-leasing.

Asked to rank 36 management tasks on a five-point scale (5 = very important; 1 = not important), survey respondents replied similarly:

▶ Tenant relations, with the greatest emphasis on tenant retention, takes top priority. In fact, the four top-rated tasks are all aspects of tenant relations. These include retaining tenants (4.59), negotiating leases (4.50), obtaining tenants (4.50) and handling tenant relations (4.39).

The lessons of the "Death Wish Paradox," the "Tenant Turnover Analysis," and the various techniques for calculating the costs of poor service to tenants and negative word of mouth, coupled with the admonitions to real estate managers contained in *Managing the Future,* make developing techniques for reducing tenant turnover an imperative for managers of commercial real estate. We suggest that there are several ways to do this. However, a preliminary step in this direction is consideration of the cost of losing customers as you develop your marketing budget.

Budgeting for Retention Marketing

The "Death Wish Paradox," so simple in concept, yet so profound in implication, deserves to be framed and placed in a prominent location in every marketer's office. Its relevance for the real estate manager is not diminished merely because such comparisons have been almost entirely overlooked in the commercial real estate business. Indeed, because the lessons of the paradox are generally yet to be learned, the trailblazing managers who do so will not only automatically ensure the success of their properties, but also achieve market leadership for their companies. Heady stuff, indeed!

If the expressway to market leadership requires vastly increased attention to current-customer marketing—what the service commentators call customer retention programs—it is vital to begin to allocate resources to the endeavor in a meaningful way. This means that the traditional leasing marketing budget, which has been the embodiment of acquisition or conquest marketing, needs to be overhauled. Here is what Laura Liswood has recommended:

▶ For starters, the marketing budget should be split into two categories: (1) dollars spent on acquiring customers, and (2) dollars spent on keeping customers. There will be some overlapping because the same dollar in any given case may serve both purposes. But it's important for marketers and senior management to quantify the two basic roles separately, both for practical budgeting purposes and to ensure that the customer-retention role is given due recognition.

Most savvy real estate managers know with great precision the costs attributable to attracting each prospect visit to the property—developing contacts, cold calling, making presentations—as well as the other marketing expenses associated with each signed lease. All of these, of course, are exclusively tenant-acquisition costs. The question is, how much does it cost to *maintain* current tenants?

Most real estate managers do not know the answer to this question. Looking to the retail environment, however, you will find an average *acquisition* cost of $118.76 per customer. On the same basis, the average annual cost to *retain* a current customer is given as $19.76. This means that it costs roughly *six times as much* to acquire a new retail customer as it does to keep a current one (see also exhibit 4.1).

The precise ratio of acquisition to retention costs is unimportant. What is absolutely essential is to earmark a certain amount of the leasing marketing budget specifically for tenant retention. A percentage of the overall budget, reflected in appropriate line-item categories, is perhaps the best way to make and display the allocation. Because it can become part of the property's standard operating budget preparation procedure, this approach tends to ensure that the retention effort will continue to receive attention in subsequent years. If the retail figures are correct, it is sensible to allot at least one dollar of the marketing budget to tenant retention for every six dollars allocated for tenant acquisition.

It is also important, as part of the budgeting exercise, to consider how the retention funds will actually be used. Market research among existing tenants and analysis of the competition are likely to be funded in this manner. Examples of these applications will be detailed in chapter 8. There are, however, retention strategies that do not require direct funding. They are what constitute the broad subject of tenant relations.

Partnering as a Technique for Turnover Reduction

One method for reducing tenant turnover at commercial properties is to consider applying the strategies that have been evolving within the retailing milieu. One of the most recent is "partnering," which recognizes that it is in the mutual interest of sellers and buyers to engage in long-term relationships, not only because the expenses associated with customer turnover—so-called switching costs—are substantial, but also because it is economically beneficial to do so. The principles that underlie partnering represent a synthesis of many of the specific customer-responsive strategies—e.g., service, satisfaction, and value, among others—and have particular application in the management of commercial real estate.

In *Business Partnering for Continuous Improvement: How to Forge Enduring Alliances Among Employees, Suppliers and Customers,* Charles C. Poirier and William F. Houser defined business partnering as "a process of improvement that brings an organization and its constituent parts to the point where special benefits not found in competing networks can be created." They then described the benefits that can be realized from partnering relationships:

▶ The interaction between the organizations [of buyer and seller] does not occur in some field of combat, but in areas of mutual interest. Within this interactive zone, resources are pooled so conversations go beyond quantity and price. Consideration is given to all the potential interactions so problems can be solved and opportunities for improvement seized. The new relationship concludes with mutual winners, not with one winner and one loser from the traditional relationship.

The concept of business partnering encompasses linkages between a firm's outside vendors and the company on the one hand and the firm's "internal" customers on the other. In addition, the value of such partnering can be extended to the ways in which the organization relates to its clients.

It is conceivable that a company might pursue a philosophy of partnering for selfish reasons. In *Winning and Keeping Industrial Customers,* Barbara Bund Jackson recommended that businesses evaluate their customers in light of the customer's "switching" costs—i.e., the degree of risk that a customer perceives in entering into a commercial relationship with a vendor and the difficulty of changing to a new vendor if the relationship is unsatisfactory:

▶ At one end of the spectrum are the customers who can easily switch products or services (e.g., buyers of commodity chemicals or shipping services). At the other end are those who have an incentive to stay loyal (e.g., customers of costly computer and office-automation systems). In the middle are the majority, who are easily swayed (e.g., fleet buyers of company cars).

William A. Band elaborated on this as follows:

▶ When the perceived risk is high, and the changing of vendors difficult, buyers respond well to strategies that emphasize a close relationship between buyer and seller. However, when switching costs
are low, buyers are less interested in a long-term commitment to vendors, and price carries more weight. Understanding switching costs
is important in order to avoid building a costly relationship with a
customer who does not need or want such a commitment, and to
provide an adequate amount of vendor support to those who are in
for the long haul.

Whether or not owners and managers of commercial properties consider establishing partnering relationships from a position of self-interest, the applicability of this notion in real estate management is apparent. Simply stated,
owners and managers of commercial properties have an ongoing stake in the
economic futures of their tenants because the financial fortunes of tenants
enable them to pay rents and absorb rate increases. What is less apparent,
though no less real, is that tenants are similarly invested in their landlords'
success, at least theoretically. When landlords prosper, chances that they will
refurbish their properties improve correspondingly. Whether that correlation
is exact, it is clear that when commercial properties encounter troubled economic times, the likelihood that their owners will upgrade them is remote.

Thus, the notion of "switching" costs is applicable to the management of
commercial real estate as well. Businesses incur substantial expenses in moving from one place to another. These expenditures go beyond the financial
burden of moving to include some or all of the costs of preparing their new
space for occupancy. In addition, there is the packing and unpacking, arrang-
ing for utility shut-off and turn-on, changing addresses with their corre-
spondents (suppliers and customers), interruption (disruption) of their business activities, and all the rest—i.e., the "hassle factor"—that adds to the
perception of high risk. This aspect of the investment in moving is well-
characterized by Donald R. Libey:

▶ Your customers don't want to go somewhere else. They have a desire to be loyal. . . . Bio-psychologically, The Customer's drive to survive is directly transferred to the supplier when the decision to trade
is made. The Customer wants you to guarantee survival. The Customer is literally trusting you with a portion of personal survival.

Note that Libey has also addressed the psychological and emotional components of "switching." Commercial tenants are, after all, represented by numbers of people who have become used to a specific work environment and a
particular commute to work. Most people truly do *not* want to change where
they work, except by their own personal choice to change jobs.

Because commercial tenants make substantial financial and "hassle" investments in their landlords' properties, they are especially suitable candidates for partnering efforts by creative landlords who appreciate the breathtaking economic impact of tenant retention and understand the overwhelming costs of tenant turnover. Managers of commercial properties need to appreciate the fact that tenants are not captive. Businesses opt to relocate for a variety of reasons:

- Large space users may choose to construct their own buildings and become landlords in the process.

- Terms of a business merger or sale may require a change of location (e.g., to another city).

- It may not be possible to expand a tenant's current space to accommodate its business growth.

- There may be a need (or desire) to provide a better array of amenities as part of their employees' "benefits" package (e.g., public transportation, access to child care).

- A move out may be a move up—relocating from a building that is Class C to one that is class B (or from class B to class A) to enhance the company's prestige.

However, in the absence of other motivating factors or mitigating circumstances, a tenant who will submit to the expense—and the hassle—of moving is really dissatisfied. That is why it is to the landlord's advantage not merely to satisfy tenants and their personnel, but to create incentives for them to remain loyal customers.

One powerful partnering weapon that savvy landlords need to employ is solicitation of complaints from their tenants. We turn to that subject in the next chapter.

The Complaint Revolution

Nobody likes to hear they've done a lousy job, but criticism from customers is more valuable than praise. You want your customers to tell you when you've screwed up, so that you can take care of the problem and take steps to ensure it doesn't happen again—to them, or anybody else. If they don't tell you, they'll just walk away shaking their heads and they'll never come back. Worse, you're likely to alienate somebody else in the future by doing exactly the same thing.

—CARL SEWELL and PAUL B. BROWN, *Customers for Life*

Ironically, complainants are often valuable customers because they're giving the company a chance to make good before they take their business elsewhere. And if their complaints are handled to their satisfaction, 90 percent of them will stay. Most of us, as customers, are afflicted with the common human condition of inertia. We don't really want to move our checking account, change dry cleaners, take a chance on a different model car, or try the chairside manner of a different dentist. We prefer to stick with what's familiar, as long as we continue to get reasonable satisfaction from it. But there's a limit, and we *will* change when the satisfaction level drops too low or when we're offered a superior alternative. Thus, in a company that's truly service-oriented, any complaint is really an *opportunity*—an opportunity to correct a problem or do something better and a second chance to preserve a valuable customer relationship.

—LAURA A. LISWOOD, *Serving Them Right*

When you become a partner you break down the walls between yourself and your customer. You make a lasting commitment, and you invest in learning everything about your customer . . . . Your organization can truly become saturated with the customer's voice. You encourage your customer to fully understand what you can do, and you create a "value chain."

—RICHARD C. WHITELEY, *The Customer-Driven Company*

Chances are, if you were to ask a roomful of real estate managers to name their best tenants, you would get responses that sound something like this:

> Simplex Computer. Or maybe Cameron Distribution. No, Simplex Computer is definitely the best. Why, they've been a tenant here for five years, they always pay their rent on time, and I never hear from them. They never complain about anything—not about other tenants' employees using their area of the parking lot, roof leaks, or overcharges on their CAM bills. And when it came time to renew their lease, they never asked for any interior remodeling or repainting. They just took the market increase after their three-year lease expired, without any bickering. I'll tell you this: If I had 10 more tenants like Simplex Computer, my job would be a whole lot easier.

On the other hand, if you asked the same group of managers to name their best *friends,* the responses would be vastly different:

> My best friend? That's easy—Nancy Jones. She was a year ahead of me in college. And when I got into leasing, she was a manager over at Center Port Industrial Park. We just naturally started comparing notes about the business. When her company put in that new Skyline accounting system, she was having lots of problems, and she'd call me up at all hours, especially when she was doing her month-end reports. Now, we talk all the time, just to see how each other is doing.

Why are personal relationships typically so different from professional ones? Why do people expect—even welcome—interactions with friends that they would resent from customers? Why is it perfectly acceptable for your friend Jim to bang on your door at midnight to complain about some aspect of his job or his boss's behavior, but a simple inquiry from a tenant about a pending maintenance request is perceived as an imposition?

Professional Complaining Is Discouraged

Undoubtedly, one of the reasons for this discrepancy is that humans have different levels of *commitment* to their relationships with one another and, therefore, varying tolerances for the level of intensity and inconvenience they are likely to require. People are, in short, *differentially invested* between and within their professional and personal relationships. We believe that a major challenge for American business is to narrow the gap between the ways all the people in the company, and most especially frontline personnel, treat their friends and treat their customers.

Until this happens in commercial real estate management, individual managers are unlikely to be motivated to ascertain whether tenants are satisfied or dissatisfied with their leasing arrangements. Karl Albrecht described it this way:

▶ Apparently, many people want to remain in a comfortable state of ignorance. "If I go around asking the customers how they feel about things," they seem to think, "they'll start complaining and I'll have to do something about it." That's exactly the point. The purpose of asking customers how they're experiencing your [product] is to find out how you can improve it and keep their business or get more of it.

Paradoxically, the U.S. Office of Consumer Affairs (USOCA) has found that the problems of noncomplainers are usually the easiest to resolve:

▶ If only given the chance, business could have retained the patronage of many of these customers. Therefore, this often large pool of noncomplainants represents a significant lost marketing opportunity.

The fact is, customers are loath to complain, even though failing to do so virtually *guarantees* that their problems will not be fixed. The reasons for this apparent paradox are many. Probably the basic reason is that most people dislike contentiousness and haggling—the minor unpleasantness that sometimes escalates to wrangling, ultimatums, and even name-calling that characterizes complaining. When customers are pushed to the point that they complain, they risk encountering defensiveness, hard feelings, and even outright lying for their trouble. Customers would rather be treated equitably the first time and not be put in the position of having to insist on their rights.

Other factors conspire to discourage customer complaints. As reported in the *New York Times* (quoting research done by the USOCA):

▶ Seventy percent of consumers do not complain because they don't know where to call, don't think it's worth the effort, or don't think companies will respond.

Unfortunately, much corporate behavior tends to confirm consumer pessimism about receiving fair treatment.

Noncomplainers Vote with Their Feet—and Their Mouths. Even if some or all of the above reasons discourage customer complaints, most consumers take decisive action when their expectations are unmet—they take their business elsewhere. Businesses that do not stay in touch with their customers are nonetheless subject to customer feedback: While buyers may choose to keep the offending vendor in the dark about their exasperation, they will not hesitate to let others know of their dissatisfaction. According to Davidow and Uttal:

▶ [Dissatisfied customers] are searching for opportunities to get even. They don't tell the retailers, manufacturers, and service providers that have served them poorly—they tell their friends and colleagues. As the bad word passes along, it creates a time bomb.

Lele summarized the deterioration of the buyer-seller relationship when customers feel disgruntled:

▶ Customer dissatisfaction presents a serious threat because many unhappy customers don't complain—at least, not to the company. Instead they tell family and friends about their dissatisfaction. A good number of them switch to other suppliers. If and when they do complain to the company, they are pessimistic about their chances of being satisfied. The company's response frequently confirms their worst suspicions.

The result is that the company and its customers become increasingly isolated from each other. Management thinks that because there are no complaints, there are no problems. Lacking information from the customer about the causes of dissatisfaction . . . the company repeats its mistakes. Customers, in turn, grow more frustrated with what they see as the company's indifference to their problems and needs, and switch to other suppliers.

Clemmer calculated the impact of the negative word of mouth from unhappy customers this way:

▶ *Category*	*Number*
The original customer who won't return	1
Potential customers not gained because the original customer didn't tell them how satisfied he or she was	8
Potential customers lost because the original customer told them how *dis*satisfied he or she was	16
Total customers lost from *one* unhappy customer	25

When we attempt to quantify the magnitude of customer dissatisfaction and its consequences, we find such disturbing statistics as these:

Approximately one in four purchases results in some type of consumer problem.

Nonetheless, nearly 70 percent of customers experiencing a problem *do not complain*. Some studies show the rate of non-complaining to be as high as 90 percent. This means that, for every complaint companies register, there are approximately three other customers with problems, some serious, that the firm never hears about.

Dissatisfied customers who don't complain are the ones least likely to purchase from the same supplier. Only 9 percent in this category do so.

Other sources confirm that the customers who actually complain represent only a minuscule portion of the number of customers who are dissatisfied. According to Davidow and Uttal:

▶ While complaints are useful in all sorts of ways, from pinpointing performance problems to selling collateral products, they're a remarkably feeble index of satisfaction levels. John Goodman of Technical Assistance Research Programs, Inc. (TARP), who has studied the complaint process at over three hundred companies and government agencies, concludes that customers who complain to headquarters . . . represent a tiny fraction of all dissatisfied customers, somewhere between 2 and 4 percent.

Complaints are Golden Nuggets

While the estimates vary, the figures from the president of TARP in Washington, D.C., suggest that there is a vast sea of unhappy consumers, churning with unspoken discontent. The point was made by Stanley Marcus, Chairman Emeritus of Neiman-Marcus:

▶ Why do you think you have so many department stores in a mall these days? It's because each of them does such a poor selling job that they survive just by taking up each other's unsatisfied customers.

While there are no national studies on the subject of tenant satisfaction, there is no reason to be complacent or to assume that the level of irritation in the commercial real estate business is lower than in other consumer trades.

Statistics also illuminate the reasons why it is vital to sellers to encourage complaints. Here is how Ron Zemke and Dick Schaaf have described the importance of customer complaints:

▶ According to John Goodman, TARP's president, complaining customers can turn into extremely loyal customers. Depending on the dollar value of their problems, only 9 to 37 percent of unhappy customers who *do not* complain will do business with the offending company a second time. But from 50 to 80 percent of those who *do* complain and subsequently have their complaint fully resolved (even if it doesn't turn out in their favor) report that they will ring the company's cash register again. Based on complaint resolution and repurchase records from a number of industries, TARP has even calculated a return on investment for successful complaint handling. The lowest ROI range is 15 to 75 percent for packaged goods companies; the highest, for retailers, is 35 to 400 percent.

Apparently, complaints—even if not resolved in their favor—can generate loyalty among customers and may eventually blossom into bottom-line benefits. Figures from TARP suggest that the *immediacy* of the seller's response to the customer's complaint increases the chances of repeat business: If the matter is resolved, as many as 70 percent of customers will do business again with the company that upset them. But if the complaint is resolved *on the spot,* 95 percent will do so.

More recently, Terry Vavra summarized the importance and vitality of customer complaints as, "the five things that can happen when a customer is unhappy." They are:

▶ *The customer suffers in silence.* The next time the customer buys the product or service, he will already have a negative attitude and will be expecting and looking for problems.

The customer switches to another marketer in silence. This is only a problem for the marketer who realizes she has lost a customer, but recognizing the loss provides no information [about] how or why.

The customer tells friends and neighbors about his dissatisfaction. In this case, the firm stands to lose several customers, the original unhappy one and all the other people he influences.

The customer talks to third parties. This is the worst outcome because it can lead to lawsuits or investigations and increased negative publicity.

The customer talks to the company. This is the only positive outcome. It gives the company a second chance, the opportunity to understand the customer's needs, identify the problem and correct it, and ultimately to win back the trust of the customer.

Because complaints are so vital to successful operations—they constitute the most valuable piece of a company's business intelligence—the best firms pay close attention to those that surface and take aggressive measures to stimulate others. This receptive attitude is reflected in the following from Milind Lele: "When one of our customers sneezes, our company catches pneumonia." Or, as Donald Libey noted, "In the extraordinary company, *every* customer problem puts the company on Red Alert."

The benefits of a strategy designed to surface and respond to complaints—i.e., what happens when complaints put a company on "Red Alert"—may be summarized as follows:

1. *It helps the company keep customers who might otherwise switch to competitors.* As Milind Lele observed:

▶ Many companies don't realize that customer complaints can be more than a grave problem. They are also a tremendous opportunity. If customers who complain are ignored or treated unsatisfactorily, they can become a threat to the company's franchise. On the other hand, if their needs are addressed effectively, these same customers represent significant future sales.

2. *It overcomes some of the effects of negative word of mouth.* As Jeffrey Disend noted, studies show that:

▶ Dissatisfied customers tell twice as many people about their negative experience as satisfied customers tell about their positive experiences.

3. *It enables the company to identify, and then eliminate, the cause of problems—what one commentator calls "ricochets"—that impede customer satisfaction.* (Ricochet-fixing—i.e., service recovery—is the subject of the next chapter.) Here's what Carl Sewell had to say about the benefit of complaints to his Cadillac dealership:

▶ Sure, we have to fix problems, but if that's all we do, we're going to keep having the same problems over and over again. It's more efficient to find out what caused the problem in the first place—we do what's sometimes described as a root cause analysis—and correct the problem once and for all.

4. *It provides a company with an opportunity to distinguish itself from the competition by demonstrating its commitment to customer concerns.* Goldzimer characterized this devotion in "moment of truth" terms:

▶ By encouraging your customers to provide feedback, particularly complaints, you are showing concern, interest, *and the desire to satisfy* your customers. The very act of soliciting feedback is a positive signal to your clients.

5. *It helps to empower a firm's employees, which in turn enhances their job satisfaction.* According to Patricia Sellers, writing in *Fortune* magazine:

▶ There is a surprising payoff for those companies that make a science of listening to the customer: When they make their customers happy, they make their employees happy, too. Contented workers make for better-served customers. And there is also mounting evidence that improvement in customer satisfaction leads directly to higher employee retention.

6. *It diminishes the feeling—and often the reality—of isolation that exists between buyers and sellers, and establishes bonds instead. The impression that a company creates of being "complaint-friendly" is an especially compelling way for a company to be responsive to its clients' concerns.* As Zeithaml and coworkers observed:

Guarantees

Retailers have long recognized that guaranteeing their products and services benefits both their external and internal customers. Guarantees encourage a company's personnel to do the job right the first time. When that does not happen, corrective action becomes expensive—whether or not the work is guaranteed: The company will not only spend money to correct the error, but it may lose additional business due to customer dissatisfaction, and it may suffer from negative word-of-mouth advertising. One advantage of guarantees, then, is that they set clear performance standards for their personnel that benefit the company overall. Indeed, guarantees strengthen performance standards because both customers and employees monitor compliance. As Christopher Hart, one of the leading authorities on this subject, has observed:

▶ A specific, unambiguous service guarantee sets standards for your organization. It tells employees what the company stands for. . . . And it forces the company to define each employee's role and responsibilities in delivering the service.

Second, guarantees have powerful marketing benefits. When they are advertised, they attract customers. As Hart said:

▶ Perhaps the most obvious reason for offering a strong service guarantee is its ability to boost marketing: it encourages consumers to buy a service by reducing the risk of the purchase decision, and it generates more sales to existing customers by enhancing loyalty.

In the text, we have noted the prevalence of customer dissatisfaction with retail purchases and the perplexing shortage of consumer complaints. Government figures indicate that some 70 percent (or more) of dissatisfied customers *do not complain,* and for every complaint brought to a company's attention, approximately three other customers also experience problems—some of which are serious—that the company never learns about. In that discussion, we emphasized the value of customer complaints and suggested techniques for surfacing them.

▶ Complaints can become part of a larger process of staying in touch with customers. In particular, they can provide important information about the failures or breakdowns in the service system. If compiled, analyzed, and fed back to employees who can correct the problems, complaints can become an inexpensive and continuous source of adjustment for the service process.

7. *It enables the company to formalize complaint-handling procedures, which in turn establishes the firm as a "learning organization" in which the customer's voice is paramount. Over time, the company is considered*

Guarantees *(continued)*

Probably the most effective strategy for revealing customer complaints is to guarantee satisfaction. Guarantees force companies to produce a high quality product because anything less will induce customers to invoke the guarantee. The capacity of service guarantees to unearth customer complaints that otherwise would escape the attention of the company gives a substantial marketing edge to the firm that employs them.

The marketing muscle of guarantees is probably most evident in connection with goods whose value depends primarily on so-called experience qualities—those intangible characteristics that can best be discovered only postpurchase. (The distinction between "experience" and "search" qualities will be discussed in chapter 7.) Because the product's suitability can best be determined only after the customer has the opportunity to experience it, the perceived risk can likely be diminished by guarantees. Here is what Berry and Parasuraman have said about the search/experience dichotomy:

▶ Customers must experience the intangible service to really know it. Intangibility makes services more difficult for customers to imagine and desire than goods. Customers purchasing professional tax advice have no knobs to turn, buttons to push, or pictures to see. Customers' perception of risk tends to be high for services because services cannot be touched, smelled, tasted, or tried on before purchase. Customers can test-drive a new automobile and kick the tires, but to try a new vacation resort they must first register as guests.

Because choosing to locate a business enterprise in a particular office building or shopping center has primarily "experience" qualities, some commercial real estate managers believe guarantees are an appropriate component of their marketing and lease negotiation efforts. Others eschew the use of guarantees in this environment, especially those involving refunds. In fact, many commercial tenants consider guarantees to be a substitute for adequate performance because such guarantees often involve a refund, and more value is placed on the refund than on corrective action—or the quality of service that precludes the need for action in the first place. This negative reaction is akin to those of prospective buyers of laundry equipment:

▶ As Whirlpool, the leader in home laundry equipment, has said, "Consumers don't want their money back. *They want a product that works.*"

by its clients to be a partner in their success. Jeffrey Disend summarized the characteristics of these organizations as follows:

▶ They can never know enough about their business. They're always trying to find out what their customers want: What problems are they having? How can our product or service be more useful to them?

Guarantees *(concluded)*

The negative consequences of guarantees were summarized by Peter Glen:

▶ Lip service is even worse than mechanical service. And we are having an epidemic. Suddenly service providers are starting to issue guarantees and pay their customers after providing them with bad service. The Marriott Hotels say that if your breakfast is delivered more than fifteen minutes late, it's free. The pizza place offers a discount if your order is not delivered within thirty minutes. The restaurant provides free desserts if entrees don't come in ten minutes, and the bank hands out five-dollar bills if customers wait in line more than five minutes.

　　This automatically gives all the employees permission to deliver your breakfast and your pizza late; free desserts are figured into the selling cost of the restaurant's shoddy operations and charged to the customer; and banks can now plan on keeping customers waiting in lines forever, as long as they come around afterwards and given them some money for their time.

Paradoxically, while guarantees are designed to ensure customer satisfaction with a product, they have the potential to institutionalize its failpoints.

　　For managers of commercial real estate, specific guarantees may be impractical, but the idea should at least be considered. If nothing else, it can be used as a basis for scheduling maintenance work and setting performance standards. Minimally, a time limit for responding to tenants' service requests becomes a yardstick for measuring the effort to satisfy tenants. You can find out whether you have succeeded by asking about the quality of the service and the timeliness of the response. (The example form in exhibit 2.1 serves this purpose.) Specific complaints about particulars—work not done well or not completed, the delay in or lack of a response—might trigger a review, and possibly a tightening, of established parameters. Clearly, favorable comments would indicate your success in satisfying—even delighting—your tenants, without making any specific promises or stating any guarantees.

Executives work on the front line and 'shop' the company. Hourly workers regularly go out to meet with customers, see how customers use their products, learn about other customer needs. Ideas for improvements come largely from listening to customers.

Before a company embarks on a course that begins with complaint-responsiveness and evolves into complaint-generation, it needs to review and, if necessary, upgrade its complaint handling policies. The self-examination prerequisite is especially important in high-touch service industries such as commercial real estate management, because the fact that a firm takes corrective action when one customer brings a complaint to the attention of the firm—and that customer gets satisfaction in return—creates the anticipation of similar results on the part of other prospective complainers. Thus, whenever a company commits itself to a policy of customer-responsiveness, the resulting positive word of mouth challenges the firm to keep promises consistent with the expectations of all of its customers. Nothing could be more damaging than asking for complaints and then *not* doing anything about them.

The essential foundational elements for an effective complaint-handling process are in place once the company has (1) hired nice people, (2) trained them in such customer-sensitive subjects as listening skills, and (3) empowered them to fix their customers' problems, whenever possible, on the spot.

The hiring-training-empowering triad was discussed in chapter 3. We turn next to service "recovery"—the end-product of customer service.

The Recovery Revolution

Customers don't expect you to be perfect. They do expect you to fix things when they go wrong.

—DONALD PORTER, Senior Vice-President, British Airways

Everything you need to know about handling mistakes you learned in nursery school: acknowledge your error, fix it immediately, and say you're sorry. Odds are, your customers, like your mom and dad, will forgive you.

—CARL SEWELL and PAUL B. BROWN, *Customers for Life*

The word "recovery" has been chosen carefully—it means "to return to a normal state; to make whole again." Though many organizations have service departments established to fix what breaks, the deliberate management of the recovery is typically a reactive, damage-minimizing function. We suggest recovery can be as proactively managed for positive outcomes as can service in general.

—CHIP R. BELL and RON ZEMKE, writing in *Management Review*

Office, retail, and industrial buildings are assets that deteriorate and lose value over time. This wasting process is accelerated—or slowed—by such factors as physical age, climate, construction quality, and level of maintenance, as well as the rate of tenant turnover. Owners and managers predicate their budgeting for preventive maintenance and capital improvements, as well as much of the routine maintenance and repairs, on their assessment of the property's rate of aging. Their goal is to preserve the value of the asset and maintain it in as nearly mint condition as circumstances permit.

Real estate managers appreciate the reality of physical obsolescence and handle it as routine. Decisions whether to replace or repair an air-conditioning unit or a roof, resurface a parking lot now or wait another year, install new carpeting in an elevator or a corridor are everyday agenda items in the management business. Budgetary conditions, marketing considerations, and economic forecasts are only some of the forces that influence the decision-maker.

It is also true—although infrequently recognized—that both current and prospective tenants are very much aware that buildings deteriorate. On the basis of their companies' experiences and what they have heard from other business contacts, tenants understand and accept the reality of breakdowns and inconvenience as an unpleasant consequence of occupying leased space. So Donald Porter's comment at the beginning of this chapter, while undoubtedly directed to the airline industry, applies to managers of commercial real estate as well: Perfection is not achievable; appropriate response when the inevitable breakdown occurs—what Ron Zemke terms "service recovery"—is therefore a necessary part of the real estate manager's arsenal.

The "Over-Promise/Under-Deliver" Trap

The resigned acceptance of the fallibility of buildings and their installed systems by both landlords and tenants is likely to be one of the few times they agree about this issue. The second portion of Porter's admonition—"[Customers] do expect you to fix things when they go wrong"—raises the issue of customer expectations about the promptness and thoroughness of the work, among others. The simple fact is that most real estate owners and managers are not prepared to *delight* their tenants when they need maintenance in their leased space. Indeed, quite the opposite is usually true: The maintenance process is the point at which real estate owners and managers most typically make promises to their tenants that they either could not possibly keep, do not intend to keep, or wish forlornly they could keep. These misguided assurances result in profound levels of discontent on the part of their customers. This damaging approach—what might be called over-promising and under-delivering—pervades the commercial real estate industry and is a prime reason for the widespread mistrust and dislike of landlords. It is, in addition, one of the causes of the generally unfavorable reputation of real estate management. Milind Lele has warned service-providers to avoid this pitfall:

▶ The majority of firms fail to understand the importance of controlling or managing customers' expectations. That's putting it mildly; in many cases companies create their own problems by generating unrealistic expectations and ruining their credibility with customers. . . . They try to manage expectations dishonestly. And they work hard to hide bad news, rather than face facts and deal with the problem.

Mack Hanan and Peter Karp made the same point more vehemently:

▶ The best rule for customer satisfaction is *to deliver*. There is a vital corollary to this proposition. It is *not to promise what cannot be delivered*. Disappointment can be a lower low than fulfillment can be a high. . . . It is commonplace to forget an expectation that has been fulfilled. Hardly any customer forgets a disappointment. In the long run, what is expected but not received counts stronger negatively than fulfillment counts positively.

As insidious and misguided—and ultimately self-defeating—as the "over-promise/under-deliver" syndrome is, its popularity is understandable. Management personnel at a commercial property are frequently confronted by angry, unpleasant, sometimes obnoxious individuals—i.e., tenants' personnel—who make extreme demands. Nonetheless, in an effort to be responsive and responsible, management employees make ambitious promises—usually in good faith and often unnecessary—to placate their customers. Unfortunately, employees' expectations of their ability to keep such promises often end up being overly optimistic, frequently for reasons that are beyond their control. For example, service requests typically involve parts and equipment in addition to labor. For a variety of reasons, these supplies may be temporarily unavailable; the "labor" component—i.e., the maintenance staff—may turn out to be equally unavailable, especially because their other duties conflict. The common situation is one in which tenants' routine maintenance needs collide with emergency situations at the site. (This was elaborated in chapter 3 in the discussion of the Pareto Principle.)

The Importance of Questioning and Listening.   Another problem is that different people attach different meanings to the same words—in this case, the phrase "right away," which is a frequently used pledge in the real estate management business. Here is how a misunderstanding might arise:

> *Tenant* (to manager): "Something's wrong with the roof: We have water leaking in our warehouse area right over our new stock. We had to put tarpaulins over our storage racks last night. We're expecting a large delivery of expensive computer parts tomorrow, and I don't want these parts to get wet. We need them to finish a critical order. This problem has to be taken care of *immediately!*"

> *Manager* (responding): "I'll send a maintenance technician to your office to assess the problem, and then we'll contact the roofer who issued the warranty on the roof *right away*." (Meanwhile thinking: "Steve's working on another call right now, and he has two more lined up. I can't pull him off those jobs, and we're really short-handed this afternoon. The only other maintenance technician on

site is Gene, and he's working on an air-conditioning unit. I'll write a service request. Maybe Gene can take a look at the roof later this afternoon. In any case, I'll make sure that either Steve or Gene handles the problem first thing tomorrow.")

Tenant requests, whether or not they are reasonable, inevitably result in expectations that often go unmet. The expectations themselves are either implicit ("This problem is obviously so serious that *anybody* would understand that it needs prompt attention!") or unexpressed ("This problem is so important *to me* that I'm sure it will be fixed immediately!")

The "IRV Curve" of Customer Satisfaction.   In retailing, the degree of fit between buyers' expectations and companies' performance is the primary measure of customer satisfaction. As Milind Lele described it:

▶   Customers judge their satisfaction or dissatisfaction with a product by comparing its performance against a reference level of expectations that they've created or that has been established in their minds. If performance is [slightly] below expectations, they're satisfied; and if performance exceeds expectations, they're very happy.

Indeed, customer satisfaction might be depicted in an equation:

$$\text{Customer satisfaction} = \frac{\text{Performance}}{\text{Expectations}}$$

Much of the antidote to the pervasive over-promise/under-deliver style that typifies many businesses is to adopt its antithesis as company policy: Under-promise and over-deliver is a sure way to satisfy customers. The singular benefit of this latter approach can perhaps be best understood from the following illustration:

The "Perception and Performance Principle"

Promise to Meet Customer Needs ⟶ Exceed Promise ⟶ Customer Satisfied

Promise to Meet/Exceed Customer Expectations ⟶ Deliver
99% or Less ⟶ Customer NOT Satisfied

Promise Less than Capacity to Meet/Exceed Expectations ⟶ Deliver
100% ⟶ Customer Satisfied

The foregoing diagram illustrates a fundamental principle that distinguishes customer-driven organizations from those that are not: These firms understand that their clients expect them to keep their word. Companies that go to the trouble to pin down customer expectations and then exceed them—while resisting the temptation to promise to deliver more than they can produce—invariably succeed. Their approach to the principle depicted above looks like this:

Promise 90% (or less) of Capacity to Meet Expectations ⟶ Deliver 90% (or more) ⟶ Customer Satisfaction

On the other hand, those firms that routinely make promises to induce customer confidence, and then fail to deliver on their commitments, are destined to fail.

The second part of the antidote, then, is to find out what customer expectations really *are*—not intuit them—and then strive to satisfy them. (We discussed ways to identify tenants' expectations in chapter 2.) Frontline servers cannot substitute their judgments for those of their clients in deciding what is an appropriate, timely response. This is especially true because satisfaction depends to a great extent on whether the customer considers the recovery to be punctual or not. As David Freemantle pointed out:

▶ As soon as a company hesitates in redressing a problem with a customer, a critical alienation will occur. Conversely, swift reparation can produce a perception of a higher standard of customer service than if the problem had not occurred in the first instance.

Speed of Response as a Component of Satisfaction.   The importance of speed as a factor in the adequacy of service recovery is attributed by Libey to an unlikely source: Federal Express.

▶ As a result of the advances in communications technology and the overwhelming acceptance and success of Federal Express, global time has been redefined and reconstituted. . . . Consider the magnitude and magnificence of that accomplishment. One visionary, Fred Smith, altered global time through the philosophy of customer-focused marketing. His creation of Federal Express and his magnificent obsession with his customers has actually altered *time!*

While it may be feasible to promise action within a certain time period, it may be unnecessary to do so: The customer may be less demanding than the service provider would have supposed. In these circumstances, delivering slightly less service than the company is capable of delivering may nonetheless "WOW!" its customers. To restate the earlier point, there is no substitute for conversations with customers to learn their expectations. Here is an example based on the situation illustrated previously (the roof leak).

Tenant (to manager): "Something's wrong with the roof: We have water leaking in our warehouse area right over our new stock. We had to put tarpaulins over our storage racks last night."

Manager: "Gene, our maintenance man, is working on an air-conditioning unit right now; we've been having some minor problems with it, and I want to get it fixed before the temperature goes up this afternoon. Steve, our maintenance chief, is working on one call and has two more waiting. Tell me: Would it be satisfactory to you if Gene takes a look at your roof later this afternoon, or would it be all right if Steve comes by tomorrow morning with someone from the roofing company? They issued the warranty on the roof."

Tenant: "Well, I don't know whether I mentioned it, but I'm expecting a large delivery of expensive computer parts tomorrow which I need in order to finish a critical order. I can't afford to let that inventory get wet. This roof leak needs to be repaired."

Manager: "You're right. I didn't understand that you had such a critical order. I'll call the roofing company immediately and come over myself to assess the problem. I'll also ask if the roofer can bring over some tarpaulins to cover the damaged areas of the roof until the rain stops and they can make permanent repairs. I'll be at your office in half an hour. Will that be okay?"

In this instance, if the manager succeeds in getting the tenant's roof leak stopped temporarily today, and if the underlying problem is resolved by the roofing company soon thereafter, the tenant will doubtless be impressed by the swiftness of the repair and the personal concern of the real estate manager. This is true even though the tenant may initially have considered an immediate roof repair to be absolutely necessary. The fact that the manager chose to pose *alternative and personal solutions* to the tenant resulted in a satisfactory outcome for both landlord and tenant. In these circumstances, it is likely that the landlord benefitted from positive word of mouth—even though the manager was not able to have the leak permanently fixed that day. Still another option, albeit one that might not have been readily available, would be to offer to relocate part of the tenant's inventory temporarily.

Avoiding Double Deviations.   Much of the success of the service recovery effort depends on whether it meets the timing requirements that customers have for it. Another imperative for a successful recovery effort is that the response actually *solve* the customer's problem. While this requisite seems obvious, recovery has the potential to exacerbate customers' distress. As Berry and Parasuraman have pointed out:

▶   When a service problem is followed by a weak recovery effort . . . the company fails its customers twice, creating . . . a "double deviation" from customer expectations. A double deviation will dramatically deflate customers' confidence in a company; when preceded by a history of unreliability, it will *devastate* customers' confidence and drive them to the competition.

Service recovery is risky. Disappointed customers are especially difficult to please, and frontline employees are peculiarly subject to burnout in these interactions although their sustained performance is crucial. The challenge facing the front line is to defuse the situation, discover customers' expectations, and renew their confidence in the company's ability to respond. Moreover, companies that disappoint their customers are particularly prone to exaggerate their ability to recover. Finally, it is vital to meet customers' expectations once a breakdown occurs and not allow the situation to further disintegrate with a feeble effort at resolution. In light of these hazards, companies need to *strategize* their recovery efforts.

For example, how do you respond to an elevator breakdown, especially if someone is trapped inside? Of course, the mechanical problem should be fixed as quickly as possible, and anyone who is injured should receive medical attention immediately. (These aspects should have been addressed in an emergency procedures manual. For purposes of this example, we will explore a strategy for dealing with such incidents that are minor and in which no one has been hurt.) However, people trapped in an elevator are likely to be scared, possibly panicky, and probably angry. At the very least, they deserve a profuse apology for the inconvenience. The form of your apology can be as simple as a telephone call or a personal visit—or, preferably, both.

You might also anticipate this kind of problem and plan different levels of response. Depending on the severity and duration of the incident, your personal apology might include a token gift of candy, flowers, or a potted plant, or you might arrange for a taxicab ride home at management company expense. Gift certificates for a lunch, a dinner, or merchandise, or tickets for the theater or a sporting event may also be appropriate considerations. Regardless of any gifts, however, you should follow up with the people involved in the incident and reassure them about the safety of the repaired equipment. It is also good public relations to let everyone else in the building know that the incident occurred and how the management team responded—others may have been inconvenienced while the problem was being fixed, and everyone will appreciate knowing that elevator service has been restored.

Aspects of Service Recovery

Recovery logistics have three components: (1) resolving the immediate problem so the customer is satisfied; (2) preventing a reoccurrence so others will not encounter the same problem in the future; and (3) planning responses for recurring breakdowns that are unavoidable.

Apologize and Empathize.   The service commentators offer several suggestions for accomplishing these tasks. First, the company needs to recognize that a successful resolution of the problem starts with appropriate, sincere treatment of the disillusioned customer. Scott Gross recommended that the frontline server, as the most immediately available representative of the seller, begin by offering a heartfelt—even outrageous—apology:

▶ When you say you are sorry, be so generous that there is no doubt that you mean it. You will create so much [positive] word of mouth that your mistake will be worth its weight in gold. An occasional screw-up handled outrageously may be just what the promo doctor ordered!

According to Kristin Anderson and Ron Zemke, the customer and the problem should be addressed separately, and a high-touch approach is indispensable:

▶ When a service provider wallows in a customer's misfortune, there are two victims instead of one. As a service professional, you need to see the clear difference between what happened and who it happened to—and work on the former to bring things back to normal.

They further recommend that the staff member display empathy for the customer in this circumstance:

▶ Showing empathy for customers actually allows you to be professional . . . . It also makes customers feel like important individuals. Empathy cannot be handed out by a machine; it's something one person does for another. There is no substitute for the human touch . . . . Use empathy to let your customers know that you—and they—are more important than machines.

Empathy is expressed in the second conversational vignette between real estate manager and tenant earlier in this chapter (the roof leak example).

The Personal Component

Because service recovery is innately a person-to-person activity, service commentators emphasize that the complaint-handling procedure hinges on staff who have exceptional human relations skills. Berry and Parasuraman put it this way:

▶ Excellent recovery requires excellence in the process dimensions of service. And this requires excellent people. . . . Employee responses to service problems cannot be left to chance. While some employees may be naturally responsive, reassuring, and empathetic in dealing with customers experiencing problems, most are not. Even employees who exhibit exemplary behavior during routine transactions may come unglued in dealing with problem situations. Inability or unwillingness of service personnel to respond effectively to exceptions is a pervasive problem.

Heskett and coworkers elaborated on this when they identified the optimum personality traits for those assigned to work at recovery:

▶ [The most important requirement] is the personal manner in which the recovery process is carried out. This requires assigning people with the best listening and human skills to the recovery process, giving them the most careful training, providing them with decision latitude for the use of good judgment, and rewarding them well for their good work.

Because these are frequently high-stress as well as high-touch endeavors, other commentators have recognized that the work of frontline staff is "emotional labor." Clemmer put it this way:

▶ Frequently, pre- or post-impact recoveries are heroic. That is, they require extra, sometimes superordinary, efforts to catch or make up to customers for problems created by ricochets. A steady routine of heroic recoveries is a prescription for stress and burnout.

Get the Boss Involved.   Gross—among others—has suggested that recovery is legitimized if the *boss* participates actively in recovery:

▶ Every problem should belong to two people: the person directly responsible and someone with at least an impressive, weight-carrying title, preferably the owner. . . . Involving the boss in setting things right has several benefits:

- It lets the employee know that getting things right is important.
- It lets the customer know that getting things right is important.
- It lets the boss know about problems so that he or she can focus attention and resources on prevention.

This latter aspect of leader involvement in the recovery process has the larger advantage of helping the boss to avoid making decisions in a vacuum without understanding the needs and wants of the customers who make the business possible. More important, the *frontline involvement of the boss* in complaint-resolution tends to sensitize company leadership in general to customer expectations, which is a vital trait of customer-driven companies. (Because leadership is central to a tenant retention revolution, the next chapter is devoted to the subject.)

Objectives of Service Recovery

In strategizing the recovery effort, it is advisable to begin by setting goals, and to do so from the perspective of the disgruntled customer. Gross summarized the destination of the process this way:

▶ Complaining customers are looking for a resolution of what they see as a conflict. They may want something fixed, an apology after slow service, or restitution for missing, damaged, or shoddy product. They want justice, and justice delayed really is justice denied. Besides, every hour that you delay in setting things right is another hour for the customer to stew in his anger, and another opportunity for him to tell someone else about how awful he's been treated.

In addition to fixing the problem for one customer, service recovery has the potential to assist the company in preventing problems for other customers in the future, a procedure that is termed "root-cause analysis." Here is what Berry and Parasuraman said about this subject:

▶ Problem-resolution situations are more than just opportunities to fix flawed services and strengthen ties with customers. They are also a valuable—but frequently ignored or underutilized—source of diagnostic, prescriptive information for improving customer service. . . . A company can and should learn as much as possible from each recovery experience. Effective learning involves searching for and correcting the underlying cause of the service shortfall, readjusting the monitoring of the service process, and implementing an information system to track problems. . . . To be fully beneficial, the recovery effort must strive to ferret out and fix the root causes of the failures.

Service recovery can also be used as a planning tactic by real estate managers. We noted earlier that preventive maintenance is actually a type of service recovery, even though it is undertaken in advance of a breakdown. A similar approach, what might be called a "failpoint strategy," enables managers of commercial properties to design responses to malfunctions before they occur. For example, despite the best efforts of maintenance personnel, HVAC systems often fail in the summertime—usually on the hottest days of the year. Recognizing the likelihood of such mishaps, savvy managers may stock their office properties with portable fans for temporary tenant relief in the case of system failures, and have sufficient staff available to service tenants' air-conditioning calls during peak periods of use. Note, however, that the situation in office buildings is further complicated by the fact that today's businesses often rely on computers, and air conditioning is needed to cool equipment as well as people—the potential for damage to high-tech equipment escalates as the period of breakdown is extended. Workers can be sent home, computers cannot.

"Failpoints" usually are system defaults. They may include late or inadequate snow plowing—the "Rose in the Snow" vignette in chapter 3 was actually a failpoint—inconvenience caused by delays in sweeping parking lots, blaring fire alarms caused by power outages, and numerous other occurrences. Whether the appropriate response is a rose personally delivered to each inconvenienced tenant or some other meaningful token that acknowledges responsibility and tenders an apology for the mishap, the management staff should brainstorm how they intend to handle predictable failpoints when they occur. (This type of brainstorming was discussed in chapter 2.)

Service Recovery Competence as a Marketing Tool

Yet another goal of service recovery—and one that is particularly appropriate in the management of commercial real estate—should be to create competency in the company's recovery efforts. The firm may have sufficient confidence in its abilities to respond to service mishaps that it is willing to market its effectiveness in this area. In *The Complete Guide to Customer Service*, Linda Lash noted:

▶ Companies may be reluctant to advertise that [they have] solutions for service or product failures. It calls attention to the reality that products or services fail, that photocopy machines break down, that overbookings may occur, that staff may not always be friendly and unrushed. Yet customers are often well aware of these problems, either from personal experience or word-of-mouth advertising from their friends. Knowing that a company has solutions to these problems creates customer confidence, both in the company's dedication to preventing the problem from occurring routinely and in the company's commitment to delivering a helpful solution when the problem does occur. To put this into advertising is a bold step but one that has won customers and market shares for those who have done it. When customers know that they will be looked after when problems occur, or that they will receive continuing service on a major item, the assurance increases their intent to purchase that product or service again.

A tenant's leased space represents a major investment and a long-term commitment to a location. The management team's ability to strategize solutions for both common and uncommon problems will be a key factor in retention of tenants—and a distinguishing feature to attract new ones.

Motivating Customers—An E-Plus Strategy

There is more to service recovery than customer satisfaction. Paul R. Timm, Ph.D., a professor at the Marriott School of Management at Brigham Young University, thinks customers need to be motivated:

▶ Most managers give at least lip service to the idea that the customer "is the boss," "is always right," and "is the reason the organization exists." But making a commitment to better customer service involves much more that mouthing a motto, slogan, or mechanical phrase. The real management challenge lies in translating the slogan into actions that create customer satisfaction and loyalty—in creating a *strategy* for implementing good service intentions.

Most commercial real estate managers think that if the service experience is positive, tenants will probably renew their leases; if it is negative, they may be inclined to move out. However, Timm offered the following caution about customers' motivation:

▶ [It] is not quite so clear cut. . . . Their satisfaction is simply an *absence of dissatisfaction,* not motivation to become a repeat customer. . . . The challenge is to move the customer beyond mere satisfaction to motivation—motivation to become a loyal repeat customer.

Like retail customers, all tenants have service expectations, and the degree to which those expectations are met determines their level of satisfaction. This was acknowledged earlier in this chapter. When the tenant's experience is worse than expected—because the problem was not fixed, the tenant had to wait too long for the response, or the attitude of the management team was unprofessional—the result will be dissatisfaction.

The issue is one of balance—customers are constantly assessing the equity between what they are giving to the buyer-seller relationship and what they are getting from it. The same is true of tenants and landlords. As Timm outlined the effort to overcome an inequity in favor of the business, the dissatisfied customer will respond by acting in one or more of the following ways:

▶ • *Ignore or rationalize the inequity.* The customer concludes that the service is poor but it's poor everywhere. . . .

• *Demand restitution.* The offended person demands fairer treatment or asks for money back.

• *Retaliation.* The offended person speaks badly of the organization or person seen as the cause of the inequity. . . .

• *Withdraw from the relationship.* The customer refuses to do further business with the organization or person.

Similarly, a dissatisfied tenant may claim never to have had a management company that was any good—obviously, service is poor everywhere. To counter the inequity, the tenant may seek to provide its own service—with a proportionate reduction in the rent. Retaliation can range from negative word of mouth to seeking a rent abatement—or, perhaps, threatening to break the lease or bring a lawsuit against the management company. The tenant may do all of these things or none of them—more than likely, the dissatisfaction will grow, and the tenant simply will not renew its lease.

The ability to "recover" requires the service provider to know how and why the customer is dissatisfied. In a worst-case scenario, the tenant will simply suffer in silence and you will never have an opportunity to make things right. Merely satisfying a tenant probably will not provide the response commercial real estate managers are striving to achieve. Timm considers satisfaction a "zone of indifference" between dissatisfaction (the E-Minus experience) and motivation (the E-Plus experience). The satisfied tenant is not necessarily singing the praises of the management company to other tenants or clients. You cannot be assured that satisfied tenants will renew their leases. The only thing certain is that your services have not yet dissatisfied them. That is why, according to Timm, the other side of equity theory must also be addressed:

▶ People who feel they are receiving *more than they deserve* from a transaction also . . . need to restore balance. . . . The challenge is to create positive imbalances by *exceeding customer expectations.* This is E-Plus.

Satisfaction is E, not E-Plus. By exceeding tenants' expectations, real estate managers will increase the probability of their tenants becoming loyal repeat customers. To create the E-Plus experience, the real estate management company must be committed to a level of tenant service that is better than tenants expect (underpromise and overdeliver) so that they will:

• Tell other tenants and/or clients of their positive experience.

• Pay a premium—additional rent or fees—for your services.

• Renew their leases at market or higher rents to maintain the level of services offered.

Implementation of an effective E-Plus strategy requires a coordinated company effort that asks each employee to continually seek out customer expectations and find ways to exceed them. Often it is the little things that mean the most to tenants. However, such "intangible perquisites" will be meaningless if the core problem is not addressed as well.

To implement an E-Plus strategy, Timm has suggested that management follow six steps:

▶ 1. Introduce employees to the E-Plus concept. Training and reading materials can get everyone in the organization thinking E-Plus.

  2. Add management attention, encouragement, and a reward system that reinforces participation in idea sharing. Hold regular E-Plus brainstorming sessions. Be receptive and imaginative to employee ideas.

3. Celebrate with hoopla. Make the effort fun and recognize people's participation and successes.

4. Constantly sharpen the picture of what customers expect. Use naive listening, open-ended questions, focus groups, and exploration teams to monitor customers' and competitors' ideas.

5. Hire people who have good attitudes toward customers. If possible, hire people experienced in dealing successfully with customers—and reward them for their efforts.

6. Make customer satisfaction an ongoing priority, not just a program.

If implemented effectively, an E-Plus customer satisfaction strategy can ensure a higher level of tenant loyalty and give the company a competitive advantage in its market. (Exhibit 6.1 summarizes customer expectations and responses in terms of satisfaction.)

The ℞ for Service Recovery

Having established the purpose of the service recovery venture, the next step is to consider the components of the process. In *Delivering Knock Your Socks Off Service*, Kristin Anderson and Ron Zemke set out the following six-step prescription for service recovery:

▶ 1. *Apologize.* It doesn't matter who's at fault. Customers want someone to acknowledge that a problem occurred and show concern over their disappointment.

2. *Listen and empathize.* Treat your customers in a way that shows you care about them as well as about their problem. People have feelings and emotions. They want the personal side of the transaction acknowledged.

3. *Fix the problem quickly and fairly.* A "fair fix" is one that's delivered with a sense of professional concern. At the bottom line, customers want what they expected to receive in the first place, and the sooner the better.

4. *Offer atonement.* It's not uncommon for dissatisfied customers to feel injured or put out by a service break-down. Often they will look to you to provide some value-added gesture that says, in a manner appropriate to the problem, "I want to make it up to you."

5. *Keep your promises.* Service recovery is needed because a customer believes a service promise has been broken. During the recovery process, you will often make new promises. When you do, be realistic about what you can and can't deliver.

Exhibit 6.1
Customer Satisfaction—E versus E-Plus

Customer Satisfaction Scale

Dissatisfied	Satisfied	Motivated

Expectations		
Negative (Worse than expected)	Neutral (About what was expected)	Positive (Better than expected)
Responses		
• Ignore or rationalize the inequity	Satisfaction is simply an absence of dissatisfaction, not motivation to become a repeat customer.	• Tell others of the positive experience
• Demand restitution		• Pay a premium for the goods received
• Retaliate		
• Withdraw from the relationship		• Become a repeat customer

Source: Paul R. Timm, Ph.D., "From Slogans to Strategy: How to Achieve Customer Loyalty," *Exchange,* Spring 1993, pp. 20–24. Adapted by permission of the author.

6. *Follow up.* You can add a pleasant extra to the recovery sequence by following up a few hours, days, or weeks later to make sure things really were resolved to your customer's satisfaction. Don't assume you've fixed the person or the problem. Check to be sure.

The quality of the service-recovery effort is one measure of the quality of the company that institutes it. It is one of the most important determinants of service quality, and it is a major driver of customer loyalty. Customer loyalty, in turn, has a direct, bottom-line impact on profitability. Nonetheless, many companies remain unaware of the extraordinary number of unhappy customers they stand to lose at any particular moment, and equally important, they treat those few who actually *do* complain with disdain or worse.

Improvements in complaint-surfacing and complaint-handling are impossible without stimulus from the top of the organization. For this reason, and because the quality of a company's service-delivery system depends on leadership, we turn to that subject in the next chapter.

The Leadership Revolution

Underneath all of the lists, rules, manuals and consumer insight is a core problem we need to address: that our spirit at the top has to change and our attitude toward front-line service be improved. Service is a spiritual and cultural issue. . . . Few on top have been frontline. American managers are still short-term, bottom-line focused. They got where they are generally without concern for spiritual values. They want competitive volume levels *today,* are often more motivated by how to look to the next job in the next company than what *this* company will be in ten years' time. Devoting energy and heart to internal morale, creating the esprit de corps, listening to each other is still considered a job for "personnel."

—MIMI LIEBER

Leaders who hope to motivate their employees to create value for their customers must also generate a spirit of excitement, pride, and *esprit de corps.* Companies with a strong, positive corporate culture have an almost tangible spirit of excitement. In these enterprises, employees know how to work together as a team toward the common aim of serving customers, and their pride comes from setting and meeting challenging goals. This kind of pride begins at the top of the organization.

—WILLIAM A. BAND, *Creating Value for Customers*

Commitment and dedication on the part of your people only happens when there's the same commitment and dedication on the part of the boss. Top management must confront the realities of the marketplace daily. I don't sit on some mountaintop, telling the American Airlines passenger service department how to deal with problems. I get out there and watch them work. I take regular trips on American—not because I have to go somewhere, but because I want to see for myself how we're doing.

—ROBERT CRANDALL, CEO of American Airlines

If the chief executive officer isn't the number one champion of The Customer, you're in trouble.

—DONALD R. LIBEY, *Libey on Customers*

Owners of commercial properties are naturally predisposed to so-called acquisition marketing, that is, finding and closing new business rather than satisfying—and thereby retaining—existing customers (the "Death-Wish Paradox" quoted in chapter 4). The defining characteristic of this strategy is the devotion of the bulk of a company's marketing budget to capturing new business, despite the fact that to do so is demonstrably more expensive and less fruitful than earmarking funds specifically for business retention.

Acquisition Marketing in the Commercial Real Estate Industry

In fairness, the preference for acquisition marketing, with its attendant, unsurpassed thrill of deal-making, is no more prevalent in commercial real estate management than it is in other enterprises. Indeed, Laura Liswood set these alternative marketing styles into a historical context as follows:

▶   In the past, acquisition and retention marketing went hand in hand. Selling and service were part of the same ongoing company-customer relationship. By doing business with an establishment, a customer was automatically entitled to certain service rights: the rights to fair, courteous, and friendly treatment and the assurance that the proprietor would make good on anything that went wrong. However, as we matured into a more mobile, industrialized, technocratic society, a distinction arose between selling and everything that came after the sale. Selling became so specialized that it got to be called "marketing," and the job of attracting attention to a company or product evolved into "advertising and promotion." With the relentless growth in population, consumer demand, and purchasing power, everybody got so busy selling, promoting, and keeping score that owners and managers began to neglect the second half of the sale: the half where customers were supposed to be happy about turning over their money. We relegated the second half of the sale to "customer complaint departments," "service departments," and "warranty departments." That situation might have turned out fine, except that the job of providing service didn't furnish the glamour, excitement, and income associated with marketing and promotion.

Your Employees Are Your Customers, Too

Some real estate management companies seem to continually advertise the same positions in the "Help Wanted" section of the classified pages, an indication of repeated employee turnover. Firms with this type of revolving-door attitude toward staffing fail to understand the linkage between contented workers and company success. This is characteristic of the leading service industries—including, and especially, commercial real estate—in which establishing bonds between customers and companies is a necessary prologue to long-term relationships and repeat business.

The antithesis of this revolving-door attitude toward a firm's internal customers is exemplified by Hal Rosenbluth. His company's objective is to delight its employees, who in turn strive to delight the firm's external customers. As Rosenbluth put it:

▶ Companies earn the bad attitudes of their people. Does anyone ever begin a new job with a bad attitude? No. They are "bright-eyed and bushy-tailed," filled with anticipation, excitement, and ambition. But companies with little regard for the happiness of their people find that their enthusiasm and open-mindedness are soon replaced by apathy and bitterness.

Employees whose enthusiasm for their work has evaporated can hardly be expected to fulfill the company mission—which, at Rosenbluth Travel, is as follows: "Our goal is to spoil our clients beyond the point where anyone else's service will do."

Employees who are apathetic and bitter quickly become disgruntled, and their attitudes taint the viewpoints of new employees as well as those of the customers they serve. In addition, as Paul Goodstadt, director of service quality at NatWest Bank, has warned:

▶ Disgruntled employees [become] terrorists. They're out there sabotaging the customer's experience by their alienation, anger, and resentment. We must get to them and turn them around. We must get them on our side, and (more importantly) on the side of the customer.

Rosenbluth admonished the business manager to remember:

▶ *Happiness in the workplace* is a strategic advantage. Service comes from the heart, and people who feel cared for will care more. Unhappiness results in error, turnover, and other evils. To strengthen happiness you have to measure it . . . . Finally, companies have to have fun. When was the last time you excelled at something you disliked?

In chapter 2, we briefly explored the Japanese concept of "shared fate," the notion that employers and employees, whatever their job titles and responsibilities, are equally invested in the success of their companies, and equally aware that success can be affected by downswings in staff performance and productivity. In companies whose personnel at every level have internalized the principle of shared fate and the truth of the axiom, "The Customer Comes First," customer service becomes the battle cry of every employee, from the CEO to the front line and back again. Because individual accountability is

---

Customer-Focused Marketing *(After Libey)*

- Must come from the top down—beginning with the policymakers
- Requires support—money, people, deep personal involvement, proper tools
- Requires knowledge—of the customer, of the product or service, of the company, in general (personal development)
- Demands speed—of response, of results
- Must be accessible—available to all, equally
- Requires personal contact—empowerment

---

intertwined with delighting customers, every employee has the authority to become a sole-source customer-satisfaction company. When this transformation occurs, as Jeffrey Disend exclaimed, "Everyone believes, 'I'm it! I'm personally responsible for the quality and service our customers get.'" Until this understanding permeates the entire organization—the notion that every employee, whether physically situated at the frontline or in the corner office, is independently responsible for the satisfaction of each of the firm's customers—the customer service ethos that the company is seeking will be a mirage. *Customer-first* behavior is a joint and several responsibility.

Service Is a Personal Undertaking

While it is important to understand that there is a distinction between internal and external customers, this differentiation between a company's clients tends to overshadow the essential quality of the attitude that the company needs to manifest to *all* of its customers. In the service culture, every employee has a customer. Every department, whether or not it has contact with the (external) paying customer, has a client who must be served if the overall mission of the company is to be realized. William Band put it this way:

▶ If there is one dominating challenge facing business enterprises in the next decade, it can be summed up in a single word: *people.* As companies struggle to become more customer-focused, they often find their organizational structure and their employees' attitudes, beliefs, and habits present the greatest barriers to success. Ironically, part of the problem is that while businesses are attempting to treat their external customers with more care and respect, they sometimes fail to put the same value on their *internal* customers: their employees.

This essential, people-sensitive aspect of customer service is imbued with the essence of the Golden Rule and the spirit of the Boy Scout Oath. Providing excellent service to customers is an everyday person-to-person activity. Delivering *exceptional* service is doing something remarkable for the cus-

tomer—whether internal or external—as a *person*. This requires seeing each
of the firm's customers as a person, as a thinking, feeling human being with
needs. It means challenging all employees to be empathetic (rather than sym-
pathetic)—i.e., to ask themselves about every customer: If I were this customer, what would *I* want? What else might this person need? How can I do
things better for this customer? As Karl Albrecht observed:

▶ The outstanding service organization is one in which all "servers"
know clearly who their customers are; they know what constitutes
value for them; and they work continually to deliver that value.
Whether a particular department serves external customers or internal customers, or both, its mission is essentially the same: to deliver
value to those customers.

In commercial real estate management, where both owner-clients and tenants are business entities, the definition of *customer* is often blurred, making
it difficult to "personalize" the delivery of customer service. In marketing
their management services and leasing commercial space, management company personnel may be dealing exclusively with company executives—the
people who are the decision-makers in their customer-companies. However,
it is in the aftermarketing of the relationships with commercial tenants that
the personal nature of customer service is greatly expanded—the commercial real estate management company's external customers include not only
decision-makers, but the tenant's employees and its clients, customers, and
suppliers.

Top-Down Customer Service

Customer reverence as well as the shared-fate philosophy—the notion that
"we're all in this together"—necessarily begins with the boss, whose gut-
level understanding of these imperatives is exemplified by the reduction (or
outright elimination) of internal-employee turnover, substituting for it a program with employee empowerment as its centerpiece. In *Business Partnering for Continuous Improvement: How to Forge Enduring Alliances Among
Employees, Suppliers, and Customers,* Charles Poirier and William Houser put
it this way:

▶ The reality of the past decade's efforts is that American managers
prefer a quick fix, often characterized by the inevitable downsizing
in personnel. They talk at length of the merits of a long-term orientation, of the importance of quality, a customer focus, and innovation
as critical to success, of their willingness to adopt successful ideas,
and the fact that people are their most important assets. Such talk
has a hollow sound to the growing thousands of displaced people
who decry the lack of any semblance of consistency in their former
organizations, where the "survive-the-month" attitude was wor-

shipped in deference to long-term success. . . . The solution to this problem requires that leaders develop a greater understanding of the criticality of their continued, oriented, and supportive posture as a factor in successful implementation of a *continuous* improvement process, which has now become a business imperative.

Creating a shared-fate, customer-focused environment should be the first priority for every employer. Jan Carlzon, one of the pacesetters who understood the pivotal role that internal customers play in achieving this company goal, described the obligation of its leadership as follows:

▶ It is up to the top executive to become a true leader, devoted to creating an environment in which employees can accept and execute their responsibilities with confidence and finesse. He must communicate with his employees, imparting the company's vision and listening to what they need to make that vision a reality. To succeed he can no longer be an isolated and autocratic decision-maker. Instead, he must be a visionary, a strategist, an informer, a teacher, and an inspirer.

Carlzon evidently took his own advice—that the boss must be a visionary—very seriously. Realizing that he was entirely powerless to control, let alone supervise or even be in attendance at each moment of truth that SAS personnel might have with the airline's passengers, Carlzon wisely chose to *empower* his employees to act on his behalf in the best interests of SAS customers. In doing so, he recast the essence of his organization to represent its revamped ranking of concerns. This transformed the organization from a hierarchy, which had prioritized the upper echelons of internal customers, to a "flattened" structure, which accurately depicted the revamped, customer-driven SAS. Carlzon described the transformation this way:

▶ Any business organization seeking to establish a customer orientation and create a good impression during its "moments of truth" must flatten the pyramid—that is, eliminate the hierarchical tiers of responsibility in order to respond directly and quickly to customers' needs. The customer-oriented company is organized for change.

While Carlzon was describing a "decentralizing" process, others characterized this change as an "inverted pyramid." Disend put it this way:

▶ In customer-focused organizations, the [hierarchical] pyramid is exactly the opposite . . . . [and] the people most important to the success and survival of the company *aren't* the owners or executives; rather they're the customers. The customer is the real boss, and these organizations recognize that fact. The people in the organization believe they "work for" the customer. The customer has the highest status, importance, and power.

Band added another dimension to the characterization:

▶ The "inverted pyramid" represents a change in attitude, whereby managers and supervisors act more as coaches or counselors than commanders.

This inversion of the hierarchy, as it might be represented in the real estate management business, is shown in exhibit 7.1.

Learning Organizations Are Localized.   Peter Senge characterized the so-called learning organization in his book, *The Fifth Discipline: The Art and Practice of The Learning Organization.* Such a firm adapts to changing circumstances as if it were actually assimilating information. It then acts on what it has discovered, thereby continually expanding its capacity to create its own future. Senge has suggested that such companies will increasingly incorporate Carlzon's organizational paradigm, including employee empowerment:

▶ Learning organizations will, increasingly, be "localized" organizations, extending the maximum degree of authority and power as far from the "top" or corporate center as possible. Localness means moving decisions down the organizational hierarchy; designing business units where, to the greatest degree possible, local decision makers confront the full range of issues and dilemmas intrinsic in growing and sustaining any business enterprise. Localness means unleashing people's commitment by giving them the freedom to act, to try out their own ideas and be responsible for producing results.

Jan Carlzon's revolutionary idea—to flatten the organizational structure of his airline so that it would be immediately responsive to its passengers—became transformed into a mission statement for SAS employees. Karl Albrecht described Carlzon's directive as follows: "If you're not serving the customer, you'd better be serving someone who is." This concept, in turn, generated an awareness of the significance of a company's so-called internal customers—i.e., its employees—which sensitized Hal Rosenbluth and others to the importance of nurturing a firm's own personnel as a means of stimulating service-delivery to its "external" customers.

While Carlzon and Rosenbluth, among others, envisioned their functions in their respective companies as decidedly secondary to, and supportive of, frontline personnel in their firms, their efforts to define the organizational missions of SAS and Rosenbluth Travel were essential to their companies' success. The personal visions of these extraordinary leaders, while different from one another, were nonetheless complementary. More important, they were metamorphosed into forward-looking, customer-responsive missions for their organizations that can prove instructive for real estate management firms today. As Donald R. Libey observed:

▶ History is very clear and loaded with common sense in one principal area of commerce: pay extraordinary attention to your customers and they will pay extraordinary attention to your business.

Exhibit 7.1
A Customer-Focused Organizational Pyramid

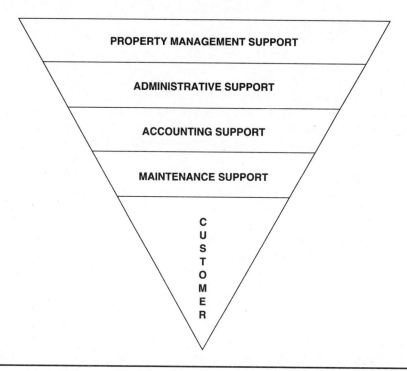

Combining this vital lesson with Carlzon's and Rosenbluth's visions yields an understanding of what commercial reality is to the top leadership of a service provider: Customers are the essence of a company's success; continuing to do business with a firm's current customers is the gist of marketing; and therefore the company needs to act in ways that demonstrate responsiveness to customer needs and preferences. Libey put it this way:

▶ The survival philosophy of the future must begin and end with The Customer for there is no other possible object of competitive primacy. If you will be first among competitors, you must first have the greatest share of The Customers. Without customers, you are but dust in the wind; with customers, you are primal.

Customer Focus in
Commercial Real Estate Management

In commercial real estate management, this reality—that tenants are the only reason for the company to be in business, and the only reason that it can stay in business—will be the defining and differentiating characteristic of the service organization, comprising its mission, its core value, through the millennium. The proper role of leaders in this environment is to express this reality in a mission statement for the organization, and thereafter to live and exemplify the mission statement in their business lives.

Michael Hammer and James Champy, authors of *Reengineering the Corporation: A Manifesto for Business Revolution,* linked corporate mission statements, leaders' actions, and company success in this powerful statement:

▶ Creating a corporate value statement alone is useless and just another faddish exercise. Without supporting management systems, most corporate value statements are collections of empty platitudes that only increase organizational cynicism. To be worth the paper it's printed on, a value statement must be reinforced by the company's management systems. The statement articulates values; the management systems give those values life and reality within the company.

And, of course, senior management must live these values themselves. If an executive says it's important to care about customers and then spends an hour a week on the phone with customers, the value of that time to customers may be minor, but its value to the organization is immeasurable. The hour is a symbol and a demonstration of management's personal commitment to the values by which they expect everyone to live.

An excellent example of how a corporate value statement can be utilized to focus the commitment of the entire company on customer service comes from Metric Property Management, whose employees created The Metric CARES Commitment resident retention program in 1992—CARES stands for Customers Always Receive Excellent Service. Kelley, Lundeen & Crawford subsequently adapted the CARES program for commercial properties they managed for Metric Property Management in the Dallas, Texas, area. When Kelley, Lundeen & Crawford became Miller Commercial in 1994, the program was formalized under the new company name.

Miller Commercial chose the word *exceptional* to characterize service that would surpass customers' expectations and represent a service level unique in the industry. Subsequently, the Miller Commercial commitment to service was embodied in the acronym *CARES*.

Customers
Always
Receive
Exceptional
Service

The acronym is supported by a written pledge (shown in exhibit 7.2), which was printed on small pocket-sized cards and distributed to each employee and manager with the challenge to read it, keep it, and practice it daily.

To reinforce the pledge, management implemented a policy of randomly asking employees what specific letters in the acronym represented. For example, a property manager meeting a maintenance engineer at a property would ask, "What does "exceptional" represent in our pledge to our customers?" In response, the maintenance engineer would recite the key points listed under exceptional. The company also instituted a CARES Ambassador-of-the-Month award, by which the managers recognize one employee who exemplified the CARES pledge during the previous month. The employee receives a letter specifically identifying the exceptional service rendered, along with a check for $50.00.

The CARES commitment provided immediate results—it solved problems between departments that previously impeded the quality of customer service rendered—because each employee assumed ownership of problems brought to his or her attention, irrespective of the department responsible for handling the problem: Maintenance personnel accepted as a personal challenge to complete tenants' service requests on the first call by making a follow-up visit to be sure the problem did not recur. Friction between managers and the accounting department ceased as both groups learned to respect each other's roles in serving customers' needs— i.e., as members of the same team.

This corporate value program focused the entire company on the importance of customer service by involving everyone in the development process. In this way, each team member accepted the commitment pledge as his or her own personal value statement. The random quizzes by managers and the CARES Ambassador-of-the-Month award reinforced the company's commitment to the pledge and provided ongoing examples of the benefits of exceptional service to Miller Commercial's customers from among the team members themselves.

Another truism that is broadly applicable in the business world—and typical of commercial real estate management—is that most companies operate in environments that have been created more by happenstance than by design. Because real estate management has frequently been an offshoot of allied activities—development and finance are but two—it has often been considered a secondary activity in relation to the central business of the firm. By becoming customer-focused, real estate management can be uniquely

Exhibit 7.2
The Miller Commercial Pledge

Miller Commercial
CARES
Our Pledge to Individual and Customer Success

Customers
- The company exists because of our *customers*. Customer service is our job, not an extension of the job.
- The *customer* is always the customer. Treat owners and tenants with respect, whether in person or over the phone.
- Our *customers* are all around us every day. Doing whatever it takes to service our immediate customers is our most important tool for creating customer loyalty and generating new loyal customers.

Always
- *Always* greet customers with enthusiasm and a smile, using their names when possible.
- *Always* be a Miller CARES ambassador inside and outside the work place.
- *Always* work as a team inside the organization to benefit customers outside the organization.

Receive
- Any employee who *receives* a customer complaint "owns" the complaint until it is resolved satisfactorily.
- When *receiving* a service request, employ the 4S formula:
    Smile
    Speed
    Solution
    Satisfaction
- All customers should *receive* a service evaluation form and be encouraged to let Miller Commercial know about their service satisfaction.

Exceptional
- The Miller Commercial Standard of *Exceptional* Service is measured by customer satisfaction.
- Perform each job function to achieve the Miller Standard of *Exceptional* Service.
- Provide for *exceptional* property appearance, tenant relations, property occupancies, and customer loyalty.

Service
- Treat each customer request as a *service* opportunity.
- Customer *service* is everyone's responsibility.

The Miller Commercial program is an adaptation of The Metric CARES Commitment developed by employees of Metric Property Management in 1992 as a resident retention program. The Metric CARES Commitment was awarded "First Place" in the category "Other Formalized Retention/Incentive Programs" in the 1993 Marketing and Communications Awards competition sponsored by the Institute of Real Estate Management.

Reprinted with permission from Miller Commercial in Dallas, Texas, and Metric Property Management, in San Francisco, California.

distinguished from a company's other real estate activities, as well as set the company apart from its competition.

The Company Culture. Historically, real estate management companies evolved in response to price-sensitive market conditions rather than according to long-range plans. However, those managing commercial properties are beginning to experience a business culture that, while perhaps somewhat less price conscious than its predecessors, has become, seemingly overnight, extraordinarily customer-responsive. Their customers—the commercial entities that are their tenants—are encountering increasing pressures to make choices in their everyday business transactions on the basis of claims that many expensive products offer superior quality, value, or service, or a combination of these features, that overwhelms mere price considerations. As Zeithaml and coworkers noted:

▶ In every nook and cranny of the service economy, the leading companies are obsessed with service excellence. They use service to be different; they use service to increase productivity; they use service to earn the customers' loyalty; they use service to fan positive word-of-mouth advertising; they use service to seek some shelter from price competition.

Moreover, competing owners and management companies, however tentatively, are beginning to introduce customer-responsive techniques into their own businesses, and are experimenting with marketing their portfolios—or even their entire firms—with a service emphasis. Having established the outlines of a service culture, these companies use it to crush their competition. Davidow and Uttal have described this phenomenon as follows:

▶ The service winners know that customer service is both a potent competitive advantage and a particularly defensible one. Because customers perceive service in relative terms, a competitor who wants to beat a company that offers relatively superior service can't play catch up. He has to leapfrog, to outdistance the competition. But since providing great service tends to be expensive, leapfrogging can break the bank.

The literature of commercial real estate management is ablaze with admonitions to practitioners to introduce service components into their marketing and leasing packages. One would almost think there is a conspiracy afoot to force owners and managers of commercial properties to reinvent their companies with a customer focus. Conspiracy or not, the ranks of commercial property management companies have only glimpsed this revolution. Frankly, when *Total Customer Service* was published in 1989, its authors considered the then-current state of customer service to be a disaster. In the mid-1990s, things have not changed much. To quote Davidow and Uttal:

▶ "Crisis" is a strong word but no exaggeration. Most customer service is poor, much of it is awful, and service quality generally appears to be falling. At the same time, the penalty is growing for companies that render inferior service. Customers . . . are getting smarter about the value of service. They're increasingly frustrated and more willing than ever to take their business elsewhere.

Strategic Planning—Stating the Vision.   Revolutionary circumstances are extraordinarily demanding of company leadership. Someone at the uppermost level of the firm—whether it is a children's hospital, a video store, or a real estate management company—must respond to the challenges that this new customer uprising poses to the company's very survival. These leaders may choose to begin their customer-service odyssey by reading some of the outstanding literature in the field (see the Bibliography at the back of this book); when they do, they will need to resist the temptation to instantly implement everything they have learned. As Jeffrey Disend has counseled:

▶ Becoming service-oriented is a process, not an event. Transforming an organization is not something that occurs quickly. Exceptional service is not something to get fired up about for a few months or a year and then forget about. It's a commitment to a lifelong approach to making customers the focal point of the organization.

The service literature, besides heightening their enthusiasm, will provide sufficient information to enable company leadership to create a strategic plan for the organization—the company's mission statement serves as the plan's foundation. Such planning is a necessary introductory step in the process of a company's becoming service-sensitive. In commercial real estate management, it is designed to answer the question, "Why should prospective office (or retail or industrial) tenants choose us, and having done so, why should they decide to stay?" Senge defined a mission statement this way:

▶ [It is] the organization's answer to the question, "Why do we exist?" Great organizations have a larger sense of purpose that transcends providing for the needs of shareholders and employees. They seek to contribute to the world in some unique way, to add a distinctive source of value.

Few managers of commercial properties have ever crafted such an ambitious plan, and fewer still have done so with the goal of generating a vision statement that will be used both as a compass and a yardstick—first to guide, and then to measure, the company's long-term progress toward meeting its goal of becoming customer-focused.

Participants in the strategic planning process may comprise the company's entire personnel roster, its management team, or a committee representing the various divisions within the firm. Because the first step, the task of developing a mission statement, necessarily involves imbuing the entire company with a personal vision, we believe that participation by as many employees as possible is crucial. This echoes remarks from Senge who recommended a broad composition of the group:

▶ The first step in mastering the discipline of building shared visions is to give up traditional notions that visions are always announced from "on high" or come from an organization's institutionalized planning processes.

The result of the process will be a collective conceptualization designed to inspire and provide direction for everyone in the firm, as Senge pointed out:

▶ A shared vision changes people's relationship with the company. It is no longer "their company;" it becomes "our company." . . . It creates a common identity.

Define the Business.   The planning group should begin by conceptualizing the nature of the company's business.

- What does our company do?
- Where is our real opportunity in the market?
- What is our special competence?
- What are our customers' real needs?
- What motivates our customers?
- What can we do with our service that our customers will really notice and pay a premium for?

The answers to these questions—whom the business is satisfying, what customer needs it is meeting, and how distinctively it is doing so—will define the nature and quality of the company's business.

Because companies have both internal and external customers who may have different expectations and needs than their counterparts, it is helpful to distinguish between a company's internal and external focuses. In addition, adopting an expansive view of the company's mission—how it intends to market itself to its external customers—helps the firm to adopt a sufficiently comprehensive approach. As Jeffrey Disend pointed out:

▶ An organization can . . . shape what people think about by deciding what business it's in. That may sound naive and blindingly obvious, but many organizations don't have a clear picture of this. The business you think you're in affects what your organization does, how it's organized, and what your people do. Identifying an organization's primary business provides focus and direction.

The importance of selecting an external focus is perhaps best illustrated with a few examples. In the early 1970s, Smith Corona fashioned a strategic plan based on the determination that the company was in the business of manufacturing typewriters. Meanwhile, IBM, whose primary product at the time was the Selectric typewriter, envisioned itself in the business of providing business solutions. Despite its recent financial problems, Big Blue has significantly outperformed its former competitor, and has done so in part because it initially formulated a vast business purpose to pursue. *Too narrow a focus can doom a company to mediocrity.*

Here are some other examples. What is Coca-Cola's business purpose? Viewed from an internal perspective, the company produces and markets soft drinks; considered more expansively, however, Coke is in the refreshment and nostalgia business. How about the American Automobile Association? Some might say that Triple-A provides emergency car repair service; a broader view is that it provides security for automobile owners. Similarly, a university continuing education department might conceive of its business as delivering college courses; the more inclusive approach would be to characterize its mission as designing vehicles for people to improve their lifestyles and thereby feel better about themselves.

Create a Mission Statement.   The variety of customers whom commercial real estate managers serve complicates the formulation of a business purpose. On the one hand, owner-clients expect the management company to maximize their properties' income and minimize its expenses, to maintain them to the highest standards, and to provide comprehensive reports of progress in meeting these goals. On the other hand, tenants require management to provide a secure, comfortable, well-maintained environment for their employees and their customers; to respond promptly to their needs; and to treat their requests with respect. Finally, on-site and central-office employees of the management company want an environment that will be conducive to their productivity, that rewards them appropriately for their efforts, respects their opinions, and recognizes them for their contributions. While these differing expectations are not internally inconsistent, they are so diverse that addressing them by means of a one-sentence mission statement presents a real challenge. Indeed, the leadership of the real estate management company must consider this proliferation of customers in developing an effective mission statement.

The process of formulating a mission statement and deriving a strategic

What Is a Mission Statement?

A mission statement is the foundation document of a company. Properly crafted, it sets out what business you are in, what market you serve, what distinctive quality you bring to the market, and the special way you approach it.

The mission statement should define the shared vision of a firm's internal customers about their professional future and how they will serve their external clients. Everyone in the company should participate in drafting the company's mission statement. If logistics make such extensive involvement impractical, the statement should at least connect the visions of people throughout the organization, rather than merely institutionalize the opinions of those at the top.

The purpose of a mission statement is to establish an overarching goal that participants in the process consider to be truly desirable. The loftiness of the target ennobles the entire enterprise, creating a spark that enlivens the organization and uplifts the aspirations of its employees. Great organizations have a purpose that transcends providing for the needs of their staffs: By means of synergistic, harmonious efforts, they seek to contribute a distinctive source of value to a particular market.

A mission statement should answer the following questions:

1. What function are we trying to fill in society? What unique capabilities does our company bring to this task?
2. For whom do we perform our functions? What do we want to communicate to our customers that will let them know how important their satisfaction is to the future of the enterprise?
3. How do we go about fulfilling these functions?

We believe the commitment to customer satisfaction as the company's ultimate product must be built into its mission statement. Indeed, *customer satisfaction must be the mission.*

---

plan for a management company—or a component of the company, such as the personnel who manage a specific office building or shopping center—is designed to assist the entity in preparing a blueprint that will guide it successfully through the competitive underbrush it will undoubtedly have to confront.

Hotel management epitomizes the demand for customer service within the real estate industry. The service opportunities with each customer are almost endless. Two national chains—The Marriott Corporation and Westin Hotels and Resorts—are striving to lead this industry in providing "exceptional" customer service as an extension of their mission statements. Both encourage their general managers to develop distinctive mission statements for their respective hotels. This provides a tremendous team-building exercise. The entire staff at the hotel works together to assess the customer needs that are served by the different departments within the hotel. Upon completion, the printed mission statement is displayed prominently throughout the hotel. This serves as a constant reminder to the team members of their individual commitment to "exceptional" service.

While visiting the Westin South Coast Plaza, Howard Lundeen, CPM®, one of the authors of this book, was impressed with the level of service within each department. His impressions are recounted here:

> After questioning the general manager to determine what made this hotel different in its commitment to "exceptional" service, I was taken to the employee dining room to experience the vision and mission statements developed by the team members. As I stood there in the middle of the dining room the answer to my question was posted all over three of the four walls. Not only were the vision and mission statements visible in the dining room, they were also on the walls in the staff corridors.

The shared values and the twenty service standards developed by Westin South Coast Plaza (see exhibit 7.3) provide a benchmark for real estate management companies as they assess their mission statement and service standards. All real estate management companies should endeavor to empower their employees *with the responsibility and authority to satisfy their customers.* Just imagine how much your service would improve if you implemented just a few of Westin's service standards in dealing with your various customers. The following are some specific suggestions.

- Escort visitors rather than pointing out directions.

- *Smile*—Maintain positive eye contact with people.

- Always provide a friendly greeting whenever you encounter tenants or their employees or customers (the *10 and 5 Rule* and the *hellozone*).

- Use proper and courteous vocabulary.

- Answer phones within three rings.

- Look out for and pick up litter *(Pick-up Club)*.

- Look out for inconsistencies and defects in the property *(Fix-up Club)*.

- Always be on the lookout for *opportunities for improvement.*

- Be knowledgeable about the property.

- Be an ambassador for the property and the management company.

- Practice energy conservation and proper maintenance and repair of the property and its equipment.

- Respond to external or internal customer requests and needs as quickly as possible. Practice teamwork and pitch-in and help. Don't wait to be asked.

- Any employee who hears of a problem, *owns* the problem. Monitor the solution process.

Assess the Competition. One starting point in developing a strategic plan is to find out the number of competitive firms or entities within the market area. Couple this with the historical demand for management of commercial properties in the same area, and these data should help the planning group arrive at a conservative forecast of future demand for the management company's services.

By focusing on the market, the group will be able to identify the new entrants providing competitive services, together with the number of firms that have emerged during the past 24 months. Moreover, it may be possible to forecast likely players that will emerge during the succeeding two-year period. An accurate assessment of the amount of competition, together with an evaluation of the company's own capabilities, will assist it in charting a new course and positioning its products and services against opposing offerings.

Identify Distinctive Competencies. Addressing the way a management company responds to the various needs of its diverse clientele of external and internal customers determines its distinctive competencies—its uniqueness in its markets—which in turn tends to create customer loyalty to the firm. The relationships that a company initiates and cultivates with its constituencies determine its peculiar positioning within the commercial real estate industry. Because each of these clients has unique expectations, company leaders can determine what they are and strategize ways to meet them. If the company consistently *exceeds* its clients' expectations, the leaders can establish a special competence for their companies. Here is an example:

> Assume that the management company has an institutional owner-client that expects its property to achieve a five-percent annual increase in net operating income—a figure that would exceed its past performance. If the company can deliver a nine-percent increase, it will have demonstrated to this owner that it possesses a "distinctive competence." Similarly, if tenants in the building have become accustomed to a one-day turnaround in work-order processing, a one-hour response time exhibits the distinctive competence of the property's maintenance personnel. Finally, for building employees

---

Exhibit 7.3
The Westin South Coast Plaza Mission Statement

At The Westin South Coast Plaza we have a vision to always be regarded as the best first-class hotel in Orange County.

In order to realize our vision, our Mission must be to achieve the highest possible levels of customer satisfaction. We will accomplish our Mission by:

Committing to our shared values*;

Being empowered with the responsibility and authority to satisfy our customers;

Continuously improving ourselves and the level of service we provide.

Customers are both external and internal and are defined as guests, the local community, employees, and owners.

*Our Shared Values

Values are the beliefs and attitudes that determine how work is accomplished, how we interact with each other. They guide our decisions.

• Integrity:	Keeping our word when we promise.
• Excellence:	An overall drive to be the best.
• Vision:	Our direction for the future.
• People:	Our most valuable asset.
• Hard Work:	Giving 100% every day/year.
• Empowerment:	Giving employees the responsibility and the authority to satisfy their customers.
• Open Communication:	Talking and listening to everyone, everyday, with words and actions.
• Growth and Financial Success:	Increased market share translates into increased revenue, profits, and return on investment for owners, and therefore funds to make improvements.

TOTAL QUALITY CORNERSTONES

1. Continuous improvement
2. Employee involvement and teamwork
3. Customer centered
4. Data-based decision making
5. Systems and support
6. Top management ownership
7. Supplier involvement

---

whose labors typically go unnoticed, if the president of the management company publicly recognizes their achievements at a monthly staff meeting or a holiday get-together, the employer's distinctive competence is also demonstrated in the minds of the staff.

This concept of "distinctive competence" is especially useful to leaders in real estate management firms that are faced with significant market pressures. The ability to develop "brand loyalty," which certain retailers have succeeded in

Exhibit 7.3 *(continued)*

SERVICE STANDARDS

1. Our Mission Statement, Shared Values, and TQ Cornerstones will be known and practiced by all employees.
2. Customers have the right of way. Always let them go first.
3. Escort customers, rather than pointing out directions to another area of the hotel.
4. *10 and 5 Rule.* A group of two or more employees will stop talking when an approaching customer is within 10 feet and greet the customers when within 5 feet.
5. *Smile.* Don't walk with your head and eyes cast downward. Be alert to things going on around you. Maintain positive eye contact with external and internal customers.
6. *Hellozone.* Always provide a friendly greeting whenever you encounter an external or internal customer. Don't wait for customers to address you. Address them first and by name whenever possible.
7. Use proper and courteous vocabulary with all external and internal customers. Ask rather than demand. Say *please, yes, hello,* and *thank you.* Eliminate *yeah, hi, thanks.*
8. Respond to external or internal customer wishes and needs as quickly as possible. Cooperate with other employees. Practice teamwork and pitch-in and help. Don't wait to be asked.
9. Any employee who hears a problem, *owns* the problem. Monitor the solution process from beginning to end to ensure satisfaction. Every employee is empowered to resolve problems.
10. *Telephone Etiquette.* Answer within three rings and with a *smile,* give greeting (Good morning, afternoon, evening), department and name. Do not screen calls. Eliminate call transfers when possible.
11. *Pick-Up Club.* Always be on the look-out for and pick up debris and discarded materials. Empty ash trays of contents.
12. *Fix-Up Club.* Always be on the look-out for inconsistencies and defects throughout the hotel. If possible, correct immediately. If not, notify your supervisor.
13. *OFI.* Always be on the look-out for *Opportunities for Improvement* throughout the hotel. Submit your ideas on an OFI form to the Quality Council.
14. Uniforms and business attire are to be clean, neat and professional looking. Wear proper footwear (clean and polished) and name tag at all times. Personal appearance, grooming, and cleanliness is to be uncompromising and immaculate.
15. Be knowledgeable of hotel information (hours of operation etc.) to answer guest inquiries. Recommend the hotel's food and beverage outlets first.
16. Be an ambassador of Westin Hotels and Resorts in and outside of the workplace. Always talk positively. No negative comments.
17. Know your role during emergency situations and be aware of fire and life safety response processes.
18. Notify your supervisor immediately of hazards, injuries, equipment or assistance that you need.
19. Practice energy conservation and proper maintenance and repair of hotel property and equipment.
20. Protecting the assets of Westin Hotels and Resorts is the responsibility of every employee.

Reproduced with permission from Westin South Coast Plaza Hotel in Costa Mesa, California.

doing, is a devastating competitive advantage that is available in commercial real estate management as well.

The customer service revolution that has begun to reach the commercial real estate industry will undoubtedly result in brand loyalty to management companies that have developed a reputation for delivering uncommon value to tenants. Its clearest manifestation will be tenants who, when circumstances require them to leave a particular property at the expiration of their lease terms, inquire whether the firm manages another property in the city to which they are moving. *Portfolio loyalty based on product differentiation* will be the defining competitive advantage in commercial real estate management in the future.

Distinguish Your Commercial Real Estate Product.   Product differentiation is the strategic goal of the planning process for the leaders of the real estate management firm. In one sense, seeking a competitive edge by devising a means of differentiating a firm's product from the thicket of competing goods is an effort to rob customers of their power to make choices. Because rents and other commercial lease terms vary within the community, and because there is usually a glut of product, tenants have a substantial amount of discretion (meaning: "power") available to them. (Such an environment has typified the commercial real estate industry in most U.S. markets throughout the early 1990s and will almost certainly be repeated at some time in the future.) These days, prospective tenants' selections of leased space are frequently made at random and determined *primarily* on the basis of price considerations. Consequently, the success of any particular office building, shopping center, or industrial site, as well as its managing entity, is more likely to be determined by chance than any other factor.

On the other hand, if the property can be successfully distinguished from its competition on the basis of some consideration *other than price*—the quality of the service orientation demonstrated by the site staff, for example—it will attain a competitive advantage, and its managing agent will achieve similar preeminence. The problem is that "service" is a difficult concept to employ as a sales proposition. Because of this fact, leaders of companies who are attempting to differentiate otherwise interchangeable products are confronted by a somewhat greater challenge than others whose goods are easily distinguished from those of their competitors.

In commercial real estate management, it can be especially difficult to distinguish one "vanilla box" from another (see chapter 2 and exhibit 2.2). This was addressed by economist Philip Nelson who has categorized products as possessing so-called *search* and *experience* qualities. The former are qualities that a consumer can evaluate *prior to* purchase, while the latter are those that can be determined only *after* the purchase. The central, albeit unfortunate, characteristic of service is that it possesses primarily "experience" qualities: Service is intangible, which means that it cannot be inspected prior to purchase; service is delivered to customers at the same time it is produced. The fact that service is an intangible quality makes it an especially difficult characteristic to market. A real estate management company may assert that it is "tenant-driven" or "tenant-oriented," yet prospective tenants cannot determine the truth of that claim until they experience the environment the firm has established, that is, until *after* they become tenants.

Because marketing service as a competitive advantage is such a formidable challenge, some may wonder whether the process of becoming a service-oriented company or entity is worth the trouble. In fact, we believe that management firms, as well as divisions of such firms, ought to undertake this arduous journey at least in part *because of its unparalleled marketing potential.* Here is what Berry and Parasuraman have written about this subject:

▶ Services are dominated by experience qualities, attributes that can be meaningfully evaluated only after purchase and during production-consumption. In services, both *post-sale marketing* through orchestrating a satisfying experience for customers during production and *word-of mouth communication* (which is surrogate and supplement for customers' direct experiences) have prominent effects in winning customers' loyalty.

Reasons Why Customer Satisfaction Is a Company's Salvation

Four factors coalesce to make customer satisfaction the driving force for an organization. First, customers are the lifeblood of a business (this has been noted at several points elsewhere in this book). Without them, a company has no reason to exist. As Donald Libey pointed out:

▶ The only path to long-term, profitable survival is customer-focused marketing. All business begins and ends with The Customer. In the beginning, there was The Customer. In the end there will be The Customer. The company with the most customers wins.

Second, when a firm establishes customer service as a "distinctive competence" it sets itself apart from, and far ahead of, its competitors. Again, as quoted from Davidow and Uttal earlier in this chapter:

▶ The service winners know that customer service is both a potent competitive advantage and a peculiarly defensible one. Because customers perceive service in relative terms, a competitor who wants to beat a company that offers relatively superior service can't play catch up. He has to leapfrog, to outdistance the competition. But since providing great service tends to be expensive, leapfrogging can break the bank.

For commercial real estate managers who operate in a marketing milieu in which devotion to customers is a rarity, constructing a credible service program will result in a competitive advantage that will be unbeatable.

Third, once it has established a reputation for delivering superior service, the firm can capitalize on the positive word-of-mouth referrals that every company craves. Because prospects seek out and rely more on information from personal sources (i.e., the experiences of others) than impersonal ones (for example, newspaper and magazine advertisements), word-of-mouth advertising over time can become the central marketing strategy for the firm, resulting in significant cost savings. As Hanan and Karp stated in *Customer Satisfaction: How to Maximize, Measure, and Market Your Company's "Ultimate Product":*

▶ At its best, [advertising] replicates an exchange of confidences between a trusted source and a trusting prospect. Who can be trusted? The most trustworthy source is never you, the manufacturer or supplier. *The most credible persuader is another customer who has already been satisfied.* This permits new customers to identify with the same satisfaction, apply it to their own situation, and rehearse their enjoyment of its benefits for themselves.

Indeed, the availability of testimonial advertising demonstrates to a prospective customer the firm's commitment to manufacturing satisfied customers, which is the company's true bottom line. *Satisfied customers are the most effective salespeople for the organization's goods and services,* in effect becoming partners who help to grow the business.

Prospective tenants of properties owned and/or managed by Chase Manhattan Bank are given an opportunity to experience this type of credible persuasion. As R. Bruce Smith, CPM®, tells it:

A truly tenant-oriented management company can let prospective tenants know in advance what kind of service they can expect. For example, I have 87 tenants in New York, Maryland, and Ohio. In each of these states, I provide a prospective tenant with the company and contact names and telephone numbers of our established tenants. I encourage the prospect to contact any or all of them, and I provide a list of questions regarding service quality that I think they should ask—along with any other questions they might have. In essence, I am telling the prospect up front how confident I am in the level of service we deliver.

Finally, providing exceptional service to a company's external clients benefits its internal customers as well. As Scott Gross pointed out:

▶ There is a surprising payoff awaiting these and other companies that imbue their customers with the service ethic: When they make their customers happy, they make their employees happy, too. Contented workers make for better-served customers, and there is mounting evidence that improvements in customer satisfaction lead directly to higher employee retention.

When the firm consistently delivers excellent service to all of its customers, a reinforcing process sets in: Small positive changes based on small positive actions tend to snowball, producing what might be called "virtuous cycles" of service that fortify and amplify each other. (See chapter 3 for a more detailed discussion of employee empowerment and satisfaction.)

For the leadership of a real estate management firm, becoming tenant-focused presents significant risks and opportunities. The metamorphosis from an inward-looking company that is preoccupied with its own narrow (often bureaucratic) concerns to a vibrant, outward-focused, customer-centered organization is an arduous, time-consuming process. Visionary leadership is the essential distinctive characteristic, as well as the driving force, of this dynamic transformation.

The
Benchmarking
Revolution

Society is always taken by surprise at any new example of common sense.
—RALPH WALDO EMERSON

Benchmarking is the continuous process of measuring products, services, and practices against the toughest competitors or those companies recognized as industry leaders.
—DAVID T. KEARNS, CEO of Xerox

If you would like to be an outstanding guitar player, cabaret singer, tennis player, sculptor, novelist, surgeon, stand-up comedian, interior designer, or anything else, it makes sense to study the best in your chosen field. How do they do what they do? What are their critical skills? How do they approach the challenge of excellence? How do they think? What are their success attitudes? How did they get to be the best?
—KARL ALBRECHT, *The Only Thing That Matters*

Benchmarking is one way to cut the ties of the past. By carefully revealing reality to the organization in digestible pieces, it inserts new views, objectives, and models into the murky waters of the past. Once gathered, benchmarking data do not go away, even if placed in a locked safe or shredded. Every individual who came in touch with the message is forever changed; they will never again see the organization in the same light. These individual revelations can build toward internal revolution, even while the security system is reporting that all is well. Change cannot be prevented or contained once it begins.
—KATHLEEN H. J. LEIBFRIED and C. J. McNAIR, *Benchmarking*

Competition, though rarely welcome, is healthy for any business. While most companies would probably prefer to have a monopolistic position in their industries, the benefits of competition are undeniable. Competition requires a firm to bring its best products to market, to price them fairly, and to service them faithfully. Competition challenges companies to stretch capacities, to refine products and pricing structures continuously, and to vie with competitors at the highest, most productive, most cost-effective levels of which they are capable. In short, competition impels a company to excellence and forces the ones that cannot meet this standard out of the market. This is not new. Rather, it is "the American way" of doing business and one of the reasons the Japanese have been so successful in recent years.

In the commercial real estate business, successful owners and managers analyze those product features and services in the competitive market that business tenants prefer—and are willing to pay premium rents to obtain—and then incorporate them into their properties. This concept, which might be termed "follow the leader," also challenges owners and managers to study rival buildings—to "go to school on the winners," as Richard Whiteley puts it—to determine suitable rent structures for their properties. Managers of commercial properties can begin to refine their rent-setting procedures by supplementing the traditional list of features and amenities and their respective price adjustments with rankings of certain "intangible perquisites" that are included in the product "bundle" in their particular market—such things as quality of staff, construction, security features, etc.

It is *competition* that drives these behaviors, after all, and competition is the foundation for "benchmarking," a novel concept pioneered by the Xerox Corporation to meet the Japanese competitive challenge of the 1970s and refined and perfected by Xerox, Avon Products, Exxon Chemical, AT&T, and others thereafter. The underlying principle of benchmarking, according to Robert C. Camp, one of the inventors of the concept, is "the search for those best practices that will lead to the superior performance of a company."

When these "best practices" are collected and analyzed, they can be incorporated into a company's own operations; the underpinnings of benchmarking are therefore similar to mimicry or imitation—i.e., copycatting. Karl Albrecht is one commentator who recognizes this implicit criticism. He explained it this way:

▶ It makes good sense for the leaders of any business organization to study the best practices of the champions in their own field. The goal is not to try to make an organization a carbon copy of any other, but to discern the truth of their success and implement that truth in their own unique way.

To this we would only add the old cliche: Imitation is the sincerest flattery.

Routine Benchmarking Applications

Consumers benchmark continuously and relentlessly—comparison shopping is benchmarking. Before purchasing an automobile, shoppers compare and contrast the features of various makes and models (domestic and foreign), try to measure values of each in economic and other terms, and routinely calibrate their findings against some "absolute"—a Mercedes, a Cadillac, or a Lexus, for example, or perhaps the first car they ever owned or the "perfect" vehicle they have conjured up in their imaginations. Whether shopping for perfume, a new suit, a VCR, or professional assistance with tax preparation, consumers weigh costs against product attributes and frequently consider the "bundle" of adjuncts that competing products offer—such as their guarantees, reputations, and ease and access of service—before they make a decision to buy. For consumers in the waning years of the twentieth century, effective benchmarking, although not identified as such, is almost second nature.

Benchmarking in the Commercial Real Estate Industry

Benchmarking is also frequently involved when real estate managers design an advertisement, seek out prospective tenants, negotiate with a vendor, or handle any one of the infinite number of moments of truth that are required in the management of office buildings, shopping centers, and other commercial properties. Consciously or unconsciously, you probably emulate people whom you believe are most effective at performing these types of routine management and marketing tasks—the styles of the leading retail managers and marketers who dominate their respective industries are seen on television or billboards, in newspaper or magazine advertisements, and are therefore readily adopted and adapted.

Although the best efforts of others may be routinely benchmarked, this does not necessarily restrict the scope of such imitation to any particular industry. You may choose to incorporate certain aspects of a rental car advertisement into one of your own ads, or to copy decorating details from an upscale hotel in the common areas of an office building you manage, or even to adapt the sales techniques of a particularly talented investment advisor as part of your own selling methodology. The opportunities to appropriate excellence from outside sources are potentially limitless. The willingness to seek out and emulate the "best of the best"—what the Japanese call *dantotsu*—extends across industries and is not restricted to any one source. "Dantotsu" is another ingredient of benchmarking.

Yet another characteristic of benchmarking is that it helps a company realize its ultimate potential in a perilous competitive battleground. Robert Camp likened its utility to warfare:

▶ In the year 500 B.C., Sun Tzu, a Chinese general, wrote, "If you know your enemy and know yourself, you need not fear the result of a hundred battles." Sun Tzu's words could just as well show the way to success in all kinds of business situations. Solving ordinary business problems, conducting management battles, and surviving in the marketplace are all forms of war, fought by the same rules—Sun Tzu's rules.

Benchmarking and Rent-Setting.   Pricing is a powerful weapon in commercial warfare, and benchmarking techniques can assist you in arriving at a proper pricing matrix for the leased space in commercial properties. The technique that is generally accepted in the real estate industry for evaluating a competitive market and ascertaining appropriate rental rates is *comparison grid analysis*. (Exhibits 8.1 and 8.2 are example grid forms for comparing office buildings and retail properties, respectively.)

This rent-setting approach, which is taught by the Institute of Real Estate Management in its core leasing and management courses, permits direct comparison of rental rates and amenities at the property that is the subject of the study with those of other properties in its immediate market that are comparable to it in size, features, and location. The left-hand column lists the features or qualities of the properties in the study, and blank columns are provided for each of the buildings to be compared. The subject property is described in the column adjacent to the features list, and the comparable properties are evaluated in successive columns to the right. [NOTE: Usually at least three comparable properties are identified. In cases where there are no comparable properties nearby, properties of similar configuration within the general trade area of the subject may be used; these are often identified as competitors (rather than comparables) on the grid.]

Note that the grids include two columns for each of the comparable properties—one to describe qualities and features and the other to adjust rental amounts upward or downward in dollar increments. The adjustments are intended to reflect whether a comparable is superior to the subject property with respect to a particular feature or quality. In effect, the rent of each comparable is adjusted up or down in an attempt to evaluate the differences between the subject and comparable properties, to quantify them in terms of rental value.

Benchmarking and Assessing Competitiveness.   Another technique utilized by many real estate managers is *market analysis*. This approach goes beyond simply comparing features, amenities, and rental rates of comparable properties to evaluate their overall *competitiveness*—a benchmarking exercise. The example market analysis grid in exhibit 8.3 employs a numerical rating scale of 1 to 5 for each category. It considers not only whether a particular characteristic is present, but also whether it is good or excellent or

Exhibit 8.1
Example Comparison Grid for Analyzing Office Buildings

Date _____

___ Renovated ___ As is	Subject	Comp #1		Comp #2		Comp #3	
Property Name							
Base Rental Rate							
− Concessions (Prorated)							
+ Expense Pass-Throughs							
+ Tenant-Paid Improvements (Prorated)							
+ Tenant's Effective Rent							
Categories	**Description**	**Descr.**	**Adj***	**Descr.**	**Adj***	**Descr.**	**Adj***
Location/Accessibility							
Age							
Reputation/Market Presence							
Building Condition: Exterior							
Grounds							
Common Areas							
Office Space							
Other							
Building Systems: Elevators							
HVAC Efficiency							
After-Hours Charges							
Life Safety							
Other							
Available Space: Location							
Floor Plate							
Window Modulation							
Other							
Parking: Open/Covered/Garage							
Visitor Spaces							
Cost to Tenant							
Other							
Amenities/Features:							
Vacancy Rate							
Total Rent Adjustments							
Adjusted Effective Rent per Rentable Sq Ft							
× R/U Ratio							
= Adjusted Effective Rent per Useable Sq Ft							

Exhibit 8.2

Example Comparison Grid for Analyzing Retail Properties

Date _____

	Subject	Comparable #1		Comparable #2		Comparable #3	
	Description	Description	Adj*	Description	Adj*	Description	Adj*
Market Minimum Rent†							
Anchor Draw							
Tenant Mix Synergy							
Parking							
Street Visibility							
Drive-by Traffic							
Vacancy Rate							
Ingress/Egress							
Signage Appearance							
Overall Appearance							
Pass-Throughs							
Total Adjustment							
Adjusted Market Minimum Rent*							
Average Adjusted Market Min. Rent							

*To approximate the minimum rent for the subject property, the comparable's rent is adjusted *downward* if the comparable is superior to the subject or *upward* if the comparable is inferior to the subject.
†Use average market minimum rent for comparable space with all rents in dollars per square foot.

This form is used for comparison grid analysis exercises in IREM Course 303, Management and Leasing of Shopping Centers and Retail Space. Copyright 1992 by the Institute of Real Estate Management. Reproduced by permission of the copyright holder.

Exhibit 8.1 *(continued)*

*To approximate the minimum rent for the subject property, the comparable's rent is adjusted *downward* if the comparable is superior to the subject or *upward* if the comparable is inferior to the subject. All dollar amounts are annual rates per rentable square foot unless otherwise noted.

This form is used for comparison grid analysis exercises in IREM Course 302, Leasing and Management of Office Buildings. Copyright 1991 by the Institute of Real Estate Management. Reproduced by permission of the copyright holder.

only fair. Note that the categories include construction quality, management staff, tenant mix, building classification, and other "intangible perquisites" that are not directly measurable but nevertheless affect rental rates and perceptions of value and, in turn, affect commercial tenants' decisions to lease space at particular properties. The aggregate score for each property is a gauge of its ability to compete in its market; the property with the highest score is the one that is most competitive.

Rating characteristics based on qualitative judgments admittedly adds greater subjectivity to a process that is inherently idiosyncratic. However, we believe there are a number of values of the type described here that tenants are likely to consider in making decisions about leasing new space or staying where they are. As a consequence, these values need to be included in any market comparison. Indeed, we believe that qualitative attributes are likely to be increasingly important in determining the distinctiveness of commercial properties.

Evaluating Rents and Assessing Competitiveness in the Future.   A grid of the type depicted in exhibit 8.3 helps to determine the actual *market leader* in a competitive market. If a comparison grid like the ones in exhibit 8.1 or 8.2 is used, the market leader—the market's "best-of-class"—is the property that emerges as the one commanding the highest "adjusted/comparable real rent." If a market analysis grid like that in exhibit 8.3 is used, the market leader is the one receiving the highest score. It should be noted that the "best-of-class" property derived from the market analysis exercise is often not the subject property. The purpose of such market analysis is usually to measure whether the subject property is performing as well as may be expected in light of market conditions that typically include at least one competitor judged to be superior to the subject property overall.

Completion of a market analysis grid helps the analyst determine the competitiveness of the subject property relative to the market leader on some particular quantifiable basis. For example, exhibit 8.3 isolates 20 "quality" and "amenity" factors that contribute to the value of an office building. Based on the five-point rating system in the exhibit, the market leader (i.e., the benchmark) can receive as many as 100 points. Conversely, the subject property—assuming it is not the market leader—will score a certain percentage amount compared to the market leader. This exercise can be used to identify areas in which the subject property is less competitive and suggest areas that can be changed to improve its competitive position.

Economic Aspects of Benchmarking.   Benchmarking quality attributes of the kinds identified in exhibit 8.3 can also facilitate measurement of the financial benefit—if any—that can be realized after making improvements to a property. It provides a useful starting point in valuing properties "as-is" versus "as-improved." Camp described the generic benchmarking process this way:

Exhibit 8.3
Example Market Analysis Grid (Office Building)

Date of Analysis _____

QUALITY ASSESSMENT*	Subject	Competitor #1	Competitor #2	Competitor #3
Construction Quality				
Management Staff				
Building Reputation				
Common Areas				
Tenant Mix				
Flexibility (Design/Space Utilization)				
Exercise Facilities (equipment, locker rooms)				
Ownership Stability				
National Credit Tenants				
Location/Accessibility†				
Neighborhood Support Services†				
General Appeal and Overall Cleanliness				
On-Site Security/Monitoring				
AMENITIES*				
Concierge Services‡				
Retail/Sundry Services				
Banking Services				
Secretarial Services				
Covered Parking				
Conference Facilities				
Freight Elevator/Loading Dock				

*For *quality assessment,* the authors rate the attributes of their properties using a scale of **1** to **5** with 5 = excellent; 4 = very good; 3 = average; 2 = fair; 1 = poor. For *amenities,* they list the number **5** if the amenity is present, **0** if it is not. The total possible rating is 100 points. Usually one of the competing properties receives the highest score; this is therefore the "benchmark." The subject property's total rating is thus a percentage of the benchmark.

†Neighborhood support services encompasses those kinds of amenities that appeal to tenant's employees (e.g., shopping, restaurants) as well as those facilities and services that might be important for business executives (e.g., nearby hotels/motels, fine dining, entertainment); location/accessibility relates to such things as traffic patterns (ingress/egress), transportation, and highways as well as general visibility.

‡Identify array of concierge services available, including travel/theater ticket services, pick-up/delivery services, etc.

NOTE: The authors developed these lists of representatives attributes and amenities based on competing office buildings within their specific markets. For any particular benchmarking evaluation, it is imperative to identify property characteristics and specific features and amenities within your competitive marketplace (i.e., what the direct competition, in particular, has to offer). This approach is useable for other types of commercial properties by modifying the list of quality characteristics and amenities appropriately. For a shopping center, this might include characteristics of the trade area, tenant placement and internal traffic flow patterns, and the quality of tenants—i.e., national versus regional versus local chains of independent merchants.

▶   Benchmarking is not just a study of competition but a process of
    determining the effectiveness of industry leaders by measuring their
    results. . . . [It] is basically an objective-setting process. *Benchmarks,*
    when best practices are translated into operational units of measure,
    are a projection of a future state or endpoint.

Once a market analysis grid is completed, the analyst will be in a position to
make decisions about specific improvements to the quality features or amenities of the subject property that will enhance its competitiveness in a measurable way and determine whether they are achievable—i.e., physically
possible and economically feasible. Such "improvements" are either those
grid features for which the market leader outscores the subject property—
but which can be improved at the subject so that it will be more competitive
at the top of its market (i.e., the benchmarks)—or those features which can
be improved at the subject property so that it can actually *outperform* the
market leader. (Here, improvements include both physical attributes and "intangible perquisites.") Note, however, that the most valuable attribute of real
estate—its location— cannot be changed and, therefore, is not correctable
by management. Thus, for a retail site, being on the "going home" side of the
street is a competitive advantage; a competing property on the other side of
the street cannot compensate for this difference.

A completed market analysis grid of the type depicted in exhibit 8.3 will
allow the analyst to evaluate the ability of the subject property to attract increased rents. The extent of this capacity can be evaluated by means of the
typical comparison grid analysis (as in exhibits 8.1 and 8.2). Assuming, for
example, that the market leader received 100 points and the subject property
received 75 points on the market analysis grid, and assuming that the market
leader rents office space for $20 per rentable square foot, it should be pos-
sible to increase rental rates for the same type of space at the subject property
based on achievable improvements in the "quality" and "amenities" listings
contained in the grid. By determining the costs of these achievable improvements, the analyst can calculate the payback period required to recoup the
investment, as well as the post-enhancement improvement in the subject
property's net operating income. However, such computations are the prov-
ince of investment analysis, which is beyond the scope of this book.

**Tenant "Psychographics" and Commercial Property Benchmark-
ing.**   We need to add a cautionary word to this discussion. As we will explain later in this section, one of the deficiencies of comparison grid exercises
in general, including the enhanced version—the market analysis grid in exhibit 8.3—is that *they fail to measure the true preferences—the so-called buy*
factors—of current and prospective tenants and instead reveal only the par-
tiality of the analyst. Any assumptions about the desirability of real estate
features and amenities are subject to errors which can render the results of

such grid analyses almost meaningless. John Sharpe, Executive Vice President of Operations for Four Seasons Hotels, has pointed this out succinctly:

▶ Customers don't buy a product, they buy what the product does for them. Quality in product or service is not what *we* think it is.

Jim Clemmer had this to add:

▶ Too often the features, attributes, or service/quality expectations of the customer are out of sync with what the organization considers to be important and is focused on delivering. As customers, we have all dealt with organizations that have done an outstanding job delivering a service or product feature we could care less about.

While traditional comparison grid analysis represents an effort to provide an objective basis for rent-setting, the exercise is innately compromised by the subjectivity of the analyst. The objection is two-sided: First, because the components of the grid analysis (the buy factors) are likely to reflect the analyst's predilections rather than actual preferences of commercial tenants and prospects, dollar adjustments based on them are likely to be inaccurate (and incomplete). Second, regardless of whether the buy factors mirror the predispositions of current and prospective tenants, the dollar adjustments for them will undoubtedly reflect values assigned by the analyst (rather than by tenants or the market), such that any adjusted rental rates are likely to be deceptive. Their value is in the comparison exercise, moreso than in the numbers they derive.

Benchmarking for Performance Measurement.   Clemmer's observations identify a short sight of most real estate management companies that focus only on market comparisons. "Service/quality expectations of the customer are out of sync with what the organization considers to be important and is focused on delivering." It is imperative that real estate managers also identify the demands and expectations of their two primary customers:

1. Building owners who hire them to provide property management services.

2. Tenants who pay rent for professionally managed buildings.

With competition for tenants at the highest level in more than 20 years, successful management companies have expanded their benchmarking activities to include performance measurement questionnaires directed to their two primary customers.

CEL & Associates, Inc., a pioneer in the field of performance measurement for real estate management companies, has developed an evaluation system called REACT:

> REACT was developed . . . in conjunction with [commercial] tenants, real estate professionals, property managers, performance measurement specialists, statisticians, and business advisors. REACT is an independent/objective, self-administered performance measurement tool that quantifies and compares the perceptions and opinions of tenants, building owners, and property managers to each other and to the scores from the best in the industry. . . . [The] performance measurement questionnaire (1) identifies those performance areas in need of improvement; (2) establishes benchmarks for future performance evaluations; (3) allows the users to compare their performance to the industry's best, between property managers, regions and portfolios; and (4) identifies potential lease renewal problems before they become unresolvable.

CEL & Associates serve as consultants and scorekeepers for their clients. Questionnaire responses are incorporated into their computer data base which contains information gathered from across the real estate industry. This allows them to prepare separate reports on the various participants' (tenants, property manager, owner) perceptions and compare them to prior results as well as to industry scores. These comparisons take the form of graphs that visually display the similarities and differences.

Implementing this type of performance evaluation requires input from both building owners and tenants. According to CEL & Associates, to be effective and achieve a maximum response, a performance measurement program should adhere to the following guidelines.

- The questionnaire should fit on one page and take less than 15 minutes to complete.

- The rating system should require respondents to express an opinion; a three-point or five-point rating scale is recommended.

- Each question should be clearly worded for maximum understanding.

- Each question should be tested for reliability.

- The format should allow for quick turnaround of results (rapid tabulation of data).

- The results should facilitate performance measurement and future benchmarking (administered, at best, on an annual basis).

Alignment with Customer Service/Quality Expectations.   Performance measurement questionnaires directed to owner-clients and to tenants at different types of commercial properties provide formats for soliciting the service/quality expectations of both owners and tenants.

An owner questionnaire should be designed to evaluate the management company's performance in key functional areas of management responsibility. The example in exhibit 8.4 measures the effectiveness of:

Exhibit 8.4
Example Performance Measurement Questionnaire—Owner

	Excellent	Adequate	Needs Improvement	Comments
Manager				
Communication				
Thoroughness				
Tenant Retention/Rapport				
Appearance and Maintenance of Properties				
Budgeting and Expense Control				
Level of Experience				
Leasing				
Communication				
Market Knowledge				
Level of Experience				
Overall Performance				
Construction Management				
Communication				
Level of Experience				
Overall Performance				
Corporate Office				
Communication				
Responsiveness				
Level of Commitment				
Accounting				
Timeliness				
Accuracy				
Accounting Package Format				
Financial Analysis Skills				
Flexibility				

Do you anticipate other properties in _____ (state area) this year? _____
What services will be required for these properties?
     Property Management _____ Leasing _____ Brokerage _____
Do you have any specific suggestions to help us improve our service to you this year? _____

Are there any additional services or support areas that we do not offer that you would like
to see? _____

Submitted by: _____   Company: _____

Reprinted by permission of Miller Commercial in Dallas, Texas.

- The property manager
- The leasing function
- Construction management
- The corporate office
- Accounting

Exhibit 8.5

Example Building Services Evaluation (Office)

Property: _____

Address: _____

_____

Tenant Name: _____

Date: _____

By: _____

	Excellent	Good	Needs Improvement
1. Janitorial Service—In your office area			
2. Janitorial Service—Rest rooms			
3. Janitorial Service—Corridors and Lobbies			
4. Maintenance of Landscaped Areas			
5. Heating, Ventilating & Air Conditioning Operations			
6. Security Procedures & Personnel			
7. Operation of Elevators			
8. Quality of Tenant Improvements			
9. Property Manager			
a. Courtesy			
b. Responsiveness			
c. Follow through			
d. Appearance			
10. Building Secretary/Assistant Manager			
a. Courtesy			
b. Responsiveness			
c. Follow through			
11. Property Maintenance Staff			
a. Courtesy			
b. Appearance			
c. Level of Experience			
d. Follow through			
12. Marketing Representative/Leasing Agent			
a. Courtesy			
b. Responsiveness			
c. Market Knowledge			

13. How do the building services compare with other buildings you are familiar with in the area? _____

14. Please evaluate the effectiveness of *[Mgmt Co. Name]* in regard to communication of information and overall effectiveness in responding to the needs of your company.

_____

_____

15. What could be done to improve the building operations? _____

_____

16. Will you need expansion space within the next 6 months? 12 months? 24 months? ___

17. Additional comments:

_____

_____

_____

Reprinted by permission of Miller Commercial in Dallas, Texas.

Exhibit 8.6

Example Building Services Evaluation (Retail/Industrial)

Property: _____

Address: _____

_____

Tenant Name: _____

Date: _____

By: _____

	Excellent	Good	Needs Improvement
1. Maintenance of Parking Lot			
2. Maintenance of Building Exterior			
3. Maintenance of Landscaped Areas			
4. Availability of Parking for Employees/Customers			
5. Effectiveness of Promotional/Marketing Program			
6. Visibility of Signage			
7. Overall Curb Appeal			
8. Quality of Tenant Improvements			
9. Property Manager			
a. Courtesy			
b. Responsiveness			
c. Follow through			
d. Appearance			
10. Building Secretary/Assistant Manager			
a. Courtesy			
b. Responsiveness			
c. Follow through			
11. Property Maintenance Staff			
a. Courtesy			
b. Appearance			
c. Level of Experience			
d. Follow through			
12. Marketing Representative/Leasing Agent			
a. Courtesy			
b. Responsiveness			
c. Market Knowledge			

13. How do the building services compare with other buildings you are familiar with in the area? _____

14. Please evaluate the effectiveness of *[Mgmt Co. Name]* in regard to communication of information and overall effectiveness in responding to the needs of your company.

_____

_____

15. What could be done to improve the building operations? _____

_____

_____

16. Will you need expansion space within the next 6 months? 12 months? 24 months? ___

17. Additional comments:

_____

_____

_____

Reprinted by permission of Miller Commercial in Dallas, Texas.

Each management function is further subdivided to evaluate such things as communication, tenant retention and rapport, appearance and maintenance of properties, budgeting and expense control, management responsiveness and level of commitment, timeliness and accuracy of accounting and reporting, flexibility, level of experience, and overall performance.

Tenant questionnaires should focus on key services valued by them as well as the job performance of those hired by the management company to provide these services. Exhibits 8.5 and 8.6 are examples (see preceding pages). As with any evaluation, it is important to provide space for respondents to include personal comments.

Benchmarking and Performance Measurement for E-Plus Service.   Benchmarking and performance measurement tools can be part of an E-Plus strategy for motivating customers (see chapter 6). In implementing E-Plus, all management company employees should be invited to ask two crucial questions consistently: (1) What do my customers (tenants and building owners) expect and (2) how can I exceed their expectations? As Dr. Timm pointed out, "Exceeding in small ways is often sufficient. Little things mean a lot to customers."

The performance measurement evaluations are important tools for assessing customer "satisfaction." The goal should be to have each customer "motivated" (exhibit 8.7 indicates the desired responses). At this level of performance, the tenants and the building owners are seeing management's service performance as exceeding their expectations. This not only leads to lease renewals and management contract renewals, but also expedites the lease-up process and generates additional management contracts.

Management's commitment to E-Plus should be supported by benchmarking Dr. Timm's six steps for implementing an E-Plus strategy:

▶   1. Introduce employees to the E-Plus concept.

   2. Add management attention, encouragement, and a reward system that reinforces participation.

   3. Make the effort fun and recognize people's participation and successes.

   4. Constantly sharpen the picture of what customers expect.

   5. Hire people who have good attitudes toward customers.

   6. Make customer satisfaction an ongoing priority.

Other suggested strategies and examples of what many real estate management companies are doing to exceed their customers' expectations will be presented in chapter 9.

Exhibit 8.7
Customer Satisfaction Scale

Customer Satisfaction Scale

	Dissatisfied	Satisfied	Motivated
Expectations			
	Negative (Worse than expected)	Neutral (About what was expected)	Positive (Better than expected)
Responses			
	• Ignore or rationalize the inequity • Demand restitution • Retaliate • Withdraw from the relationship	Satisfaction is simply an absence of dissatisfaction, not motivation to become a repeat customer.	• Telling others of the positive experience • Paying a premium for the goods received • Becoming a repeat customer

Source: Paul R. Timm, Ph.D., "From Slogans to Strategy: How to Achieve Customer Loyalty," *Exchange*, Spring 1993, pp. 20–24. Adapted by permission of the author.

The Benefits of Benchmarking

In this chapter, we have suggested several applications for benchmarking in commercial real estate management. Here, in conclusion, is what Robert C. Camp, one of its inventors, has suggested as its utility:

▶ Benchmarking can benefit a company in several ways:

- It enables the best practices from any industry to be creatively incorporated into the processes of the benchmarked function.
- It can provide stimulation and motivation to the professionals whose creativity is required to perform and implement benchmark findings.

- Benchmarking breaks down ingrained reluctance of operations to change. It has been found that people are more receptive to new ideas and their creative adoption when those ideas did not necessarily originate in their own industry.

- Benchmarking may also identify a technological breakthrough that would not have been recognized, and thus not applied, in one's own industry for some time to come, such as bar coding, originally adopted and proven in the grocery industry. In these instances it is more important to uncover the industry best practices than to concentrate on obtaining comparative cost data. The business unit can determine for itself what cost levels could be achieved if it incorporated the benchmark practices in its own operations.

- Finally, those involved in the benchmarking process often find their professional contacts and interactions from benchmarking are invaluable for future professional growth. It permits the individuals to broaden their background and experience. It makes them more useful to the organization in future assignments.

All real estate organizations need to know who they are, what they do best (or at least what they do well), how they distinguish themselves in the marketplace, and what value-added services and/or amenities will garner the most customers—i.e., property owner-clients and tenants. Without a clear vision and correctly defined business practices and processes, an organization is doomed to lackluster performance and loss of business.

Strategizing the Tenant Retention Revolution

The key success factor, where the service system is concerned, is the "customer-friendly" system. Service systems that are low on the friendliness scale tend, by their very design, to subordinate convenience and ease of access *for the customer* in favor of the convenience of the people who work within the system. A customer-friendly system, on the other hand, is one whose basic design makes things easy for the customer.

—Karl Albrecht and Ron Zemke, *Service America!*

Benchmarking processes bring about an awareness of the external world. Its greatest value is in learning about practices used by others that are better than those currently in place internally. The outside findings are used directly or used to modify, improve, or adapt external practices to provide useful internal change and improve efficiency and effectiveness. It is a process to find a better way, rather than an attempt to reinvent the proverbial wheel.

—Robert C. Camp, *Benchmarking*

How many times would service have been improved if the salespeople or front-line employees had the responsibility and authority to make decisions on the spot? Instead we often have red tape, rules and regulations, and a detached, "You'll have to see the manager" attitude. Instead of flexibility and accountability we often have a bureaucratic approach to service. Is it any wonder we cannot get good service?

—D. Keith Denton, *Quality Service*

It's not enough for senior executive team members to be "committed" to service/quality improvement; they must be *visibly seen* to be *obsessed* with this as their top priority. Since we all know that actions speak much louder than words, senior managers need to work hard on *visibly signaling their commitment* so strongly and *consistently* that there can be no room for doubt about how critical service/quality is to the organization's future.

—Jim Clemmer, *Firing on All Cylinders*

Americans expect—indeed, demand—immediate gratification. They assume there will be instantaneous and dramatic results whenever energy is expended—and the greater the expenditure of energy, they reason, the more spectacular the results. Pursuing the goal of a customer-driven company culture is a process, rather than an event, and runs counter to this belief system. The work is arduous, the results are not necessarily immediate, and the required commitment is life-long. Because the evolution is also potentially both expensive and revolutionary, many organizations may undertake it, but few have the staying power to succeed. Jeffrey Disend has forewarned those about to begin to transform their companies:

▶ [Being customer-focused] means changing the way all the employees in your organization think about themselves and their customers. It must be an organization-wide process from the top down and from the bottom up. It must be ongoing. And it takes time. Anything else is a waste of your people's time and your organization's money.

Measure the Intensity of Your Commitment to Change

A successful metamorphosis demands focused, daily commitment on the part of every member of the organization. It is useful to remember, however, that the entity involved need not be an entire company, although the task is significantly easier when it is. Sometimes one portion of the on-site management staff—e.g., the accounting personnel or a maintenance crew—provides extraordinary service to tenants, while the rest of the team lags slightly behind, perhaps concentrating on internal processes.

The commercial real estate industry typically operates in what might be termed "self-directed work groups," functioning in a behaviorally autonomous fashion. Because service, in its essence, is a marketing strategy implemented by one frontline server for the benefit of one customer at a time, a particular organizational atom may develop a service culture different from, larger than, and independent of, any other in the company. In such circumstances, the owner or the real estate manager might be a tyrant—even customer-toxic—but the on-site management team delivers superlative customer service nonetheless.

A logical first step in developing a customer-focused culture is to dissect and study operating systems piecemeal. The real estate management business is one in which various outmoded ideas have unfortunately endured well beyond their useful lives: Forms and manuals may be duplicated for decades without anyone ever asking whether they still serve the purpose for which they are being used. Reporting requirements are often added or expanded without any consideration of whether existing, duplicative, inferior ones might be scuttled. The list is endless.

Champion Your Tenants, *Not* the Status Quo

It is time to investigate the way you do business to see how you can help your tenants win. All employees should ask this question as they proceed through each workday: "Is the system (task, form, etc.) that I'm involved with right now in the best interest of our customers?" Or more broadly, "Are our customer service policies, procedures, protocols, and principles designed to serve the customer—or were they really constructed to make things more convenient for the company?" A scrupulously honest answer to this question can serve as a fruitful first step in launching your firm's tenant retention revolution.

The undertaking is further complicated by the fact that real estate management operations suffer an ever-increasing administrative burden. Too often they are paper-driven rather than customer-driven—Monday-morning reports tend to be ranked ahead of happy customers. To have a successful tenant retention revolution, these priorities will have to be forcefully reordered to put your customers first in line.

The late Sam Walton, founder of Wal-Mart and one of the great champions of the customer-driven company, put it this way:

▶ There is only one boss, and whether a person shines shoes for a living or heads up the biggest corporation in the world, the boss remains the same. It's the customer! The customer is the person who pays everyone's salary and who decides whether a business is going to succeed or fail. In fact, the customer can fire everybody in the company from the chairman on down, and he can do it simply by spending his money somewhere else.

Henry Ford made the same observation: "It is not the employer who pays the wages. Employers only handle the money. It is the customers who pay the wages."

As you review your business practices, remember that nothing about your present way of operating should be considered sacred—or even appropriate. For example, how tenant-friendly are the various provisions in your lease agreement? Are your rules "red" rules—that is, are they essential to the health and safety and security of your tenants and their employees and customers, or for the protection of the property? Or have you created so many "blue" rules—those designed for the convenience of the on-site management team—that your tenants will be insulted? Albrecht and Zemke have pointed out how this happens:

▶ There is, in most organizations, a conspiracy of accolades and incentives that tie people to the rules of the system first and the needs of the customer second.

When you examine your procedures from a wide-angle, customer-sensitive perspective, you may discover to your chagrin that they were either designed or have evolved in such a way that company interests come first and customer interests a distant second. Richard C. Whiteley has prescribed an aggressive pruning of the company rulebook as one of the first steps in the transformation:

▶ Review the policies of your company, department, or business unit. The first goal is to eliminate all policies that are "unnecessary" and "not customer friendly." Often old, out-moded, customer-irritating policies remain in force for no other reason than "It's the way we've always done it." Get rid of them.

Second, examine the "unfriendly" but "necessary" policies. Challenge them. Are they really necessary? Ask yourself: What would be the consequences of eliminating this policy? Would the resulting problems outweigh the aggravation we're causing our customers by retaining the policies?

Are the stock responses of company employees to tenants—for example, "Sorry, that's our policy," or "I understand what you're saying, but we've always done it this way"—the messages you truly want to convey to your customers? As a matter of fact, do you really *know* what's going on out there at the front line? Do you personally and regularly watch and listen to the interactions that take place between your internal and external customers? "Management by Walking Around," Tom Peters' shorthand description of the optimum way for company leadership to get close to their customers (and stay there), means that managers need to devise ways to leave their plush corner offices and check out what is happening on the front line. The quality of those server-to-customer "moments of truth" will determine your tenants' satisfaction—and decide your company's fate.

Adopt Your Customers' Perspective on Your Company's Frontline Servers

Look at your staff from the vantage point of your tenants and their employees and customers. How amiable are your frontline servers? Are they people *you* would be eager to do business with? Most important, are they the kinds of folks you feel comfortable entrusting with the future of your business? You can provide technical training that can make virtually any competent candidate a productive employee, but it is very difficult—if not impossible—to retrofit people with the congenial attitude that you want your company to display to your customers. That is a matter of genes or upbringing or a combination of the two; in any event, the socialization process was completed long before a candidate approached you for a job.

Here's the truth of the matter: Service is an affair of the heart; for service to touch the mind of the consumer, it must come from the heart of the server.

People are the epicenter of the customer-driven company. Goods and services are generally brought to the market by people, and customers are happiest when they are being attended to by nice people. The great customer service companies overflow with friendly employees. Your job as a revolutionary is to find, hire, train, and retain the nicest people available. Too often in the past, the people hired for real estate management positions have been efficient, bottom-line driven, and skilled at enforcing rules. With few exceptions, they tend not to be genuinely congenial people—all too often, they sell apathetically, they smile reflexively, and they manage primarily by fear. These kinds of people do not belong in a customer-passionate business. Laura Liswood has underscored this problem:

▶ Many employees in customer-contact jobs are ill-suited by nature to deal with people. They may be trained to work the cash register, know the merchandise, and parrot the words, "May I help you, please?" and "Thank you." But they lack the outgoing personality, enthusiasm, and honest desire to serve.

Folks like these are so entrenched in their outmoded marketing and management styles that they probably are not capable of embracing the notion of *delighting* customers. They are easy to recognize. Their litany goes something like this: "If you give tenants an inch they will take a mile," and "If we offer something to one of them they'll all want it."

Such beliefs are ruinous to a customer service culture. Each of your tenants is unique, precious, and irreplaceable—and deserves to be treated as such. Because the happiness of commercial tenants is the indispensable foundation of the real estate management business, everyone in your company needs to renew their pledge to the satisfaction of your tenants every day. Management personnel might choose to benchmark Donald Libey by adopting this *mantra* as their daily devotion:

▶ [Customer focus] has no vacation, no time off, no afternoon away. It takes no break during the morning or the afternoon, has no lunch hour, and is incapable of leaving its place of duty. It is forever and always, eternal, and ever-vigilant.

Many of the service writers' sentiments are echoed by William G. Jankovich, CPM®, of Towne Realty Inc. in Milwaukee: "Our secret program that we use to service our tenants [and] our best method and motivating factor has been our operating policy manual which we put together [several] years ago. . . . Each employee has a copy in which we have tried to outline our goals, strategies, job descriptions, etc." The following are excerpted from some of the individual job descriptions.

TENANT SERVICES COORDINATOR: [This] individual becomes
Towne's personal contact with our tenants . . . .

BUILDING SUPERINTENDENT: The appearance and attitude of the individual must reflect the highest standard set by the industry. The tenants of our buildings are the people paying our salaries and should be treated as [though] they were guests in a hotel.

LOBBY ATTENDANT: Your primary duty is to position yourself in the building lobby and to courteously assist people having business in the building.

It is interesting to note that most of the job descriptions begin: "As the representative of Towne Realty in the building, . . ." Even more important, Towne's operations manual includes a mission statement for its Commercial Division and a list of five specific objectives to be accomplished, the first of which is: "To properly maintain all properties of Towne Realty so as *to retain existing tenants* and provide [the] proper environment to assist [the] Leasing Department in securing new tenants." This objective is further reinforced by being incorporated specifically in the job descriptions of the Vice President of Operations and the Operations Manager, thus assuring that tenant retention is the goal of everyone on the staff—from the top down.

Your Goal: Let the Tenant Win!   Managers of office buildings, shopping centers, and other commercial properties regularly hear owners say, "I know what I should be doing, but I have a manager who has been with me 20 years. He's doing what he was taught to do back then, but he refuses to do this (tenant retention) stuff. I can't fire him for that."

Unfortunately, managers such as these are ubiquitous. We recommend that owners give them a chance to change. Make it clear to them that a revolution is underway. Challenge them to become excited about—and involved in—this new approach to your tenants. Make them a central part of the transformation. Invite them to take the lead. Meanwhile, you may have to redefine the reward system and clearly explain the change and mean it. Managers need to be confident that your perspective has changed and that they will not be judged by both standards. However, if they cannot genuinely play an active role, you will have no choice but to hire someone else who will: Heeding the call to "Let the Customer Win!" means that those who cannot do so will lose.

As you assess how tenant-passionate each of your employees is, you may find yourself having to fill some vacated positions. When that happens, ensure that in your revamped hiring procedure, just as in every other company function, you put your customers' best interests first. This is the message once again: Do everything you can to *hire the nicest people you can find*. If you are forced to choose between a candidate with a great attitude and one with great technical skills, pick the great attitude. Skills can be taught; attitude is inbred. Here's what William A. Band had to say about the importance of demeanor at the front line:

▶ When respondents [in a 1988 ASQC/Gallup survey of American con-
sumers] were asked what they considered to represent high quality
in services, the characteristics most frequently mentioned were:
"courtesy, promptness, a basic sense that one's needs [were] being
satisfied, and the attitude of the service provider." In other words,
American consumers are not expecting accuracy and convenience
so much as they are saying, "treat us nicely."

In chapter 8, we suggested revising the traditional comparison grid analysis
form, proposing one that will allow managers of commercial properties to
arrive at appropriate pricing levels by including for consideration such intangible factors as the quality of security, building construction, and staffing (exhibit 8.3). We believe that tenants' leasing decisions are based at least as
much on these elements as on the traditional array of features and amenities
(the dollar value adjustment and totalling exercise) that has characterized
comparison grid analysis previously. Equally important, managers of commercial properties need to focus their attention on the cheerfulness, helpfulness, and overall friendliness of *all* of the team members who come in contact with their customers—tenants and owners. In overbuilt markets where
competition for commercial tenants is fierce, the "intangible perquisites"—
such subjective issues as tenant-friendliness—can be an important additional
consideration in the prospective tenant's choice of a business location. Thus,
the "likability quotient" derived from the types of "company report cards" in
exhibits 8.5 and 8.6 can become a significant element in evaluating staff
members' performance and bonuses, even their continued employment.

Make Your Company Tenant-Friendly
(Customer Ergonomics)

Companies that decide to improve the quality of the service they offer their
customers need to appraise early on what we call "customer ergonomics"—
that is, how friendly their customers perceive them to be. One example of
ergonomics, of course, is the "red" rule/"blue" rule distinction. Another is the
company's dedication to "hiring nice." (Both of these topics were addressed
in detail in chapter 3.) Those companies that are *customer-driven* routinely
and rigorously assess how easy and how pleasant it is for their customers to
do business with them and relentlessly tear down any barriers they encounter
that complicate things for their clients.

The measure of the customer-driven firm is its attitude toward complaints. Ergonomically designed companies recognize two essential truths:

1. The absence of complaints means that underlying company-customer
   relationships are actually unhealthy, and

2. Complaining customers are either a gold mine of future business or a
   blueprint for disaster.

The first step in creating a complaint-friendly environment is to seek out and welcome customer input, be it positive or negative. As Michael LeBoeuf has remarked:

▶ [Complaints] aren't annoyances but opportunities to get better and build customer loyalty. Be wary of long-term customers who never complain. Nobody is ever totally satisfied for an extended period of time. Either they aren't being candid or they aren't being asked the platinum questions.

We recognize that it is counter-intuitive to welcome complaints. Human nature perceives an unhappy customer as a troublemaker at best or, more likely, as a lost customer. Many businesses adopt the attitude that unhappy customers are annoying squawkers, nitpickers, or outright thieves. Such labels get stuck on practically everyone who complains, which means that disaffected customers become more vulnerable to poor treatment, without regard for the real merits of their problems.

This attitude is entirely misguided: Complaining customers are, in effect, inviting the company to earn their continued business; their complaints are actually camouflaged requests for service. As Heskett and his colleagues have noted:

▶ Managers either purposely or unwittingly suppress complaints, viewing them as negative marks on short-term performance rather than what one breakthrough service manager has called the "golden nuggets of information" that provide the basis for recovery. As a result, some of the most important information available to a service company is lost.

The management company and the property owner must establish an atmosphere that is conducive to surfacing and resolving complaints. There is no point in punishing someone who receives twenty complaints; what should be punished is having complaints that are unresolved.

The absence of complaints means that the company has gotten out of touch with its customers. The consequences are dire: The firm almost certainly will continue to lose more of its current clientele—without knowing why—and will likely forfeit additional business with potential customers because of negative word-of-mouth advertising. As Milind Lele remarked:

▶ Customer dissatisfaction presents a serious threat because many unhappy customers don't complain—at least, not to the company. Instead they tell family and friends about their dissatisfaction. A good number of them switch to other suppliers.

How many noncomplainers will actually defect? D. Keith Denton, citing a study conducted by the White House Office of Consumer Affairs, quantified the magnitude this way:

▶ [The study] found that for every complaint at company headquarters the average business has another 26 customers with problems, at least six of which are serious. The cold facts are that anywhere from 65 to 90% of those noncomplainers will not buy from that business again.

On the other hand, soliciting customer complaints can provide abundant benefits. First, if company leadership becomes involved in actually fielding the complaints, invaluable information will be made available to the top of the organization. Michael LeBoeuf made this recommendation:

▶ *Get people at the top actively involved in both listening to and helping resolve customer complaints.* This is an excellent way for top management to learn customer wants and then respond with action to meet those wants. Too many managers make decisions in a vacuum without understanding the needs and wants of the customers who make the business possible.

Second, the complaint procedure can stimulate company leadership to *empower* its frontline employees to respond effectively to the concerns of its clientele. According to Linda Lash:

▶ Most companies have found that empowering the front-line saves money in the centralized customer service department because it reduces the number of complaints received. [Conversely,] disgruntled customers who harbor their complaints until they get time to write or call the company's headquarters office intensify and embellish the complaint, making it more costly to handle and allowing time for dangerous word-of-mouth advertising.

Complaints Document Your Failpoints and Provide Profit Centers. The third impetus for a company to surface customer complaints is that the outcome of the process is essentially a report card of service failpoints: A system that documents and classifies complaints pinpoints the areas of greatest customer irritation that need immediate attention. When faithfully recorded and carefully catalogued, customer complaints can provide worthwhile guidance for company management in areas ranging from personnel selection and staffing needs to preventive maintenance.

CIP Property Management Services, Inc., in Austin, Texas, catalogues their service requests (tenant complaints) and work orders by property each month. Not only is the information carefully analyzed to monitor overall maintenance performance, but the chart (exhibit 9.1) is actually included in the monthly report to the property owner. (Over time, the charts become a visible measure of improvement while also showing where problems persist.) As a customer-driven company, CIP is committed to sharing with its

Exhibit 9.1
Sample Service Calls Report

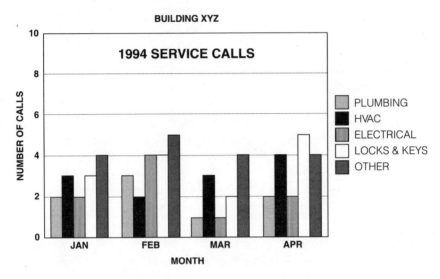

This type of graphical chart of service calls is completed for each managed building and incorporated into the monthly reports to the owner.

Reproduced courtesy of CIP Property Management Services, Inc., in Austin, Texas.

owner-clients their system directed toward reducing tenant complaints and enhancing tenant satisfaction.

Another approach to tracking responsiveness to customer requests is a grid format. Exhibit 9.2 is one of a series of forms used by Stein & Company of Chicago, Illinois, for tracking responsiveness, which they view as a strategy for obtaining lease renewals. In addition to a tenant survey questionnaire, they utilize a series of logs to record interactions with tenants. A Tenant Contact Log, which is used to track personal visits, entertainment, and phone calls during the month, includes columns for the tenant name and suite number, plus one column each for the four weeks of the month, and another one for comments. Their Maintenance Request Log, also completed each month, has columns for the date and time, the names of the tenant and the person making the service request, the location, and an explanation of the problem.

Whether you use a graph, a grid, or some other technique, monitoring service calls and staff responsiveness helps you identify problems and ways to overcome them. As Zeithaml and coworkers have noted:

Exhibit 9.2
Sample Tenant Request Report

Building _____ Week of _____

Category	No. of Calls	Same Day	Next Day	Two or More Days	No. of Call Backs*
HVAC					
Light bulbs					
Electrical					
Plumbing					
Cleaning					
Locks and Keys					
Other					

Comments:

*Please comment on all call backs and those items that take two or more days.

Adapted from "Tracking Retention Efforts," by William D. Norwell, CPM®, and Victoria A. Stevens, CPM®, *Journal of Property Management* 57(2): 24–28, March/April 1992. Reprinted courtesy of the *Journal of Property Management.*

▶ Complaints can become part of a larger process of staying in touch with customers. In particular, they can provide important information about the failures or breakdowns in the service system. If compiled, analyzed, and fed back to employees who can correct the problems, complaints can become an inexpensive and continuous source of adjustment for the service process.

The real incentive for companies to become complaint-friendly, however, is that it is financially sensible to do so. As Linda Lash spelled it out:

▶ The paramount reason for a company or organization to spend money on resources to handle complaints and inquiries is to get repeat business. Repeat business generates revenue and profit and turns what is typically viewed as a cost center into a revenue-generating and profit-generating business activity.

Complaints often identify voids in current services provided. These service voids, when filled, can provide new profit centers. Some examples of "new" services that might fit into this category are construction management, in-house security, additional janitorial or maintenance services, concierge services, expanded accounting services, and tax protest assistance, among others.

Remedying service failpoints also lessens the "hassle factor" of customers' dealings with the company. Reducing customer hassles is another way to make the firm ergonomically sound. Berry and Parasuraman had this to say about the subject:

▶ Whenever customers experience a service problem, they are forced to sacrifice something they would not have to if the service had been performed right the first time. . . . An excellent service recovery effort must make amends for the hassle factor. Companies must do more for the customer than merely reperforming the service.

Another source of complaints from tenants at commercial properties is the number and frequency of billings for common area maintenance (CAM) and other pass-through expenses. Weingarten Realty Investors, which owns and manages many neighborhood, community, and strip shopping centers throughout the Southwest, has addressed this by providing a single year-end statement package to their tenants. The package consists of rental coupons (to be returned with their checks), self-addressed envelopes for mailing them, and a change letter that spells out adjustments to the tenant's escrow account for pro-rated pass-throughs (CAM, taxes, insurance). Also included is a manager's overview of the property that addresses current issues (marketing, security) as well as the coming year's expenses. This has been most favorably received by independent retailers as it mirrors everyone's common experience with home mortgage payments.

Not All "Complaints" Are Negatives.   In chapter 2, we recommended techniques for brainstorming "failpoints" as a way to anticipate and prevent service problems. Then in chapter 5, we admonished you to invite your tenants' complaints so that you can overcome (recover from) problems that do occur. It is also important to recognize, however, that some of the feedback from your tenants may constitute a pat on the back (positive) or contain comments or suggestions unrelated to service (neutral).

Sometimes the way the invitation to complain is structured may get in the way. Respondents to telephone and mail surveys are often asked to rate different items on a scale of "1" to "5" or "1" to "10" with the top of the scale signifying the best and the bottom the worst. Such a rating scale might characterize the best quality as superior or excellent and the worst simply as poor. A rating for service might range from very or extremely satisfactory to very or extremely unsatisfactory.

The problem with these types of scales is that they are focused on the product or service rather than the purchaser or recipient. A product or service that is itself excellent may receive low ratings from the company's customers. What is needed is a way to measure the customer's *personal* reaction. Here is an example of what we mean: G & S Typesetters, Inc., in Austin, Texas, includes a preaddressed, stamped, postcard with the final package of type art sent to its customers. The card asks respondents to rate five product quality and adjunct service components so the company can improve its work. How-ever, in place of the usual rating scales, customers are asked if they were delighted, satisfied, dissatisfied, or upset. There is also space for additional comments. This simple response postcard clearly *invites* a pat on the back as well as any complaints.

Comment forms or cards are a way of generating "neutral" comments or suggestions as well as inviting customers to state their expectations or wishes. They are a commonplace in shopping centers where anyone who enters the property is a "customer" of the management company. As consumer pur-chasing patterns and demographic profiles are ever-changing, continuous feedback from retail customers is important to the shopping center manager. The information collected in this way is used to analyze customer percep-tions, both as a measure of the effectiveness of tenant retention programs and as a basis for planning needed improvements in tenant mix, services, and amenities.

As one who uses comment forms or cards routinely, Robert D. Oliver, CPM®, who manages shopping centers for Urban Retail Properties Co. out of Copley Place in Boston, shared the following with us:

> At shopping centers we manage, comment forms are displayed at the Customer Information Booths. Each mall takes a slightly differ-ent approach (as can be seen in exhibits 9.3, 9.4, and 9.5), and the forms are often used by customers to share constructive sugges-tions rather than make complaints. For example, we also sponsor senior citizen "mall walkers" exercise programs before the stores open. Recently an elderly participant used a suggestion form asking us to place rollaway coat racks in the mall corridors so the mall walk-ers can hang their coats instead of laying them on benches, plan-ters, and other surfaces. The rollaway coat racks could be put away out of sight prior to store openings and would not impede shoppers.

As a result of declining retail sales and increasing competition from discount merchandisers and manufacturers' outlets, shopping centers and malls have been forced to compete more effectively for consumer traffic—customers and sales dollars are critical factors in retaining retail tenants. The goal of satisfying shoppers is one way to address this. Other changes at shopping centers include longer shopping hours, increased security in parking lots and garages, center-wide promotions and entertainments, and community-related events and activities.

Put Your Frontline Servers *In Charge*

Even the friendliest, most highly trained employees will fail unless they are empowered to solve your tenants' problems on the spot. Because the man-agement of commercial real estate is rule and policy driven, enforcing rules

Exhibit 9.3
Sample Comment Card—Moorestown Mall

WE CARE ABOUT YOU AND YOUR OPINION OF US

In an effort to make your shopping experience more pleasurable, we would appreciate your taking a moment to comment on the questions below. Thank you.

1. Is there any service, product or store you would like to have at Moorsetown Mall?

2. How did our merchants' salespeople and mall staff treat you?

3. What can we do to make your visit to "The Menu" (the mall's food court area) more enjoyable?

4. Any other comments or suggestions?

Please drop this form in the mall suggestion box at the Information Booth in Center Court.

NAME _____ PHONE _____

ADDRESS _____

CITY/STATE _____ ZIP _____

This form asks open-ended questions, inviting shoppers' input. [According to Rick Polley, General Manager of Moorestown Mall in Moorestown, New Jersey, signage at the Information Booth informs shoppers that the mall will issue a $20.00 Moorestown Mall gift certificate to any shopper whose suggestion is implemented, and a number of gift certificates have, in fact, been issued.]

Reproduced courtesy of Urban Retail Properties Co. and Moorestown Mall, Moorestown, New Jersey.

Exhibit 9.4
Sample Comment Card—Saratoga Mall

Dear Customer

Customer satisfaction is our goal at Saratoga Mall. You can make our task a little easier by simply completing and returning the questionnaire below. Your suggestions will assist us in creating a pleasant shopping environment for you and your neighbors. Be assured that we will take action on your ideas, concerns, and criticisms. Thank you for helping us to serve you better.

Saratoga Mall Management

How would you rate your shopping experience at Saratoga Mall?
    [ ] Excellent   [ ] Good   [ ] Average   [ ] Poor
Comments:

_____

Please rate the level of customer service in our center.
    [ ] Excellent   [ ] Good   [ ] Average   [ ] Poor
Comments:

_____

Please rate the level of cleanliness at Saratoga Mall.
    [ ] Excellent   [ ] Good   [ ] Average   [ ] Poor
Comments:

_____

What store or service would you like to see at Saratoga Mall?
_____

What was your most pleasurable experience at our center today?
_____

Do you have any general comments or suggestions that would make Saratoga Mall a better place for you to shop?

_____

Name: _____ Telephone: _____
Address: _____ Time: _____ Date: _____
City: _____ State: _____ Zip Code: _____

This form facilitates a response by asking shoppers to rate specific items as well as make general comments. Note the inclusion of space to indicate the date and time of the shopper's visit and the question regarding cleanliness.

The reverse of the form says "Help Us To Serve You Better" and includes a return address so customers can take it home if they wish and respond at their leisure.

Reproduced courtesy of Urban Retail Properties Co. and Saratoga Mall, Saratoga Springs, New York.

Exhibit 9.5
Sample Comment Card—Dover Mall

WE   VALUE   YOUR

OPINION

Dover Mall is committed to making your shopping experience enjoyable and convenient. We would appreciate it if you would just take a moment to let us know how we're doing by responding to these few questions. Please deposit your opinion card in the drop box in the Food Court. Thank you for your help.

Date _____ Time: _____ am/pm

1. What store(s) did you shop today?
   _____
   _____

	Yes	No
2. Were you greeted promptly?	☐	☐
3. Were the salespeople friendly?	☐	☐
4. Were the salespeople knowledgeable about the merchandise or service?	☐	☐
5. Are you satisfied with the overall service you received?	☐	☐
6. Were mall employees (cleaning, security, customer service, etc.) friendly, helpful, knowledgeable?	☐	☐
7. Can you usually find what you want at Dover Mall?	☐	☐
8. Would you favor a mallwide "No Smoking" policy?	☐	☐

9. What stores would you like to see at Dover Mall?
   _____
   _____

10. Where have you seen or heard Dover Mall advertising?
    _____
    _____

11. Comments: Any likes/dislikes about the store(s) or mall?
    _____
    _____
    _____

Optional: Name _____
              Address _____
              _____
              Zip _____

and regulations is a necessary part of the job description of each member of the building management team. Unfortunately, employees are usually required to get permission from one or more of their supervisors each time they believe that a rule should be bent or a policy broken. Because tenants and their employees often have pressing needs that demand a quick response, they feel frustrated and angry when they have to wait while staff members consult their superiors about what should be done.

In reality, most solutions to tenants' problems are simple, inexpensive, and based on common sense. Let your tenants *win* by empowering your employees to fix what is broken on the spot. As Zemke and Bell have pointed out:

▶ [The internal clout of empowerment] results in the service deliverer acting with responsible competence and assertive confidence to take actions not covered by the firm's rules, regulations or procedures. Empowerment is the self-generated exercising of judgments. It's doing what needs to be done rather than doing what one is told.

Indeed, if your hiring and training procedures are sound, you should have confidence in the capability of your employees to take action for your customers on behalf of the company without the need for close supervision.

Empowered employees understand their company's commitment to customer satisfaction and display this positive message to their clients. This has beneficial consequences for both employee morale and repeat business. According to Heskett and coworkers:

▶ The effective response to service failures and complaints not only has a high payoff in terms of long-term business, it sends positive signals to both customers and employees that the service company's policy is to encourage corrective action and achieve customer satisfaction, enhancing the company as a place to work in the minds of its employees.

Linda Goldzimer has explained how complaint-solicitation improves customer relations:

▶ By encouraging your customers to provide feedback, particularly complaints, you are showing concern, interest, *and the desire to sat-*

Exhibit 9.5 *(continued)*

This form is more comprehensive. Asking for yes or no answers makes it easy for customers to respond. Note the questions regarding smoking (personal preference) and advertising (measure of marketing) as well as the time and date and specific store(s) shopped.

Reproduced courtesy of Urban Retail Properties Co. and Dover Mall, Dover, Delaware.

isfy your customers. The very act of soliciting feedback is a positive signal to your clients.

Customer Ergonomics in Office Buildings.   A common occurrence in office buildings is that tenants' employees often complain about unacceptable office temperatures—too hot in the summer months, too cold in the winter. Such temperature fluctuations are often the result of equipment breakdowns or maintenance problems. These circumstances require fuming tenants to track down a member of the management staff and recount their problem in an effort to resume working under acceptable temperature conditions. In addition to their physical discomfort (which may be minimal), there is the loss of work time and people's patience (almost always substantial). Yet typically, no one bothers to compensate the tenant for this type of hassle. There are alternatives to this, however, as the following examples indicate.

> DIHC Management Corporation, based in Atlanta, Georgia, also manages properties in Boston, Charlotte (North Carolina), and Washington, D.C. When air-conditioning equipment breakdowns occur in their buildings, DIHC provides portable fans on loan to each tenant. The fans are delivered personally by the manager and a member of the maintenance crew, with an apology. For example: "We're sorry you are having these temperature problems. We'll let you know when the problem has been resolved. Meanwhile, please use these fans to help minimize your employees' discomfort while we make repairs."
>
> If the air conditioning breaks down in a building managed by The Allen Morris Commercial Real Estate Services Company in West Palm Beach, Florida, and elsewhere, Häagen-Dazs ice cream and sodas are delivered to each tenant as a "pardon the inconvenience" gesture. This assures the tenants that management is "on their side and on top of the problem."

Here is another approach to consider: It is certain that tenants do not relish suffering through equipment failures, but they also know such failures are inevitable. A 30-minute response guarantee from the management company combined with complimentary after-hours air conditioning (or heat) can defuse the typical "us against them" attitude that often develops in office buildings. More than likely that company's tenants would not locate their businesses in a building managed by any other firm. This illustrates a simple truth about tenant retention and customer service in the management of commercial real estate: A successful approach requires a combination of the Golden Rule ("Do unto others . . . . ") and the Boy Scout Oath ("Do a Good Turn Daily"). Such an attitude has the cumulative benefit of "wowing" tenants, which increases the chances of attracting their continued patronage and creating positive word-of-mouth, which increases the chances of attracting the patronage of others.

Encourage Your Tenants' Positive Word-of-Mouth

Beneficial word-of-mouth is essential to the success of a commercial property, just as it is to anyone in the business of selling services. James Heskett and his colleagues have explained why:

▶ [Products possess] search qualities and experience qualities. Search qualities are qualities that a consumer can determine prior to purchasing a product; experience qualities are those that can be determined [only] after the purchase.

Tenants are able to judge their satisfaction with a commercial location only after they have actually experienced it—that is, after they have searched for the right location, negotiated acceptable lease terms, made arrangements for the transfer, and actually moved in (all the while keeping the business operational)—i.e., lived through all the hassles that are inherent in relocating an established business. In other words, the "experience qualities" of commercial properties overwhelm "search qualities" as a way of evaluating tenants' overall satisfaction. Consequently, prospective tenants are much more likely to seek out and rely on information from personal networking sources (business associates, clients, and vendors) than from impersonal sources (e.g., advertising) before making the decision to lease space at a particular commercial property. Word-of-mouth recommendations are, therefore, an invaluable underpinning of the marketing program for office buildings, shopping centers, and other commercial properties.

Because word-of-mouth advertising is so vital to success, managers of commercial properties ought to strategize techniques to encourage it. An example from the realm of apartment management provides a potential benchmark.

> WilsonSchanzer Real Estate Services in San Antonio, Texas, has devised an unusual way to reward residents for prospect referrals. Because Texas prohibits remuneration for unlicensed referrals (as many other states also do), the company had to craft a bonus program that would be consistent with Texas law. The WilsonSchanzer "Home Improvements Program" awards points for resident referrals (in 25-unit increments). Residents can either collect apartment upgrades immediately after making a successful referral or stockpile them and receive a higher-value bonus. The choice of improvements includes redecorating, new carpeting or wallpaper, ceiling fans, alarm systems and the like. (The roster may be customized for the particular property.) Perhaps the best feature of the Home Improvements Program, however, is that the reward is essentially a

capital upgrade that remains with the apartment on a long-term basis.

Applied to commercial properties, this idea might take the form of landlord-paid upgrades to existing tenants' leased space in return for their help in expediting initial lease-up or eliminating existing vacancies by referring prospective tenants to the leasing team. However, COMPASS Management and Leasing, Inc., has instituted a different type of reward program to encourage tenant referrals. Anytime a tenant refers another business that signs a lease, the management company treats the established tenant's employees to a luncheon at a top local restaurant.

Partner With Your Customers to Reduce Their Hassles and Build Your Business

The "hassle factor" crops up in many real estate management situations. Establishing and nurturing creative partnering arrangements between sellers and buyers—i.e., between commercial properties and the tenants who occupy them—is primarily an attempt to cut down on the hassle that is inherent in continually developing new relationships. Partnering is the optimal economic arrangement because it establishes long-term "win-win" professional interdependencies. Here's what Donald Libey has written about the subject:

▶ Your customers don't want to go somewhere else. They have a desire to be loyal. . . . Bio-psychologically, The Customer's drive to survive is directly transferred to the supplier when the decision to trade is made. The Customer wants you to guarantee survival. The Customer is literally trusting you with a portion of personal survival.

Zemke and Bell echoed this sentiment:

▶ More and more of the world's economic work gets done through long-term relationships between sellers and buyers. It is not a matter of just getting and then holding on to customers. It is more a matter of giving the buyers what they want. Buyers want vendors who keep promises, who'll keep supplying and standing behind what they promised. . . . Under these conditions, success in marketing is transformed into the inescapability of a relationship. Interface becomes interdependence.

Regardless whether the mutual attachments advocated by Zemke and Bell will develop between commercial properties and tenants, the "bio-psychological" partnering relationship that Libey describes is unquestionably present in the real estate management environment. (Partnering with tenants was discussed in chapter 4; partnering with employees was addressed in chapter 3.)

While it might seem surprising to some to describe landlords and tenants as "partners," consider this: When landlords are financially successful, they

Appealing to Tenants' Personnel

A company's line employees may not be involved in lease nego-tiations or make service requests directly. However, their welfare will be part of the package business tenants seek in leasing com-mercial space. If a company is planning to relocate, the happi-ness of its employees could (in fact, should) be a vital considera-tion. It is only human to want comparable or better amenities at a new business address, and if the current location includes fea-tures and amenities that serve their employees, the tenants are less likely to want to leave.

It may not be practical to add an outdoor sports complex as one Chicago-area property did recently. A suburban location with available land and a large tenant base whose employees pursue golf, volleyball, and other outdoor sports make that particular amenity workable. However, managers of office buildings can seek out new tenants whose businesses would become amenities of the building. Child care (day care facilities) is a very important amenity for employees who are parents. Fitness or workout facili-ties are popular, too. As more and more businesses create non-smoking environments for their workers, a designated smoking area or a smoking lounge can be a welcome amenity for those who still indulge.

Dry cleaners (valet services) and travel agencies would attract their own retail customer base as well as serve tenants and their employees. Eating facilities (fast food or a sit-down restaurant) and a place to buy newspapers, magazines, and candy bars would save steps. (Often workers at suburban locations have to drive a distance just to have lunch.) A concierge who will arrange for theater tickets, a special dinner, local transportation, etc.—for a fee, if necessary—is a popular addition to many properties. Many of these types of services and amenities are equally desir-able to employees of retail and industrial tenants.

A branch bank or an automated teller machine (ATM) is a welcome amenity for any type of commercial property. Office supplies, greeting cards, and books are other examples of retail amenities that will appeal to tenants' employees and attract the general public to the property. While it may not be possible or practical to have these types of facilities or services on site, hav-ing them nearby is often a desirable alternative because they can be cited as part of the larger array of features and amenities of a location in general.

are more likely to staff their properties with top-quality personnel, provide superior maintenance and janitorial services, and implement desirable capital upgrades, all of which benefit their tenants by adding to the actual (and per-ceived) quality of the property. Because the landlord-tenant relationship is continuous—unlike the typical seller-buyer association in the retail milieu, which is generally intermittent, commercial leases are for a period of years and sometimes decades—tenants are "invested" in the success of the suppliers of their office, store, or warehouse space. (This mutual "investment" is reflected financially in the additional rent they pay as their pro rata share of the common area expenses—retail tenants often pay merchants association dues or contribute to a marketing fund in addition to percentage or overage rent.) Conversely, if prospective tenants were shrewd enough to know the detrimental consequences of receivership or bankruptcy for a commercial property, it is exceedingly unlikely that they would choose to lease space at a property experiencing either situation. They would rightly suspect that their lease experience would be unfavorably affected by the negative financial and legal status of the property and preferentially lease at a property that is economically healthy.

Landlords and tenants are necessarily affected similarly by the fiscal performance of commercial properties. Because this is so, landlords and tenants are *inevitably* partners—a well-managed property attracts financially sound tenants who help management maintain the property's fiscal condition and reputation. This perspective of the landlord-tenant relationship is radically different from the traditional view of the parties as adversaries, but viewing them in this light is helpful in designing tenant retention strategies that can be beneficial to all.

Laura Liswood has summarized the importance of the partnering relationship, emphasizing that companies need to be accommodating to the personal needs of their customer "partners":

▶ A good and long-standing customer expects a reciprocal relationship with the company. The customer demonstrates good will through repeat buying and on-time payments, and the company is expected to reciprocate with some good will of its own. It might be an overstatement to call this arrangement a "friendship," but most of us *do* feel more kindly toward a company that treats us like a friend. We like to think that our business is appreciated and that we represent something more than a speck on a computer chip or a name on a mailing list. That's why it's important that a company's delivery chain or customer-interaction process—no matter how much it is automated and computerized—be designed to allow for the personal touch, to accommodate exceptions, and to show real responsiveness to the unique needs of individual customers.

Such creative partnering can result in a multifaceted tenant retention "program," as R. Bruce Smith, CPM®, Second Vice President and Manager of Corporate Real Estate Administration for The Chase Manhattan Bank, N.A., learned:

The death of the proprietor of Nate's Shoeshine had a profound impact. Nate was known as the "Mayor of the Concourse" at Chase Tower in Rochester, New York. His work with underprivileged lo-

Exhibit 9.6
Sample Shoe Shine Coupon

This coupon entitles the bearer to one
free shoe shine at:

Griff's Shoe Shine
Chase Tower Concourse

No. **1349**

The coupons were printed in black ink, on heavy white paper (card stock), and trimmed to 3½ inches wide by 2 inches deep (about the size of a standard business card). They were also numbered sequentially to keep track of who received which coupons and who actually used them.

Reproduced courtesy of The Chase Manhattan Bank, N.A., and Chase Tower in Rochester, New York.

cal youngsters was legendary, as was his being named Rochester's "Citizen of the Year." While we could easily find another shoeshine operator, we knew it would be impossible to replace Nate.

There was no need to advertise for a shoeshine operator. News of Nate's passing had spread throughout Rochester, and I was approached by numerous people who had an interest in taking over Nate's business. After meeting with nearly a dozen parties, I felt that I had found the right type of person to run the shoeshine stand. Griff, as he is nicknamed, was quiet but friendly, unassuming yet quick with a smile. As a learning-disabled adult, he was embarking on his own business with the aid of his counselor.

The shoeshine stand was basically set up and ready for business. There was, however, the problem of supplies and inventory of ancillary items (shoelaces, shoehorns, etc.). Griff needed "seed" money to get started.

To solve this problem, I asked another of the Concourse merchants, Lincoln Quickprint, to make up 200 coupons, each good for one free shoeshine at Griff's stand (exhibit 9.6). [NOTE: Because the proprietor of Lincoln Quickprint felt that more traffic in the Concourse would be good for his business, too, the coupons were prepared as a "courtesy" at no charge.]

I pre-purchased all 200 coupons from Griff, for the sum of $800, with the understanding that he would honor these coupons as they were redeemed. (Griff was asked to return the "used" coupons to me.) I then composed two different letters—one to bank department managers and the other to key contacts among the building tenants, each to be accompanied by several of Griff's numbered coupons. The first letter stated that we wanted bank employees to be aware of the fact that we had a new merchant in the Concourse and asked the bank managers to give a coupon to someone in their department who had shown a little initiative or "gone the extra mile" in serving a customer. The tenants' letter expressed our thanks for their being such good tenants and let them know just how much the relationship with them was valued. The coupons were our way of allowing them to reward certain of their employees who might have done something a little bit special recently. Thus, for an investment of only $800, I was able to:

- Further an ongoing business relationship with Lincoln Quickprint,

- Capitalize Griff's start-up business and allow him to buy all the inventory he needed,

- Remind our tenants that their tenancy was valued and something we worked hard every day to keep,

- Allow tenants and bank department managers, alike, to say thank you to their valued employees, at no cost to them, and

- Make nearly every one of Chase Tower's 1,700 workers aware of the fact that there was a new shoeshine stand operator doing business in the Concourse, which resulted in new business for Griff.

As Bruce commented in closing, "With a little creativity, it is not difficult to reap multiple benefits from your efforts to establish long-term relationships with your tenants and reinforce in their minds that they made the right choice when they decided to make your building their business home."

Benchmark Ideas of Others that You Can Put to Work for You

Benchmark other organizations both inside and outside your industry. Appropriate as many great ideas as you can find, and put them to work in your own company. For example, the "royal" treatment you received as a dinner guest at a local restaurant might suggest ways to provide more personal attention as your staff members interact with tenants. Just as important, one or more of the personnel working at the restaurant may be so dazzling you will want to interview them for frontline positions in your company. The "Not Invented Here" syndrome—the notion that any idea that did not originate with us cannot be any good—is destructive of excellence and detrimental to innovation. The wisdom of benchmarking is that it helps to avoid reinventing the wheel in a surprising variety of different ways. Indeed, Robert Camp, one of the experts on the subject, summarized its purpose this way:

▶ *Incorporate the best.* Learn from industry leaders and competition. If they are strong in given areas, uncover why they are and how they got that way. Find those best practices wherever they exist and do not hesitate to copy or modify and incorporate them in your own operation. Emulate their strengths.

Zeithaml and her colleagues illustrated the use of benchmarking to motivate customers to complain, commending inventive use of technology as a way to stimulate customer feedback:

▶ British Airways . . . installed customer-complaint booths at Heathrow Airport where disgruntled passengers could air their grievances on videotape. Besides giving customers immediate relief from their annoyances, British Air found that the complaint videotapes gave vivid information to management about customers' problems and expectations.

The British Airways example is illustrative for managers of commercial properties: It is entirely appropriate to borrow an idea from another enterprise—for example, the hospitality industry—to help you become complaint-friendly. In *Delivering Knock Your Socks Off Service,* Kristin Anderson and Ron Zemke included an admonition from a poster they had seen hanging in an automobile repair shop: "Every job is a self-portrait of the person who did it. Autograph your work with excellence." In effect, an employee's signature becomes a guarantee that the work is satisfactory. It not only verifies that the condition has been inspected and determined to be adequate, but invites the customer to complain if the work is at all deficient. (Exhibit 9.7 is an example of this type of tool.) Real estate management companies and service providers that are "customer-focused" provide additional examples.

SunLife of Canada owns and manages Airport Executive Park in Richmond, British Columbia. Working with their janitorial service provider, they developed a door hanger "report card" as a means for tenants to provide direct feedback to the janitorial company as well as make special service requests. The two-copy door hanger also provides the management company with a means of monitoring tenant satisfaction.

Exhibit 9.7
Example Service Follow-Up Questionnaire

**PLEASE LET US KNOW HOW WE HANDLED YOUR SERVICE REQUEST.
(RETURN QUESTIONNAIRE TO THE MANAGEMENT COMPANY OFFICE.)**

SUITE/STORE NUMBER/ADDRESS _____

DESCRIPTION OF WORK DONE _____ (Date)

_____

_____

_____

_____

Management Staff Name/Signature

	YES	NO
WERE WE PROMPT?	☐	☐
WERE WE FRIENDLY?	☐	☐
WAS THE REPAIR ADEQUATE?	☐	☐
IS THERE ANYTHING ELSE WE CAN DO?	☐	☐

COMMENTS: _____

_____

_____

_____

Tenant Signature   **Date**

This type of follow-up questionnaire can be printed on brightly colored card stock (about 5″ wide x 8″ deep) or made part of a work order/authorization form for tenant sign-off. Any requests for additional work produce more work orders which, in turn, yield more completed questionnaires.

Weingarten Realty Investors in Houston, Texas, manages retail properties in eight states. They rely on local contractors to perform most maintenance services for their tenants because the properties cannot support an on-site staff. Because such long-distance management tends to hamper communications, they developed a series of "note cards" that acknowledge the service request, thank the tenant for taking time to make the request, and provide a confirmation number for subsequent follow-up after the work is performed.

Several management companies (Transwestern Property Company in Houston and Newmark Realty, Inc., in New York City among them) employ another service modeled after the hospitality industry to encourage new tenants to complain if the condition of their leased space does not meet their expectations—they appoint a tenant liaison. The person in this position is responsible for visiting all tenants regularly, beginning prior to occupancy and continuing each month after they move in. The purpose of the tenant liaison position is to ensure that services provided to the tenant are continually at the highest level possible, as well as communicate needed information to each tenant in a timely manner.

Other management firms charge the property manager with direct responsibility for measuring and maintaining tenants' satisfaction. According to Gary R. Sligar, CPM®, President and CEO of COMPASS Management and Leasing, Inc., in Atlanta, "Tenant relations begin before the lease is signed," and the company strives to communicate throughout its many regional offices and managed properties one simple message: "The tenant is king."

To measure how well (and consistently) they are communicating this message, tenants are asked periodically to complete a "tenant satisfaction survey." (The COMPASS survey forms are similar in content to the questionnaires in exhibits 8.4 and 8.5.)

After the lease is signed, but prior to move-in, the property manager visits the new tenant's existing office to discuss details of the move—including such things as tenant signage, parking, directory strips, etc.—so that everything will go smoothly. New tenants are welcomed with an appropriate gift, which may take the form of coffee and sweet rolls served to the new tenant's employees on move-in day.

After move-in, property managers are encouraged to establish a one-on-one working relationship by frequent contacts or meetings (at least twice a year) with key decision makers and others who will represent the tenant to the management company. Critical to COM-

PASS's tenant relations is a form that identifies the individual contact, his or her position in the tenant company, and the anniversary of the tenant's lease. Personal information such as marital status, spouse's name, children's names and ages, club memberships, and interests is also gathered on each one to facilitate planning and co-ordination of tenant-focused programs. Property managers are expected to establish and maintain a follow-up system designed to recognize lease anniversaries with a token gift and acknowledge media recognition or company achievements with a note.

Leverage *KAIZEN* Regeneration of Your Company for the Long Term

As you transform your firm, recognize that this activity is not a static enterprise, nor is it a one-time thing with a particular endpoint. If the work is to be lasting, it must be continuous. Ask yourself daily, weekly, monthly, and in formalized annual review processes: "Why do we do this? Is it still a good idea?" Always be in the business of pruning and sharpening your operations by having uppermost in your mind the goal of delighting your tenants and their personnel.

Remember, too, that not all of the customer service deficiencies you may unearth in your firm need to be remedied the instant you discover them: The *evolution* to service excellence should be a KAIZEN process, an operation that occurs day-by-day, a little bit at a time. As Professor Theodore Levitt pointed out:

▶ Trying routinely to get better one step at a time is a far better way to get better than shooting constantly for the moon . . . . Sustained success is largely a matter of focusing regularly on the right things and making a lot of uncelebrated little improvements every day. Getting better and better one step at a time adds up.

The KAIZEN approach, besides being gradual, can also involve rather insignificant improvements that prompt more pivotal ones. For example, during the metamorphosis to the customer-driven company, you might choose to benchmark T. Scott Gross:

▶ There is no greater way for a business to demonstrate status to customers than to know them by name. . . . Make it a habit to learn the name of at least one new customer every day. Just walk right up and introduce yourself. This may be more difficult than you expect, but only with regular customers that you should already know.

Donald Libey, one of the most thoughtful and provocative of the service commentators, underlined the importance of knowing customers' names:

▶ Every customer you will meet has a name. . . . [T]he person's name is intensely personal and distinguishing.

    In every regard, according a person's name the proper dignity brings proper dignity to the process of commerce. People want to be treated with dignity. People want to feel as if they are respected for who they are. And who they are is, first and forever, the unique name they possess within the family structure.

    Differentiation of customer treatment begins with a policy of names. If a company will adopt a policy of referring to every customer as Mr., Mrs., or Ms., in *every* instance, *always,* that company will immediately and permanently improve its image with the entire customer base.

The exhortation to learn customers' names gradually is an example of leverage—that is, initiating an improvement in one area that is likely to stimulate more substantial benefits elsewhere—in this instance, the hope that useful personal interchange will develop from personal greetings. Peter Senge linked leverage with KAIZEN more directly:

▶ The bottom line of systems thinking is leverage—seeing where actions and changes in structures can lead to significant, enduring improvements. Often, leverage follows the principle of economy of means: where the best results come not from large-scale efforts but from small well-focused actions.

Indeed, small changes tend to build on themselves, to become self-reinforcing. Positive movement is amplified, producing more—and more substantial—movement in the same direction. Action snowballs, with more and more and still more of the same. Some service observers have compared this to the Pygmalion effect, describing it as a "virtuous cycle."

    Sometimes, the way things are named connotes the feelings people have—or should have—toward them. Karl Albrecht has commented about the leverage gained by correcting the way servers refer to their customers:

▶ Centering on the customer is easier said than done. In an organization, the language that people use when referring to customers, or
when describing service-quality programs, signals very clearly how
they view their customers and how they see themselves as relating
to them. Many organizations have evolved a special terminology that
enables them to *avoid* referring to people as customers.

Managers of residential properties invoke personal feelings of warmth and
friendliness by referring to their tenants as residents and by calling their rental
apartments homes. In the realm of commercial real estate, there are no comparable euphemisms even though managers of retail properties refer to store
owners and managers as "merchants." However, there are opportunities to
leverage other types of benefits. Buildings that are named for the property
owner or for a major tenant—e.g., the First National Bank Building, the Stone
Container Building—resonate with prestige and have an implied history.
Those whose addresses include "place" or "mall" or "plaza" (e.g., Copley
Place, Nicollet Mall, Three First National Plaza) suggest open spaces where
people are welcome to gather. By leveraging language—by updating the terminology you employ when referring to your properties—you may also be
enhancing the perception of a building's quality, location, and character in
the minds of existing and prospective tenants.

The piecemeal strategy to improvement is especially appropriate in an
environment in which the goal is innately a shifting target. As David Freemantle has observed:

▶ Customer service is a moving horizon, the high standards of today
can be the low standards of a few years time. Constant improvement
is a necessity.

One way to invigorate your company's customer focus is to streamline operations so as to meet your tenants' expectations of punctual performance.
Savvy retailers are increasingly aware of their customers' need for *immediacy*. According to Libey:

▶ The expectation for immediacy is so high that the merchant is measured less on value and quality and more on convenience and the
ability to satisfy the immediate whim. . . . The increased level of dis-
posable income contributes to immediacy. Coupled with the rise of
quantitative values and the acceptance of credit financing, the capacity exists to afford immediacy. Customers will pay more to get
what they want immediately, and they have the resources to spend.
If you want a new car tonight, you can have a new car tonight. . . .
We can afford to be instantly gratified.

Lead the Revolution
and Reward Your Revolutionaries

Once you are satisfied that your firm blooms with nice people, both old employees and new, you need to coach them to deliver spectacular customer service. Recall that people learn in different ways. Some adults learn new skills best when they read about them; these employees should have access to the extraordinary variety of cutting-edge service literature (such as the books and articles cited in the Bibliography). Others master techniques by listening to people talk about approaches; for these employees, a number of the customer service-related texts may be found on audiotapes. (Another possible option for them is personal training.) Still others comprehend best by mimicking the behavior of others—most especially, the leaders in their own companies. This latter model—what might be termed "benchmarking leadership"—is an essential inspirational wellspring of the service culture. As Scott Gross observed:

▶ Excellent customer service occurs only when employees have an excellent, visible standard that they can imitate and against which they can compare their own behavior. The good news is that the standard is always visible. The bad news is that the visible standard is not always a *visible standard of excellence.* . . . As the owner, CEO, or manager, you bear the special responsibility of being the most visible standard. If you are in any way unsatisfied with your employee's customer service behavior, there is only one first step to take. Look in the mirror!

Karl Albrecht also commented on the significant role that leadership plays in the regeneration process:

▶ If there is one lesson [I have learned] . . . , it is that leadership is the crucial ingredient in achieving service excellence on the part of organizations. There needs to be an element of executive evangelism in operation; not only the chief executive but the other senior managers must preach, teach, and reinforce the gospel of service quality.

Effective leadership in the customer-driven company requires that these trailblazers completely immerse themselves in the company's transformation. As Richard Whiteley has noted:

▶ Successful managers who carry out these customer-focused principles are creating a new view of leadership. Today, top corporate leaders . . . have shown what real leaders must do. They personally put the customer first. They promote their companies' visions. They become "students for life," constantly seeking new ways to learn. They believe in and invest in their people. They build customer-focused teams, celebrating successes and encouraging collaboration. And, finally, they "lead by example," personifying the organization's purpose.

"Preaching," "teaching," and "reinforcing" the service gospel—three of the activities that the service teachers challenge company leadership to undertake—should be supplemented by one other: "Rewarding." Michael LeBoeuf has outlined the importance of including rewards as a means of challenging internal customers to become involved in the transformation of their companies:

▶ Make it a contest, complete with rewards and recognition for those persons or groups with the best answers. If an idea makes or saves money, consider giving a piece of the profits to the creator. And most important, when you get a good idea, put it to work and let it be known that it's an employee-generated idea. People like to be proud of what they do and will support what they help create. Once employees see that you are serious about putting their ideas to work, you'll get plenty of them.

Poirier and Houser expanded on LeBoeuf's idea, urging that employee bonuses be funded from the company's increased earnings generated by their recommendations:

▶ The process of cultivating workers' input can be called employee involvement, participative management, or employee participation. The labels are unimportant. The idea is to tap the creativity and knowledge of the human resources of an organization. Mutual benefits can include increased profits from lower costs. They should also include making the job of achieving those results less arduous and more satisfying. . . . Since their work ultimately brings the desired results, workers have a right to know how they affect the chosen course of action and to have some measure of control over what they do or, at least, over how they do it. The final, perhaps most crucial, link occurs when management ties worker performance directly to the fortunes of the organization by creating a pool from earnings that can be distributed to those creating the necessary improvements.

Although the subject of designing a reward system for company employees is beyond the scope of this book, it can be helpful to benchmark the models employed by successful companies. One of these, The Ryan Companies, a Minneapolis-based construction and property management firm, has developed a program "based on immediate verbal and written recognition for exemplary performance." As a commitment to their Quality Improvement Process, "this program encourages continuous acknowledgment of quality performances."

> The "Ryan Recognition Program" employs shamrock designs as a basis for company awards. All employees are eligible to receive *and* distribute shamrocks, which are certificates of recognition that recognize performance that "goes above and beyond normal expectations." Employees collect shamrock forms, which can be redeemed for merchandise awards selected from a gift catalog.
>
> Employees are encouraged to reward their peers for recommending "value ideas" and performing exemplary customer service. For the customer service category, for example, the "award application" reads as follows:

1. Write the name of the employee deserving the recognition.

2. Briefly describe the commendable performance.

3. Identify when it happened.

4. Sign your name.

5. Date when you issued the Shamrock.

6. Fill in the recipient's supervisor name.

7. Send the original Shamrock to the award recipient!

8. Send the yellow copy to the supervisor listed on the certificate.

9. Submit the pink copy to a member of the Recognition Team for program records.

> In addition to rewards for outstanding customer service, the Ryan program recognizes employees on their birthdays and employment anniversary dates, as well as those who either "[exemplify] respect, integrity, community involvement, and other qualities" or propose "an innovative idea that promotes COST SAVINGS, TIME SAVINGS, OR ADDED VALUE."

"Co-Produce" Service With Your Customers' Help

Shrewd companies involve their customers in delivering the service they receive. This concept, known as service "co-production" or "self-service," has been employed for several years in many retail fields. As Heskett and co-workers have observed:

▶ Self-service concepts employ customers as part of the service delivery system. The most effective insure that customers are trained, through clear instructions, in how to be good "helpers." The range of activities in which customers are willing to engage is rather remarkable. Whether they pump their own gas, as a majority of U.S. consumers do; bus their own dishes; or haul their own furniture purchases, customers enable service providers to reduce demand on the delivery system during peak periods, thereby providing incentives in the form of lower prices to encourage customers to increase their participation further.

The commentators applaud self-service as a means of making service-delivery less expensive for the service purchaser, and easier and more convenient for the service provider. Davidow and Uttal, for example, had this to say:

▶ To more market-oriented managers, involving the customer is the key to increasing service productivity. While admitting that the more high touch a service is, the less efficient and controllable it tends to be, members of this school point out that self-service is often better service. Designing self-service operations that encourage and support customer participation, they contend, is the only way to achieve big leaps in service productivity without sacrificing quality and effectiveness. Striving to isolate customers from the production system is woefully misguided.

The notion of encouraging purchasers to become involved in producing their own service—e.g., by recycling certain materials that supply raw materials for other products while simultaneously providing environmental benefits—is an essential aspect of what we have described as "partnering," that is, the process of developing relationships between buyers and sellers. As we shall demonstrate later in this chapter, partnering alliances can have positive economic consequences for suppliers and consumers; such affiliations can be beneficial to landlords and tenants as well.

In the management of commercial properties, the concept of self-service may be employed to assist tenants in becoming more responsible building occupants, which provides direct benefits to themselves and assists their landlords and other tenants as well. The following is an example:

In addition to providing new tenants with a thorough information packet at move-in, The Allen Morris Commercial Real Estate Services Company holds monthly tenant meetings to solicit suggestions or concerns from tenants. Coffee and donuts are served to create an informal atmosphere and encourage attendance. As a follow-up, the meeting is summarized in the next monthly newsletter. The goal is to assure the tenants that management is listening to their concerns and is committed to problem resolution.

Other management companies have taken a different approach to meetings with tenants. The following was shared by Joseph W. Karp, CPM®, of Weingarten Realty Investors in Houston, Texas:

In our experience, meetings with groups of retailer-tenants often have the potential to deteriorate into nonproductive gripe sessions. To prevent this, we implemented a strategy we call the "roving town hall" meeting. Rather than invite our tenants to a central location, members of the management team—usually the manager, leasing agent, marketing representative, and accounting supervisor—visit with the retailers in their stores (meeting with all the tenants at one location in a one- or two-day session). These "meetings" are carefully timed to avoid conflicting with peak sales periods or lunch hours.

Although a lease for commercial space may be fairly standard, the people who negotiated and signed the lease may not be involved in the day-to-day operations of the tenant's business in the new location. This is especially true when someone from a corporate headquarters handles the lease arrangements for all of the company's operating units. The occupants of the leased space may be familiar with the broad terms of the lease (things like rent amount and payment schedule) but not fully cognizant of all the nuances. This can be a particular concern if a business has relocated from another state or even a different city. Building rules and regulations often differ in the details, as do components of the pass-through expenses and how they are billed, definitions of the common area and its maintenance, and on and on. Information about the building equipment and facilities, move-in scheduling and procedures for unloading, as well as directions to the property and details about employee parking and nearby service amenities are among the items that might be presented to tenants *before* move-in—i.e., a "welcome" package.

To facilitate compliance with the lease terms and maximize the benefits of the property services offered, several management companies provide an orientation session for new tenants. (Koll Management Services, Inc., in San Diego, Trammell Crow Company in Dallas, Hiffman Shaffer Anderson Inc. in

Chicago, and COMPASS Management and Leasing, Inc., in Atlanta are just a few examples.) The orientation typically introduces each member of the management team—including the maintenance and accounting staffs—and covers building rules and regulations, janitorial services, and service request procedures, as well as information on how to reduce common area service charges.

In truth, some form of "tenant orientation" is fairly common, even if it only reviews the lease terms. However, additional information and training is often desirable from both managers' and tenants' perspectives. This is an area where the real estate management company can and should take the lead.

> Transamerica Corporation in Miami, Florida, uses tenant meetings as training sessions for its retailer tenants. Prior to a recent holiday season at one retail property, the management company held a meeting of the retail store managers to provide training on customer safety and security. The program was put on by the local police department and provided an excellent forum to develop a unified security program for the upcoming holiday. Other training sessions covered the tenants' responsibility for maintenance of package HVAC units, reducing utility bills, and maximizing marketing results (getting the most customers for their advertising dollars). These tenants know the company that manages the retail center is committed not only to the property's success, but to the success of each individual tenant.

As the foregoing examples indicate, informed participation in co-producing service for themselves benefits not only the tenants and their personnel, but also the management staff and the property owner. It also contributes to tenants' pride in their office or store location.

Technological advances offer still other ways to foster self-service. For example, USAir has different telephone numbers for reservations, depending on the level of frequent-flyer miles their customers have attained: The "regular" reservation number is for nonfrequent flyers; Priority Gold is for those who have accumulated more than 30,000 miles in the previous year and Priority Gold *Plus* for those with more than 60,000 miles the previous year. Thus, USAir knows how important a customer you are by what number you call.

Other technologies also have direct applications in the realm of real estate management. Computerized, menu-driven building directories that allow the user to select options for finding specific information have been used in some hotels and retail businesses. A series of prompts guides the searcher much as voice mail systems guide callers to the person or function that will best serve their needs. Although many people will opt for such "convenience" because it can save time and expedite straightforward inquiries, we offer a word of caution about these types of systems: Ultimately, customers prefer to interact with another human being, and any high-tech self-service system must include as an option a quick exit to a living person who can respond directly to his or her inquiry.

Brainstorm the Course of Your Revolution

Because the transformation from company-driven to tenant-responsive demands the active involvement—indeed, the *passion*—of everyone in the company, it makes sense to involve everyone in the process of designing the renovated firm. Whether you call it "brainstorming," "think tank," "outer-circle thinking," or something else, your team needs to be involved in a formalized group exercise. Band described this as:

▶   . . . an unrestrained and creative process for generating ideas and suggestions by all members of a group for solutions, especially non-traditional ones, to customer satisfaction problems.

Effective brainstorming consists of the following steps. First, the session leader defines the scope and direction of the issues to be discussed. Group members are then given time to write down their ideas, after which each person is called upon to contribute one idea. The process is repeated until all ideas have been heard. The group leader simply records the ideas on a flip chart or blackboard; evaluation or criticism is not allowed at this stage. Once the ideas have been listed, the discussion is opened up to generate and record new thoughts.

Band goes on to describe a somewhat more refined brainstorming exercise known as "nominal group technique":

▶   This method begins the same way as brainstorming does, generating and combining ideas. The surviving ideas are numbered for identification, then each member privately ranks the top five ideas. The rankings are compiled from each person's rating to form a collective score for each idea. (The supervisor's vote is taken last to avoid prejudicing of the group.) The winning idea emerges from the voting.

However elegant the technique you employ, your purpose is to cultivate maximum employee participation in the planning process. The goal is to stimulate the imagination and tap the creativity of the human resources of your organization. Participants in the process might include the site manager, leasing personnel, accounting staff, maintenance personnel, and security staff. It is imperative that the team who will execute the customer service program participate in designing it. During the initial planning stages, meet as often as weekly, and no less than monthly. Because your brainstorming sessions are valuable learning exercises as well, staff members can teach each other all your company needs to know about "WOW!" tenant service.

Michael LeBoeuf created an interesting parallel between designing a service strategy and keeping score at a sporting event:

▶ Here's a good rule of thumb: When it comes to service quality, customers know the score but employees know how it got that way. Ask customers to tell you what your level of service quality is and what to work on to improve it. Then ask employees why your level of service quality is what it is and how to go about improving it.

To carry the sports analogy one step further, the customer is the scorekeeper, but the employees are the players and coaches that can tell you why things are going the way they are and how to make them better. While you need to know what the score is, you also need to know why it got that way and how to go about improving it. And employees are your best source for this type of information. The person who does the job every day usually has the best insight about why things do or don't work and the best ideas for making improvements. Simply asking employees for their ideas provides a tremendous, but often overlooked, reservoir of knowledge and creativity. Why not tap it?

You can begin the exercise by vividly characterizing for the participants your commitment to delivering superior service to tenants. Tell the staff that what you are after is not good—or even great—tenant service. These aren't enough: You're looking for service that will "WOW!" tenants, service that will "knock their socks off," service that will make the company not just the best, but *legendary*.

If you get off to a slow start, you might invite the participants to respond to two questions. These come from LeBoeuf:

▶ What's the biggest, most frequently occurring problem that you face in trying to serve the customer?

If you were the president and could make only one change to improve the quality of customer service, what would you do?

Because the group may need a jumpstart, here are some of the ideas that have come from Miller Commercial's brainstorming:

• A regular *newsletter,* sent to tenants monthly or quarterly, can be used to announce upcoming events, inform them of security/safety concerns, and introduce new tenants.

• A *suggestion box* provides a real partnering system if management is seen addressing the specific suggestions.

- Tenant *gifts* for specific holidays.

- Designate a *special parking space,* adjacent to the main entrance door, to be awarded to a different tenant each month (to be used by any employee of that tenant during the month as employee of the month).

- *Spontaneous activities* by the building management team—periodic windshield cleaning for cars in the building garage or parking lot, fresh flowers in the restrooms, a jar of candy placed on each reception desk and periodically refilled.

- *Sporting leagues* (bowling, baseball, etc.) organized by the real estate management company with competing teams fielded by single tenants (or a group of tenants) from among their employees.

- Semiannual *"Principal Mixer"* (group get-together) to bring decision makers together with other executives in a professional atmosphere.

- For a building renovation, invite tenants to a *construction party* to keep them informed and part of the action—hand out hard hats and tools, and take pictures of their participation in the demolition phase. Follow-up with refreshments.

- Sponsor a tenant *golf tournament.*

- Recognize tenants' *lease anniversaries* with a card or gift.

- Organize tenant *theme parties* related to specific holidays or events: a Fourth of July barbecue, an ice cream social, a cross-selling of services luncheon, a hot dog social, a "Toys for Tots" function, an Easter Seal walk-a-thon.

- *Welcome gifts,* given to new tenants and those renewing leases.

- Put on a *move-in party* (management and maintenance staff) with a deli tray or pizza for the new tenant's personnel on the day of the move.

- Hold *tenant education sessions* on such topics as life safety, CPR, self defense, personal wellness, tax planning, and other topics of interest to tenants and their personnel. (Ask tenants to identify the topics.)

- When you conduct a *building evacuation drill* (life safety practice), follow up with a small complimentary first aid kit given to each tenant participating.

- Use the lobby to *showcase the arts* by sponsoring a holiday gift bazaar (crafts), jazz concerts during the lunch hour, an opportunity for local artists to exhibit their works.

Many of these suggestions have been implemented successfully by other real estate management firms. Newsletters are a common means of communication—for example, SunLife distributes *The Grapevine,* a four-page quarterly newsletter, at Airport Executive Park in Richmond, British Columbia; The Allen Morris Company issues two-page quarterly newsletters—*The Cypress Pointer* at Cypress Point in Tampa and *Tower Talk* for tenants at United National Bank Tower in West Palm Beach. Westcor Partners in Phoenix sponsors an annual golf tournament (players are asked to pay a less-than-cost entry fee as a guarantee of their participation).

Tenant gifts—to welcome new occupants, to acknowledge lease anniversaries, to say "thank you for your business"—are also a common component of tenant retention programs. Jerome A. Sand, Jr., CPM®, tells how Northco, a Minneapolis-based real estate company, created an ongoing program using M&M candies.

> Each holiday season, it has become somewhat traditional to provide each of our tenants in each of our commercial buildings a small token of appreciation for not only their tenancy but also their commitment to the particular property and the ownership. These tokens might be flowers, candy, cheese packs, or similar items. The costs are absorbed by the landlords of the properties and are not escalatable (i.e., recoverable from the tenants). One year, we gave each of our tenants a large glass jar filled with two pounds of cashews. (Large space users were given more than one jar.) Tenants were encouraged to keep the jars with a promise of a refill sometime in the future. They were not told how often the jars would be refilled or what goodies would be delivered. As it turned out, a three-pound package of M&M candies was slightly more than one jar would hold. At a nominal cost per tenant—we were able to purchase the three-pound bags at a substantial discount—each jar could be refilled several times in a year, and we were surprised at how many tenants held onto the jars in anticipation of refills. On the other hand, many of the tenants were surprised that owners (or our company on behalf of the building ownership) were willing in this day and age to give a gift of whatever caliber as a thank you to tenants.

Going in still another direction, COMPASS Management and Leasing sponsors a variety of holiday parties, barbecues, and sporting events for their tenants. In their "Tenant Relations and Tenant Retention Program," a separate section lists ideas for special events:

1. Valentine's Day—Heart-shaped box of chocolates delivered to appropriate tenant contacts.
2. St. Patrick's Day—Hand out Shamrocks, Irish music in lobby.

3. Secretary's Day—Rose buds/carnations delivered to secretaries.

4. Spring picnic and barbecue.

5. Summer ice cream party.

6. Halloween—Deliver pumpkin baskets with candy; sponsor Jack-o-Lantern contest with prizes.

7. Christmas—Decorations; lobby music, carolers, string quartet, piano, etc.; community food drive; Christmas gifts to key decision makers.

8. Pro-Sports Night—Arrange for block of tickets, bus and refreshments on the bus.

9. Sponsor meetings and seminars on life safety issues, personal security and defense, health fair, etc.

10. Sponsor blood drive.

Implementation of these or any similar tenant retention ideas should be a function of the property size and type and its position in the marketplace. Also to be considered are input from tenants, the tenant makeup, and ownership's objectives for such programs. Note how many of the ideas include food. That is because food of any kind—whether candy, snacks, or elegant meals—enhances relationships when the experience is shared.

Regardless of the content, the truly superlative ideas are those that surprise the customer. Events that are regular tend to get boring; because they are recurring, they lose their capacity to "WOW!" customers. Worse still, when truly unique ideas become predictable because they are delivered routinely, they become a part of the expected product. As Scott Gross has cautioned:

▶ "Unexpected" is key to the definition of truly Positively Outrageous Service. It's the element of surprise and novelty that jolts the attention of the customer or patron and creates an experience that's memorable because it is so different from the expectation. Even if you are expecting the unexpected and don't know exactly *what* to expect, I guess you could call that the unexpected!

To get started with your brainstorming, turn back to chapter 2 of this book and use or adapt one or more of the strategies outlined there: The Levitt paradigm exercise utilizes concentric circles to focus on enhancements to the "plain vanilla box"—each circle incorporates more quality-based components as you progress outward from generic to expected to augmented and then contemplate the potential "product" or service. Market research techniques can also serve as "brainstorming" tools—focus groups help surface tenants' expectations; questionnaires measure how well their expectations are being met. The goal of brainstorming should be, first and foremost, to generate ideas; however, it is the adoption of these ideas—and the results of their implementation—that are the starting point for your revolution.

Go Out and Start a Revolution!

The extraordinary variety of customer service techniques that have been developed, tested, and refined in the retailing and consumer services environment provide a vivid benchmark for the real estate management milieu. Activities, however, are merely a reflection of, and not a substitute for, the fundamental attitudinal metamorphosis which has to precede a revolution that would revamp a company's approach to its customers.

Yet, we believe a revolution in the way real estate managers treat their customers is predestined—and desirable. This is true in part because the owners of commercial properties will increasingly demand that managers demonstrate responsiveness toward tenants as a way not only of maintaining and improving the value of the real estate assets under their care, but also as a means of reducing expenses in an economically unsettled climate. This view is exemplified in the following excerpt from *Managing the Future: Real Estate in the 1990s:*

▶ As the net income from managed properties slips in response to rising taxes and sagging real rents, [property] managers will be pressed to fill vacant space while at the same time cutting expenses and improving their controls. Those who can procure new tenants and retain the old ones without compromising property economics will do better than the rest.

The IREM Foundation study accentuates the need to devise ways to improve the volume and quality of business that owners of commercial properties are doing with their current tenants. So-called retention marketing represents an awareness that service industries are actually in the business of *manufacturing satisfied customers*. Michael LeBoeuf, one of the most provocative of the service commentators, made this point:

▶ Stop for a moment and consider just how valuable customers are. They alone make it possible for you to earn your livelihood in the way that you do. Treat them well and satisfied customers will be your best source of advertising and marketing. Give them good value and they will continue to reward you with their dollars year after year. All the slick financial and marketing techniques in the world are no substitute for an army of satisfied customers. Don't ever make the mistake of thinking of buildings, computers, consultants, or even employees as your company's greatest assets. Every company's greatest assets are its customers, because without customers there is no company. It's that simple.

As the management of commercial real estate evolves from tenant-tolerant to tenant-responsive to tenant-driven and beyond, it will be interesting to see whether the owners of major holdings of investment real estate will be willing to embrace the practical consequences of this fresh outlook toward tenants. We believe, for example, that retention efforts merit budgetary considerations and dollar allocations separate from, and in addition to, those accorded to marketing—which, after all, is simply business acquisition. Moreover, it is our opinion that the success of retention efforts will be determined in large part by the friendliness and overall people skills of the on-site management team, rather than by their dexterity in handling paperwork. Whether asset managers will defer to these revamped priorities remains to be seen. At the very least, it is likely that the admonition to property managers to reduce tenant turnover *(Managing the Future)*—if it is to become a true marketing strategy—will require behavioral changes in both managers and owners of commercial real estate.

Another reason for an adjustment in attitude toward tenants is that office, retail, and industrial properties are often indistinguishable from their competition. Successful real estate managers will be able to differentiate their product primarily by means of the personal touches their team members display to their customers. Albrecht and Zemke summarized the importance of this approach succinctly:

▶ [Service] is the new standard used by customers and consumers to measure organizational performance. Increasingly, the marketplace is opting to do business with those who serve, and declining involvement with those who merely supply.

Yet another reason for the real estate management industry to follow the customer service lead of retailers is that many of those who initiated and implemented the revolution in the retail trades are, themselves, tenants at commercial properties. They understand from their everyday business experiences that customers are entitled to an elevated level of treatment, and they expect similar attention from their landlords.

This unique confluence of external pressures from major owners of investment real estate, the commercial environment in which real estate managers function, and commercial tenants themselves, makes it inevitable that managers begin by reexamining the way they deal with tenants, with a view to completely revamping their approach. Indeed, these are the hoofbeats of a revolution, and as Donald Libey warned, "When you hear hoofbeats, expect horses."

The customer-retention techniques derived from retailing and summarized in this book go well beyond the sloganeering that has been characteristic of many of the "self-improvement" cycles American business has suffered during the past two decades or so. One of the reasons the customer service revolution has endured is the fact that its progenitor was Jan Carlzon, an especially intelligent, thoughtful, and dynamic individual. Carlzon's genius lay in his ability to recognize certain interconnected realities of management, most prominent among them the fact that SAS customers formed indelible impressions about the quality of his company in 15-second increments, well beyond his—or any manager's—ability to influence (or even supervise) these decisive "moments of truth."

The "moments of truth" concept, in turn, led Carlzon and others to explore such ancillary concepts as empowerment, benchmarking, internal and external customers, the role of leadership, employee rewards, and much more. Here's an example of one of the implications of *empowerment* from Carlzon's seminal book, *Moments of Truth:*

▶ If we are truly dedicated to orienting our company toward each customer's individual needs, then we cannot rely on rule books and instructions from distant corporate offices. We have to place responsibility for ideas, decisions, and actions with the people who *are* SAS during those 15 seconds: ticket agents, flight attendants, baggage handlers, and all the other frontline employees. If they have to go up the organizational chain of command for a decision on an individual problem, then those 15 golden seconds will elapse without a response, and we will have lost an opportunity to earn a loyal customer.

One offshoot of Carlzon's thinking, in our view, poses intriguing possibilities for the future of service in American business in general and the management of commercial properties in particular. This concept, known as "partnering," recognizes that there is a commonality of interest between a company's "internal" and "external" customers—that is, between its owners, managers, line staff, and clients. Because these apparently dissimilar parties are uniformly invested in the success of the company as a going concern, opportunities arise that may benefit all of these seemingly diverse and incompatible participants.

Many management companies are potentially the best customers of their suppliers—most firms are very good customers in terms of the quantity of business they do, year after year, with their vendors. They purchase huge quantities of products, ranging from cleaning supplies and plumbing parts to carpeting and wallcoverings. Despite evident opportunities to make bulk purchases, many managers buy piecemeal, meeting only their immediate needs. In truth, real estate managers often approach these business dealings as if they were merely sporadic, despite the fact that their relationships with their suppliers are ongoing.

The principles of partnering would recommend that purchasers who enjoy a "best customer" status with their suppliers ought to leverage this advantage, while not creating a corresponding disadvantage to the seller. Here is a hypothetical example.

In reviewing its purchasing history and its current budgetary projections, a management company may determine that it purchases hundreds of thousands of dollars' worth of HVAC replacement parts annually, including pumps and motors. Some years, the expenditure on this commodity approaches three quarters of a million dollars. Nonetheless, in accordance with the owners' directives, the management company routinely purchases these parts from the low-bid vendor. Indeed, low-bid contracting is a hallmark of commercial real estate management.

Suppose, however, that the manager decides to explore the possibility of partnering with one vendor. He might say to the supplier, "You know, we buy a lot of HVAC replacement parts each year, and we have to keep backup motors and pumps on hand. We've consistently done several hundred thousand dollars of business with HVAC parts vendors, including your company. I'd like to find out whether it would make sense for your firm to become the sole-source supplier for us. I'm thinking that if you knew, in advance, the volume of business we would do, say, by time period and location, maybe we could do better on price, and with more consistent quality, be able to minimize the disruption of HVAC service at the properties we manage."

The supplier might respond, "I know that we've done a lot of business with your company, but I had no idea that you spent so much on HVAC replacement parts every year. I'll tell you this: We don't have many customers that do that kind of volume with us. Offhand, it seems to me that if we could do some advance planning, I'll bet we could save us both some money. I think we ought to sit down and sketch out your needs, especially as they relate to specific equipment at each of your locations. If we could plan to store some of the parts as well as a couple of extra backup pumps and motors at a central location, the savings could be *enormous*."

The supplier might even make additional suggestions: "Why don't we also investigate the possibility of standardizing some or all of the HVAC components at your properties—or at least establish a range of compatibilities. Either of these approaches could allow you to reduce your overall inventory of HVAC stock items."

As this hypothetical discussion illustrates, some conventional rules (confidentiality of information, multiple-bidding requirements, and the like) need to be modified—or discarded—if partnering is to work. The long-term benefits of such relationships can be expected to be generally lower costs to both partners and an overall heightened awareness of each partner's needs by the other. More important, when business is awarded on a basis other than mere price, and when buyers and sellers are equally invested in one another's long-term profitability, both parties are bound to realize unexpected benefits from the relationship. Alliances constructed on "best-customer" foundations, rather than on price alone, may revolutionize American commerce. [NOTE: The suggestion to partner with a vendor is not a recommendation to forego competitive bidding. Rather, it is a suggestion to look beyond the bidding process, to build a relationship that will benefit the property owner, the management company, and the vendor by exploring possibilities, inviting recommendations, and capitalizing on the vendor's specialized expertise.]

Another aspect of partnering, called "aftermarketing," recognizes that acquisition marketing—deal-making—needs to be subordinated to retention marketing—that is, long-term customer satisfaction. Terry Vavra, an advocate of aftermarketing, has made this distinction and underlined its validity:

▶ Marketing must change its mentality from completing a sale to beginning a relationship; from closing a deal to building loyalty. Yet in the daily planning of marketing effort, more attention is generally directed at conquest—winning new customers to one's brand, product, or service. It is much rarer to find a company also devoting attention to maximizing the satisfaction of current customers. In such a company, the customer would not only be right, but his or her opinions would be actively sought out. This is the spirit of aftermarketing activities.

Whether the tenant retention movement in your firm will be a "revolution," albeit one that matures and deepens over time, depends on the transformation of the attitude of your company's leadership toward its internal and external customers. The impact on internal customers of a business approach that looks outward to the satisfaction of its clients rather than inward to its own bureaucratic processes has been described by Davidow and Uttal:

▶ First of all, driving a company to produce outstanding service flies in the face of conventional wisdom. Instead of being told to keep their eyes glued to the bottom line of the income statement, employees are asked to forget purely financial considerations and pursue customer satisfaction at all costs. Few employees will respond unless they see that top managers are irrevocably committed to achieving a service vision.

In this same vein, Karl Albrecht has described the depth and breadth of the transformation that companies must undertake:

▶ There must be a fundamental revision in our way of thinking about customers, about service, about leadership and management, and about the culture of organizations if we are to build and maintain the kind of competitive customer-winning capability that will be able to survive and thrive into the twenty-first century. That change in think-ing will take the form of a basic relearning of most of what we know about those subjects, and a reconceptualization of that knowledge.

Company leaders will lead the customer service revolution if there is to be a revolution at all. Their words and deeds are, in Davidow and Uttal's phrase, "the touchstones of [company] culture." Although the transformation is greatly facilitated if internal customers are responsible for planning and monitoring it, "customer service" and "tenant retention" will be but dust in the wind unless company leadership is fanatically committed to the revolu-tion. The importance of top-level commitment was pointed out by Richard Whiteley:

▶   The companies making real progress in serving their customers are led by people who themselves put the customer first. More than that, they believe passionately in giving the customer what he or she wants. They spend much of their time with their customers and they become the voice of the customer within their organizations.

However, while company leadership is obligated to launch the revolution, the people responsible for implementing it are found at the front line: The firm's "internal customers." As we have noted earlier, *customer service is a marketing strategy implemented by one frontline server for the benefit of one customer at a time.* Because implementation occurs in a multitude of random ways in a multiplicity of locations, frontline servers must have the necessary authority to act on behalf of the company in order to serve their external customers. In these circumstances, as Laura Liswood has observed:

▶   The best managers try to meddle as little as possible in the jobs their subordinates are doing. They strive to do their own jobs right the first time, while instilling that same ethic in their subordinates and peers. In customer-retention management, this philosophy of "let-ting go" is especially important. It means letting go enough so that the people closest to the customers can do their jobs right.

After "empowering" its frontline servers, company leadership needs to sup-port and encourage them in a variety of person-to-person ways. As Zeithaml and coworkers have noted:

▶   Service leaders lead in the field, where the action is, rather than from their desks. They are visible to their people, endlessly coaching, praising, correcting, cajoling, sermonizing, observing, questioning, and listening. They emphasize two-way, personal communications because they know this is the best way to give shape, substance, and credibility to the service vision and the best way to learn what is really going on in the field.

This "in-the-field" leadership style pioneered by Jan Carlzon and executives of major American corporations has the potential to reorganize the company, as Carlzon had to do at SAS:

▶   In a customer-driven company, the distribution of roles is radically different. The organization is decentralized, with responsibility delegated to those who until now have comprised the order-obeying bottom of the pyramid. The traditional, hierarchical corporate structure, in other words, is beginning to give way to a flattened, more horizontal, structure. This is particularly true in service businesses that begin not with the product but with the customer.

Effective, energized leadership. Empowered, excited frontline servers. The company is now ready to do business with and for its external customers, its tenant-"partners."

The course of the revolution will undoubtedly require the firm at some point to institute a tenant-feedback system; assess and implement techniques to reduce hassles that tenants encounter in dealing with their leased space (offices, stores, warehouses, etc.); study ways for tenants to become involved in their own service-production, and much more. Benchmarking other companies, both inside and outside the commercial real estate environment, may provide useful guidance.

The scope of revolutionary activities seems to be daunting, even overwhelming. Yet it is possible—and certainly desirable—for the company to proceed with its revolution in its own way and at its own pace. At the outset, then, it is useful to keep two Japanese concepts in mind. *Dantotsu*, or "shared fate," means roughly, "We're all in this together." In fact, the companies that have had the most success in transforming their businesses for the benefit of their customers have involved their own internal customers in every aspect of the transformation. *KAIZEN*, on the other hand, is an admonition to "take it slowly." Revolutions need to be made manageable. As Davidow and Uttal have cautioned:

▶   Since the task is so large, you have to decide which elements to stress first, where to place the heaviest bets. And that decision hinges on the evolutionary stage of competition in your industry and on the competitive position your company occupies.

Finally, to the managers of office buildings, shopping centers, warehouses, etc.: Those are hoofbeats you are hearing; the horses are not far away. Get out and lead *your* own tenant retention revolution.

The Roads to a Tenant Retention Revolution

Launching the Revolution

Appreciate the primacy of your tenants. Do whatever it takes to earn—and deserve—their loyalty. They are the lifeblood of your company.

Hire nice. The most important consideration in selecting new hires is to find the nicest people you can, and put them on the front lines. How helpful and friendly are *your* company's ambassadors?

Hire partners. Your employees, and the quality of their contacts with your customers, will determine whether or not you stay in business. Do you have confidence that your frontline servers are the people you want to entrust with the future of your company?

Know the costs of "conquest" marketing and tenant turnover. After you have calculated the cost of gaining signed leases at each of your properties, compute the expenses associated with each piece of lost business. Do you know the economic costs associated with tenant turnover at your properties?

Market for retention. Acquisition marketing is enormously expensive. Set aside dollars to keep current customers. Designate an item in each property's annual budget as "retention marketing." Do some staff brainstorming to plan how to spend the allocation. Make sure you spend every penny of the money you have budgeted for retention marketing.

Seeing the Revolution Through Your Employees' Eyes

Focus on the front line. Because frontline personnel have the most frequent—and often the most unpleasant—interactions with commercial tenants and their people, they *are* the property's human "moments of truth." Do you hire the best people you can find for these positions? Do you compensate them commensurate with their responsibility? Do you give them all the authority they need to perform? Do you support them without hesitation?

Train your staff to understand your company's ethos BEFORE you teach job skills. "Acculturation" is the process of familiarizing new employees with a company's values and goals. Premier service providers concentrate on acquainting new hires with the company mission before they teach job skills. Do *your* employees understand your company's ethos, its attitudes toward your customers, and its reason for being in business?

Staff for "request rhythms." The accessibility of management team members to tenants, at times that are convenient to the tenants, is an important ingredient in commercial property management. Have you attempted to match your staff's availability—especially the availability of your maintenance personnel—to the needs of your tenants?

Empower your staff. Let your employees know that one of their most important responsibilities is to *LET YOUR TENANTS WIN!* They need the authority to solve their customers' problems *on the spot;* equally important, they need to know that the organization will uphold their decisions and provide whatever assistance they may need.

Reward the behavior you want to encourage. Do you compensate employees for improvements in a property's overall economic performance or incremental increases in its value? Or is their pay tied, even indirectly, to tenant turnover?

Reward everyone who contributes to improved economic outcomes. Because reduction of tenant turnover is the business of all personnel at a commercial site, the entire management team should participate in the building's bonus program.

Treat your internal customers like gold. The most successful retailers recognize that their ability to serve and satisfy their external customers—those clients who pay the bills—depends entirely on the dedication of their own employees or "internal" customers. Do *you* pay attention to the job satisfaction of your "internal" customers?

Lead the Revolution. The evolution to a tenant-focused company requires vision and mission statements that direct the attention of the entire company toward customer (tenant) retention. Success is contingent upon responsible company leaders planning the course of the revolution and being totally committed to a customer focus before they set out to transform their companies.

Evaluating the Revolution from Your Tenants' Perspective

Remember the value of speed. Retail customers expect expeditious service. They're increasingly willing to pay extra for it; their loyalty to particular retailers increasingly depends on speedy response. As a real estate manager, do you know what your tenants consider to be "timely" service? And do you consistently meet their expectations?

Be complaint-friendly. At any one time, many—maybe even *most*—of your tenants are dissatisfied with the quality of the services they receive and ready to move elsewhere, perhaps to a competitive office building, shopping center, or industrial site. Have you made it easy for them to let you know what you need to do to keep their business? Do you regularly survey your tenants to find out their level of satisfaction, dissatisfaction, and motivation?

Make up for the "hassle factor." When tenants experience a problem with their leased space, they expect the situation to be resolved promptly to their satisfaction. They also deserve some additional benefit, something unexpected, to make amends for the annoyance. What do *you* do to compensate for the "hassle" factor?

Improve your customer "ergonomics." How easy is it for prospective tenants—as well as your current tenants—to do business with you? Streamline your procedures from the perspective of your tenants so that your company is ergonomically *friendly.*

Make your service visible. When service is visible to customers, it is likely that they will consider it more valuable; in the absence of visibility, customers are often unaware that service is being provided at all. Have you strategized techniques for making the service you supply to your tenants—even routine service, such as common area maintenance and cleaning—*apparent* to your tenants?

Guarantee your product. Guarantees can convey a powerful marketing message to prospective tenants. They illustrate confidence in the product, and they bring to light customer dissatisfaction. Have you brainstormed ways to guarantee your commercial services?

Recover from service deficiencies. Service "recovery"—fixing problems once they are uncovered—is an essential component of a property's service image. Is your service recovery program consistent with the quality of your product?

"Co-produce" service. Many retailers involve their customers in producing the service they receive. Self-service reduces expense. Some managers of commercial real estate are beginning to engage tenants in generating their own service, which also benefits the property in general.

Under-promise/over-deliver. A frequent complaint of retail customers is that their suppliers have promised things they either could not deliver or did not intend to deliver. The "over-promise, under-deliver" syndrome is also prevalent in the real estate industry. Do *you* manage your tenants' expectations by promising something *less* than what you intend to deliver to them, or do you set them up to be disappointed by performance that doesn't meet your promise?

Build a "customer-in" organization. Ultimately, the future of your company depends on the long-term loyalty of your tenants. When you pay attention to your tenants' needs—when you listen to their *voices*—you are in the process of constructing a "customer-in" organization that merits the loyalty of its clients. Does *your* company react when it hears the voices of its tenants?

Thin the rulebook. It is human nature to over-regulate the behavior of others. Decide what rules are *absolutely essential* to protect human safety and the property as a whole. Keep them, and get rid of the unessential rules.

"WOW!" your tenants and their people. *Dazzle* your tenants with an occasional, unexpected, "moment of truth" that you have scrupulously planned to delight them. Serve them coffee, juice, and rolls in the lobby or provide a jar of candy for their reception desks and refill it periodically. Sponsor an impromptu picnic for tenants and their employees. Whatever you do, let your tenants and their employees know that you *love* them!

Motivate your tenants to become repeat customers. Develop and implement E-Plus strategies so that your service will not only exceed tenants' expectations, and thus increase the probability of their renewing leases with you, but also compel them to tell others about their experiences. Such positive word-of-mouth advertising from them will also attract new tenants.

Looking Outward for Revolutionary Guidance

Benchmark. Analyze how the best companies attract customers, market to them, and keep them coming back, year after year. How do they do it? Take the best ideas you discover, and put them to work for *you!*

Partner. Win-win commercial relationships provide benefits to buyers and sellers that they can find nowhere else. Strategize ways to make your tenants—and perhaps your suppliers—your *partners.*

Manage "moments of truth." Little things—the freshness of your signage, the friendliness of your management team members, the appearance of the building lobby—determine whether a commercial property will be successful. These individual "moments of truth" need to be identified, understood, and then managed.

Test failpoints. Building systems break down over time, and they do so in very predictable ways. Have you analyzed how individual leased spaces, common areas, and amenities in particular properties fail, and have you taken preventive measures to avert such failures?

Do some "outer-circle" thinking. Designing an office suite or store space that is the *ultimate* in tenant efficiency is challenging work. Equally important is the need to set aside some time to meet with your entire staff, and perhaps a supplier and one or two representatives from tenants, to brainstorm strategies you can use to provide the high-touch, personal value that will *immortalize* your commercial property in the minds of your prospective and current tenants.

Devise a mission statement. Has your company formulated a statement that describes its distinctive competence? Have your employees tackled the task of describing why you are in business and what is special about your firm? Mission statements contain the graphic depiction of a company's uniqueness as seen from inside the company.

"Flatten" the company's structure. The most customer-responsive firms realize that the typical bureaucratic organization distances customers from the top of the company. Those businesses that cater to their customers are blessed with leaders who personally get out on the front line to meet and serve their customer-clients face to face.

Approach the revolution with a spirit of KAIZEN. Companies that undergo the transformation to a customer focus understand that a successful revolution must be a metamorphosis, rather than a cataclysmic event. One possibility is to approach the task with an attitude of patience, rather than one of immediacy.

Epilogue

As one last comment on what a tenant retention revolution is all about, we share with you the following, albeit apocryphal, story:

> There was once a property manager who, as all of us eventually do, left behind his worldly woes and passed on to a higher plane. Upon arriving at the Pearly Gates, he was greeted by St. Peter with a choice of where he wanted to spend eternity, in heaven or in the nether world. He would be allowed to spend a week in each location, and then he would have to tell St. Peter where he wanted to reside.
>
> The property manager was instantly whisked away to Lucifer's domain, where he was greeted by the devil himself, wearing white tie and tails. From the very start, Satan was the highest caliber of host. He showed the rather unsettled guest to a magnificent suite of rooms, exquisitely decorated in the style that the property manager himself would have chosen. Every conceivable convenience and luxury was but a few steps away. To top it all off, there were several beautiful attendants who were at his beck and call, bringing him sumptuous meals that he could only think of as heavenly.
>
> When the week was up, the property manager found himself once again facing St. Peter who asked if he was ready to spend the next week in heaven. The property manager did not think twice. Telling St. Peter that if what he had just experienced was hell, he would have no reservations whatsoever about spending the rest of eternity there.
>
> At that, the property manager was instantly transported back to hell, only to find an entirely different environment. Gone was the beautiful suite of the week before. In its stead was a tiny, cramped cell with a pile of straw to sleep on, and he was served a bowl of

gruel and a crust of bread each day by the most hideous creature he had every seen.

When he finally saw the devil, the property manager ran to him exclaiming that there must have been a dreadful mistake. He implored Satan to explain what had happened.

Looking quite perturbed at the interruption, the devil told the property manager, "Apparently you just don't have a clue: Before, you were a prospect; now you are a tenant."

Too often in the past, relations with tenants have been founded on this type of attitude. What we are proposing as *THE Tenant Retention Solution* is that signing the lease is not the conclusion of the challenge. Rather, it is the beginning of a long-term relationship, and managers of commercial properties must strive every day to meet—and exceed—their tenants' expectations in order to keep them into the future.

C. C. Sullivan, Associate Editor of *Buildings* magazine summarized the situation this way:

▶ Tenant retention is the name of the game. . . . Whatever the retention strategy, it is vital that the tenants are aware of the efforts. . . . The road to successfully retaining tenants is a long one, but two lanes can help speed the process: On one hand, good relationships are vital; on the other, upgrading to avoid obsolescence is the fast lane to a competitive building. Tenant retention is the most fundamental operations concern of the '90s, and one that happens, quite literally, every day.

We could not say it better!

Endnotes

The sources of quoted materials are indicated here in the order of their presentation within the text of each respective chapter, beginning with chapter opening quotations and ending with citations within sidebars (boxed text examples), using authors' last names and shortened versions of book titles. Full publication data are presented in the Bibliography. (Sources of select illustrations are indicated within individual exhibits.) Permission to reprint selected excerpts from books is acknowledged in the Bibliography. Periodical sources and permission to reprint selected excerpts from them are cited in full in this Endnotes section.

Prologue (pages 1–3)

Liswood, *Serving Them Right,* p. xxxii.

Chapter 1, The Customer Service Revolution (pages 4–18)

Henry Ford quoted in *The Oxford Dictionary of Modern Quotations,* p. 82

Harvey Lamm quoted in Band, *Creating Value for Customers,* p. 49.

Libey, *Libey on Customers,* p. 104.

Ford Motor Company figures from *Market Share Reporter: An Annual Compilation of Reported Market Share Data on Companies, Products, and Services [1993]* (Detroit: Gale Research, Inc., 1993), pp. 308, 309, and 311.

Flock of geese analogy is from Schonberger, *Building a Chain of Customers,* p. 34.

Elephant analogy is from Albrecht and Zemke, *Service America!* p. 169.

Office vacancy statistics are from ONCOR International, cited in *Statistical Abstract of the United States: 1993* published by the U.S. Department of Labor, Bureau of the Census; 1994 data are from "Office Vacancy Index of the United States—September 30, 1994," published by CB Commercial Real Estate Group, Inc. Information on shopping centers and industrial properties is from *ULI Market Profiles: 1993* published by the Urban Land Institute and *Emerging Trends in Real Estate: 1995* published by Real Estate Research Corporation and Equitable Real Estate Investment Management, Inc.

Thrift downfall figures from *Business Week,* March 8, 1993, p. 80.

IREM Foundation, *Managing the Future,* pp. 2 and 3.

IREM Foundation, *Managing the Future,* p. 45.

Conclusion of "Survival for 21st-Century Buildings: The Key Is Happy Tenants," by C. C. Sullivan, *Buildings* 88(1):32, January 1994. Reprinted by permission of the publisher.

Carlzon, *Moments of Truth,* p. 3.

Albrecht, *At America's Service,* p. 26.

Carlzon, *Moments of Truth,* p. 5.

Carlzon, *Moments of Truth,* p. 26.

Carlzon, *Moments of Truth,* p. 5.

Carlzon, *Moments of Truth,* p. 43.

Carlzon, *Moments of Truth,* pp. 52–53.

The message regarding internal service is from Albrecht, *At America's Service,* p. 134.

Carlzon, *Moments of Truth,* p. 3.

The story of the sultan and the wizard is from "Beware the Study of Turtles," an essay by Charles Krauthammer in *Time* 141(26):76, June 28, 1993. Copyright 1993 Time Inc. Reprinted by permission. (Emphasis added.)

Carlzon, *Moments of Truth,* p. 24.

Changing Demand for Commercial Space (pages 10–12)

The impact of "officing technologies" on businesses is summarized in "New Office Technologies Affect Demand for Space," *Mortgage and Real Estate Executives Report* 27(12):5–6, August 15, 1994, and "Alternative Officing: Revolution or Merely Redesign?" by Katherine Anderson, *Journal of Property Management* 60(1):32–35, January–February 1995; some of their economic implications are outlined in "Food for Thought: Trimming the Fat—Thrifty Concepts and Technologies Whittle Down Costs" by Julie Eisele, *Buildings* 88(1):36 and 38, January 1994.

Technology's impact on retailing is outlined in "The Technological Revolution in Retailing—From Mall to Cyberspace" by Nina J. Gruen, *Journal of Property Management* 59(6):20–23, November–December 1994, and "Retailing Looks To A New Century" by Meg Whittemore, *The Nation's Business* 82(12):18–24, December 1994.

In "Long-Term Space Planning as a Retention Tool," *Journal of Property Management* 56(2):48–51, March–April 1991, Sharon K. Mount reports on a direct application of computer technology to commercial tenant retention.

Chapter 2, The Roads to Revolution (pages 19–44)

"High touch" as related to service means, "lots of flexible, warm, human interactions." Davidow and Uttal, *Total Customer Service,* p. 56.

Disend, *How to Provide Excellent Service,* p. 210.

Rick Johnson quoted in Disend, *How to Provide Excellent Service,* p. 101.

Donald Porter quoted in Albrecht and Zemke, *Service America!* p. 32.

Rosenbluth and Peters, *The Customer Comes Second,* p. 52.

Rosenbluth and Peters, *The Customer Comes Second,* p. 25.

Reference to "lighthouses for change" is from Zeithaml et al., *Delivering Quality Service,* p. 145.

Rosenbluth and Peters, *The Customer Comes Second,* p. 39.

Rosenbluth and Peters, *The Customer Comes Second,* pp. 51–52.

Rosenbluth and Peters, *The Customer Comes Second,* pp. 55–56.

"Mike" Morita quoted in Albrecht, *At America's Service,* pp. 118–119.

William Ouchi quoted in Zemke and Bell, *Service Wisdom,* p. 155.

Positively Outrageous Service (P.O.S.) is defined in general terms in Gross, *Positively Outrageous Service,* p. 1; specific components are listed on p. 63.

Davidow and Uttal, *Total Customer Service,* p. 1.

Dunckel and Taylor, *The Business Guide,* p. 15.

Discussion of the Levitt paradigm (four levels of attributes of products) is adapted from the characterization in Disend, *How to Provide Excellent Service,* pp. 105–107.

Ted Levitt quoted in Disend, *How to Provide Excellent Service,* p. 107.

Freemantle, *Incredible Customer Service,* p. 48.

Service Visibility and "Getting Your Hands Dirty" (pages 22–25)

Zemke and Schaaf, *The Service Edge,* p. 3.

McCann, *The Joy of Service,* p. 86.

LeBoeuf, *How to Win Customers,* p. 57.

Davidow and Uttal, *Total Customer Service,* p. 98.

Soichiro Honda quoted in Whiteley, *The Customer-Driven Company,* p. 200.

What Is Service? (pages 36–37)

Attributes of service adapted from Albrecht and Zemke, *Service America!* pp. 36–37.

Zemke and Schaaf, *The Service Edge,* pp. 13–14.

Heskett et al., *Service Breakthroughs,* pp. 153–154.

Business Intelligence—Finding Out What Customers Expect (pages 41–42)

Sam Walton quoted in Zeithaml et al., *Delivering Quality Service,* p. 63.

Chapter 3, Revolutionary Hiring and "Zapping" (pages 45–69)

Zeithaml et al., *Delivering Quality Service,* p. 152. (Emphasis added.)

Vavra, *Aftermarketing,* p. 251.

Whiteley, *The Customer-Driven Company,* p. 11.

Zemke and Bell, *Service Wisdom,* p. 166.

Gross, *Positively Outrageous Service,* p. 159.

Sewell and Brown, *Customers for Life,* p. 68. (Emphasis added.)

Gross, *Positively Outrageous Service,* p. 161.

Berry and Parasuraman, *Marketing Services,* p. 153.

Clemmer, *Firing on All Cylinders,* p. 128.

Rosenbluth and Peters, *The Customer Comes Second,* pp. 51–52.

Band, *Creating Value for Customers,* p. 196.

Freemantle, *Incredible Customer Service,* p. 109.

Tom Peters quoted in Clemmer, *Firing on All Cylinders,* p. 149.

Gross, *Positively Outrageous Service,* p. 172. (Emphasis added.)

Shannon Johnston quoted in Zemke and Bell, *Service Wisdom,* pp. 158–159.

Davidow and Uttal, *Total Customer Service,* p. 126.

Albrecht, *At America's Service,* p. 54.

Disend, *How to Provide Excellent Service,* pp. 170–171.

Libey, *Libey on Customers,* p. 218.

Zeithaml et al., *Delivering Quality Service,* p. 152. (Emphasis added.)

Disend, *How to Provide Excellent Service,* pp. 92–93.

Carlzon, *Moments of Truth,* p. 5.

Byham, *Zapp!* ® *The Lightning of Empowerment,* pp. 9–10.

Zeithaml et al., *Delivering Quality Service,* p. 94.

Disend, *How to Provide Excellent Service,* p. 20.

Hervey Feldman quoted in Davidow and Uttal, *Total Customer Service,* p. 114.

Hart et al., The Profitable Art of Service Recovery, *Harvard Business Review,* July–August 1990, quoted in Clemmer, *Firing on All Cylinders,* p. 45.

Albrecht, *At America's Service,* p. 224.

Jan Carlzon, "The Art of Loving" (*INC,* May 1989, p. 6) quoted in Heskett et al., *Service Breakthroughs,* pp. 110–111.

Beer et al. quoted in Clemmer, *Firing on All Cylinders,* p. 54.

Glen, *It's Not My Department,* p. 53.

Anderson and Zemke, *Delivering Knock Your Socks Off Service,* p. 106.

A. S. Neill quoted in Zeithaml et al., *Delivering Quality Service,* p. 153.

Pre-Employment Psychological Testing (page 53)

For implications of the Americans with Disabilities Act of 1990 (ADA) regarding psychological testing in pre-employment screening, see 42 U.S.C. Sec. 12101–12213 (1992).

The decision in *Soroka v. Dayton Hudson Corporation* can be found at 1 Cal. Rptr. 2d 77 (Cal. Ct. App. 1991).

"Firing" Customers: The Pareto Principle (pages 61–64)

Berry and Parasuraman, *Marketing Services,* p. 19.

Albrecht, *At America's Service,* p. 114.

Berry and Parasuraman, *Marketing Services,* p. 50.

Albrecht, *At America's Service,* p. 113.

Chapter 4, The Retention Revolution (pages 70–83)

The "Death Wish Paradox" is from Clancy and Shulman, *The Marketing Revolution,* p. 238.

Advertising expenditures reported in Vavra, *Aftermarketing,* pp. 11–12.

Clancy and Shulman, *The Marketing Revolution,* p. 237.

Statistics from a survey on "Why Customers Quit" quoted in Leboeuf, *How to Win Customers,* p. 13. The same data were reported in Morgan, *Calming Upset Customers,* p. 6.

Anderson and Zemke, *Delivering Knock Your Socks Off Service,* p. 8.

TARP statistics cited in Albrecht and Bradford, *The Service Advantage,* p. 199; also in Zemke and Schaaf, *The Service Edge,* p. 4.

IREM Foundation, *Managing the Future,* p. 3.

Interviewee results from IREM Foundation, *Managing the Future,* p. 45.

Survey respondent results from IREM Foundation, *Managing the Future,* p. 45.

Liswood, *Serving Them Right,* p. 115.

Average acquisition and retention costs are from Morgan, *Calming Upset Customers,* p. 6.

Poirier and Houser, *Business Partnering,* pp. 57.

Poirier and Houser, *Business Partnering,* pp. 58.

Barbara Bund Jackson quoted in Band, *Creating Value for Customers,* p. 38.

Band, *Creating Value for Customers,* p. 38.

Libey, *Libey on Customers,* p. 38.

Chapter 5, The Complaint Revolution (pages 84–94)

Sewell and Brown, *Customers for Life,* p. 40.

Liswood, *Serving Them Right,* pp. 6–7.

Whiteley, *The Customer-Driven Company,* p. 64.

Albrecht, *The Only Thing That Matters,* p. 109.

USOCA figures from Disend, *How to Provide Excellent Service,* p. 199.

USOCA research, as reported in the *New York Times* (March 26, 1988), quoted in Goldzimer, *I'm First,* p. 69.

Davidow and Uttal, *Total Customer Service,* p. xviii.

Lele, *The Customer is Key,* pp. 209–210.

Clemmer, *Firing on All Cylinders,* p. 16.

Research data from the USOCA reported in Disend, *How to Provide Excellent Service,* pp. 72–73.

Davidow and Uttal (citing John Goodman), *Total Customer Service,* p. 15.

Stanley Marcus quoted in Liswood, *Serving Them Right,* p. 1.

Zemke and Schaaf (citing the TARP study and John Goodman), *The Service Edge,* p. 8.

TARP data on customer behaviors reported in Albrecht and Bradford, *The Service Advantage,* p. 199.

Vavra, *Aftermarketing,* p. 127.

Lele, *The Customer is Key,* p. 55.

Libey, *Libey on Customers,* p. 237.

Lele, *The Customer is Key,* p. 209.

Disend, *How to Provide Excellent Service,* p. 73.

Sewell and Brown, *Customers for Life,* p. 28.

Goldzimer, *I'm First,* p. 72.

Patricia Sellers' article in *Fortune* magazine cited in Gross, *Positively Outrageous Service,* p. 37.

Zeithaml et al., *Delivering Quality Service,* p. 54.

Disend, *How to Provide Excellent Service,* p. 20

Guarantees (pages 91–93)

Christopher Hart quoted by Zemke and Bell in *Service Wisdom,* pp. 280 and 282. Reprinted by permission of *Harvard Business Review.* Excerpts from Christopher W. L. Hart, "The Power of Unconditional Service Guarantees," *Harvard Business Review,* (July–August 1988). Copyright 1988 by the President and Fellows of Harvard College. All rights reserved.

Berry and Parasuraman, *Marketing Services,* p. 7.

Whirlpool quotation from Hanan and Karp, *Customer Satisfaction,* p. 36. (Emphasis added.)

Glen, *It's Not My Department,* pp. 70–71.

Chapter 6, The Recovery Revolution (pages 95–109)

Donald Porter quoted in Anderson and Zemke, *Delivering Knock Your Socks Off Service,* p. 87.

Sewell and Brown, *Customers for Life,* p. 164.

From "Service Breakdown—The Road to Recovery," (*Management Review,* October 1987), quoted in Zemke and Bell, *Service Wisdom,* p. 269.

Lele, *The Customer Is Key,* p. 142.

Hanan and Karp, *Customer Satisfaction,* p. 101.

Lele, *The Customer Is Key,* p. 139.

The Perception and Performance Principle is an adaptation of a formula in Nykiel, *You Can't Lose if the Customer Wins,* p. 99.

Freemantle, *Incredible Customer Service,* p. 36.

Libey, *Libey on Customers,* p. 102.

Berry and Parasuraman, *Marketing Services,* p. 40.

Gross, *Positively Outrageous Service,* p. 95.

Anderson and Zemke, *Delivering Knock Your Socks Off Service,* p. 25.

Anderson and Zemke, *Delivering Knock Your Socks Off Service,* pp. 25–26.

Berry and Parasuraman, *Marketing Services,* p. 47.

Heskett et al., *Service Breakthroughs,* p. 108.

Clemmer, *Firing on All Cylinders,* p. 46.

Gross, *Positively Outrageous Service,* pp. 97–98.

Gross, *Positively Outrageous Service,*p. 133.

Berry and Parasuraman, *Marketing Services,* p. 52.

Lash, *The Complete Guide,* pp. 136–137.

The E-Plus strategy is from Paul R. Timm, Ph.D., "From Slogans to Strategy: How to Achieve Customer Loyalty," *Exchange* (a publication of the Marriott School of Management, Brigham Young University), Spring 1993, pp. 20–24. Excerpts reprinted by permission of the author.

Anderson and Zemke, *Delivering Knock Your Socks Off Service,* p. 89.

Chapter 7, The Leadership Revolution (pages 110–133)

Mimi Lieber quoted in Zeithaml et al., *Delivering Quality Service,* p. 138.

Band, *Creating Value for Customers,* p. 180.

Robert Crandall quoted in Zeithaml et al., *Delivering Quality Service,* p. 62.

Libey, *Libey on Customers,* p. 113.

Liswood, *Serving Them Right,* pp. 14–15.

Rosenbluth and Peters, *The Customer Comes Second,* p. 35.

Rosenbluth and Peters, *The Customer Comes Second,* p. 121.

Paul Goodstadt quoted in Albrecht, *The Only Thing That Matters,* p. 91.

Rosenbluth and Peters, *The Customer Comes Second,* pp. 227–228.

Disend, *How to Provide Excellent Service,* p. 19.

Band, *Creating Value for Customers,* p. 173.

Albrecht, *The Only Thing That Matters,* p. 11.

Poirier and Houser, *Business Partnering,* p. 7.

Carlzon, *Moments of Truth,* p. 5.

Carlzon, *Moments of Truth,* p. 60.

Disend, *How to Provide Excellent Service,* p. 158.

Band, *Creating Value for Customers,* p. 187.

Senge, *The Fifth Discipline,* pp. 287–288.

Albrecht, *At America's Service,* p. 134.

Libey, *Libey on Customers,* p. 5.

Libey, *Libey on Customers,* p. 94.

Hammer and Champy, *Reengineering the Corporation,* p. 75.

Zeithaml et al., *Delivering Quality Service,* p. 2.

Davidow and Uttal, *Total Customer Service,* p. 41.

Davidow and Uttal, *Total Customer Service,* p. 1.

Disend, *How to Provide Excellent Service,* p. 244.

Senge, *The Fifth Discipline,* pp. 223–224.

Senge, *The Fifth Discipline,* p. 213.

Senge, *The Fifth Discipline,* p. 208.

Disend, *How to Provide Excellent Service,* p. 126.

The distinction between search and experience qualities, as made by Philip Nelson, is described in Heskett et al., *Service Breakthroughs,* p. 37.

Berry and Parasuraman, *Marketing Services,* p. 7.

Libey, *Libey on Customers,* p. 60.

Davidow and Uttal, *Total Customer Service,* p. 41.

Hanan and Karp, *Customer Satisfaction,* p. 83.

Gross, quoting from *Fortune* magazine (June 1990 issue), in *Positively Outrageous Service,* p. 98.

Customer-Focused Marketing (page 113)

A succinct summary of the attributes described by Libey in *Libey on Customers,* pp. 94–107.

Chapter 8, The Benchmarking Revolution (pages 134–150)

Ralph Waldo Emerson quoted in LeBoeuf, *How to Win Customers and Keep Them for Life,* p. 23.

David T. Kearns quoted in Camp, *Benchmarking (Search),* p. 10.

Albrecht, *The Only Thing That Matters,* pp. 63–64.

Leibfried and McNair, *Benchmarking (Tool),* p. 330.

The admonition to "go to school on the winners" is from Whiteley, *The Customer-Driven Company,* p. 16.

Camp, *Benchmarking (Search),* p. xi.

Albrecht, *The Only Thing That Matters,* p. 64.

Sun Tzu's rules are from *The Art of War* as quoted in Camp, *Benchmarking (Search),* p. 3.

Camp, *Benchmarking (Search),* pp. 11 and 15. (Emphasis added.)

John Sharpe quoted in Clemmer, *Firing on All Cylinders,* p. 27.

Clemmer, *Firing on All Cylinders,* p. 27.

Clemmer, *Firing on All Cylinders,* p. 27.

The REACT performance evaluation and benchmarking process is from CEL & Associates, Inc., a Los Angeles-based real estate consulting firm. Excerpt reprinted by permission of CEL & Associates, Inc., (310) 571–3113.

The E-Plus strategy is from Paul R. Timm, Ph.D., "From Slogans to Strategy: How to Achieve Customer Loyalty," *Exchange* (a publication of the Marriott School of Management, Brigham Young University), Spring 1993, pp. 20–24. Excerpts reprinted by permission of the author.

Camp, *Benchmarking (Search),* pp. 9–10.

Chapter 9, Strategizing the Tenant Retention Revolution (pages 151–202)

Albrecht and Zemke, *Service America!* p. 77.

Camp, *Benchmarking (Search),* p. 34.

Denton, *Quality Service,* p. 5.

Clemmer, *Firing on All Cylinders,* p. 105.

Disend, *How to Provide Excellent Service,* p. 1.

Sam Walton quoted in Glen, *It's Not My Department,* p. 137.

Albrecht and Zemke, *Service America!* p. 84.

Whiteley, *The Customer-Driven Company,* p. 135.

"Management by walking around" is characterized in Peters and Waterman, *In Search of Excellence,* pp. 121–125.

Liswood, *Serving Them Right,* p. 50.

Libey, *Libey on Customers,* p. 96.

Band, *Creating Value for Customers,* p. 8.

LeBoeuf, *How to Win Customers,* p. 135.

Heskett et al., *Service Breakthroughs,* p. 105.

Lele, *The Customer is Key,* p. 209.

Denton, *Quality Service,* p. 1.

LeBoeuf, *How to Win Customers,* p. 135.

Lash, *The Complete Guide,* p. 123.

Examples of the log forms and survey questionnaire can be found in "Tracking Retention Efforts" by William D. Norwell and Victoria A. Stevens, *Journal of Property Management* 57(2):24–28, March–April, 1992.

Zeithaml et al., *Delivering Quality Service,* p. 54.

Lash, *The Complete Guide,* p. 152.

Berry and Parasuraman, *Marketing Services,* p. 51.

Zemke and Bell, *Service Wisdom,* p. 175.

Heskett et al., *Service Breakthroughs,* p. 104.

Goldzimer, *I'm First,* p. 72.

Heskett et al., *Service Breakthroughs,* p. 37.

Libey, *Libey on Customers,* p. 38.

Zemke and Bell, *Service Wisdom,* pp. 7–8.

Liswood, *Serving Them Right,* pp. 112–113.

Camp, *Benchmarking (Search),* p. 4.

Zeithaml et al., *Delivering Quality Service,* p. 55.

Anderson and Zemke, *Delivering Knock Your Socks Off Service,* p. 128.

Theodore Levitt quoted in Clemmer, *Firing on All Cylinders,* p. 54.

Gross, *Positively Outrageous Service,* p. 99.

Libey, *Libey on Customers,* pp. 24–25.

Senge, *The Fifth Discipline,* p. 114.

Albrecht, *The Only Thing That Matters,* p. 9.

Freemantle, *Incredible Customer Service,* p. 123.

Libey, *Libey on Customers,* pp. 28 and 29–30.

Gross, *Positively Outrageous Service,* p. 202.

Albrecht, *At America's Service,* p. 224.

Whiteley, *The Customer-Driven Company,* p. 17.

LeBoeuf, *How to Win Customers,* p. 170.

Poirier and Houser, *Business Partnering,* p. 164.

Heskett et al., *Service Breakthroughs,* pp. 153–154.

Davidow and Uttal, *Total Customer Service,* pp. 147–148.

Band, *Creating Value for Customers,* p. 161.

Band, *Creating Value for Customers,* pp. 161–162.

LeBoeuf, *How to Win Customers,* p. 169.

LeBoeuf, *How to Win Customers,* pp. 169–170.

Gross, *Positively Outrageous Service,* p. 3.

IREM Foundation, *Managing the Future,* p. 9.

LeBoeuf, *How to Win Customers,* p. 23.

Albrecht and Zemke, *Service America!* p. 18.

Libey, *Libey on Customers,* p. 104.

Carlzon, *Moments of Truth,* p. 3.

Vavra, *Aftermarketing,* p. 14.

Davidow and Uttal, *Total Customer Service,* p. 95.

Albrecht, *The Only Thing That Matters,* p. 2.

Touchstones of culture reference is from Davidow and Uttal, *Total Customer Service,* p. 96.

Whiteley, *The Customer-Driven Company,* p. 182.

Liswood, *Serving Them Right*, p. 123.

Zeithaml et al., *Delivering Quality Service*, p. 7.

Carlzon, *Moments of Truth*, p. 5.

Davidow and Uttal, *Total Customer Service*, p. 211.

More information on the implications for real estate management companies of some of the workplace innovations noted in "The Roads to a Tenant Retention Revolution"—organizational design, reward systems, customer service—can be found in the Winter 1991 issue of *AMO® Perspectives* (Volume 6, Number 1), published by the Institute of Real Estate Management.

Appealing to Tenants' Personnel (page 171)

Many examples of people-focused amenities are described in "Getting the Most from Your Amenities" by Kathie Rategan, *Journal of Property Management* 56(1):22–26, March–April, 1991.

Epilogue (pages 203–204)

C. C. Sullivan, "Survival for 21st-Century Buildings: The Key Is Happy Tenants," *Buildings* 88(1):30 and 32, January 1994. Reprinted by permission of the publisher.

Bibliography

The following service books were used as resources in the writing of this book. Citations of data and direct quotations are identified in the Endnotes.

Karl Albrecht, *At America's Service: How Corporations Can Revolutionize the Way They Treat Their Customers* (Homewood, Illinois: Dow Jones-Irwin, 1988). Excerpts reprinted by permission of Irwin Professional Publishing.

Karl Albrecht, *The Only Thing That Matters: Bringing the Power of the Customer into the Center of Your Business* (New York: HarperBusiness, 1992). Copyright 1992 by Karl Albrecht. Excerpts reprinted by permission of HarperCollins Publishers, Inc.

Karl Albrecht and Lawrence J. Bradford, *The Service Advantage: How to Identify and Fulfill Customer Needs* (Homewood, Illinois: Dow Jones-Irwin, 1990).

Karl Albrecht and Ron Zemke, *Service America! Doing Business in the New Economy* (New York: Warner, 1985). Excerpts reprinted by permission of Irwin Professional Publishing.

Kristin Anderson and Ron Zemke, *Delivering Knock Your Socks Off Service* (New York: AMACOM, 1991). Copyright 1991 Performance Research Associates, Inc. Published by AMACOM, a division of the American Management Association. All rights reserved. Excerpts reprinted with permission of the publisher.

William A. Band, *Creating Value for Customers: Designing and Implementing a Total Corporate Strategy* (New York: John Wiley & Sons, Inc., 1991). Copyright 1991 by Coopers & Lybrand (Canada). Excerpts reprinted by permission of John Wiley & Sons, Inc.

Leonard L. Berry and A. Parasuraman, *Marketing Services: Competing Through Quality* (New York: The Free Press, 1991). Copyright 1991 by The Free Press. Excerpts reprinted with the permission of The Free Press, a Division of Simon & Schuster.

William C. Byham, Ph.D. (with Jeff Cox), *Zapp!® The Lightning of Empowerment: How to Improve Productivity, Quality, and Employee Satisfaction* (New York: Fawcett Columbine, 1988). Parts of Joe Mode's Notebook reprinted courtesy of Development Dimensions International, Inc.

Robert C. Camp, *Benchmarking: The Search for Industry Best Practices That Lead to Superior Performance* (Milwaukee: ASQC Quality Press, 1989). Excerpts reprinted by permission of the publisher.

Jan Carlzon, *Moments of Truth* (Cambridge, Massachusetts: Ballinger Publishing Company, 1987). Copyright 1987 by Ballinger Publishing Company. Excerpts reprinted by permission of HarperCollins Publishers, Inc.

Kevin J. Clancy and Robert S. Shulman, *The Marketing Revolution: A Radical Manifesto for Dominating the Marketplace* (New York: HarperBusiness, 1991). Copyright 1991 by Kevin J. Clancy and Robert Shulman. Excerpts reprinted by permission of HarperCollins Publishers, Inc.

Jim Clemmer, *Firing on All Cylinders: The Service/Quality System for High-Powered Corporate Performance* (Homewood, Illinois: Business One Irwin, 1992). Excerpts reprinted by permission of Irwin Professional Publishing.

William H. Davidow and Bro Uttal, *Total Customer Service: The Ultimate Weapon* (New York: HarperPerennial, 1989). Copyright 1989 by William H. Davidow and Bro Uttal. Excerpts reprinted by permission of HarperCollins Publishers, Inc.

D. Keith Denton, *Quality Service* (Houston: Gulf Publishing Company, 1989). Copyright 1989 by Gulf Publishing Company. Quoted material used with permission of the publisher. All rights reserved.

Jeffrey E. Disend, *How to Provide Excellent Service in Any Organization: A Blueprint for Making All the Theories Work* (Radnor, Pennsylvania: Chilton Book Company, 1991). Copyright 1991 by the author. Excerpts reprinted by permission of the publisher, Chilton Book Company.

Jacqueline Dunckel and Brian Taylor, *The Business Guide To Profitable Customer Relations* (Vancouver: Self-Counsel Press, 1988). Note to readers: This book has been revised and retitled. The excerpt appearing in this book is reprinted from *Keeping Customers Happy* by Jacqueline Dunckel and Brian Taylor, page 42. Copyright 1994 by Self-Counsel Press. Reproduced courtesy of the publisher.

David Freemantle, *Incredible Customer Service: The Final Test* (London: McGraw-Hill Book Company, 1993). Excerpts reprinted by permission of the author.

Peter Glen, *It's Not My Department! How to Get the Service You Want, Exactly the Way You Want It!* (New York: William Morrow and Company, Inc., 1990). Copyright 1990 by Peter Glen. Excerpts reprinted by permission of William Morrow & Company, Inc.

Linda Silverman Goldzimer, *"I'm First:" Your Customer's Message to You* (New York: Rawson Associates, 1989).

T. Scott Gross, *Positively Outrageous Service: New and Easy Ways to Win Customers for Life* (New York: Mastermedia, Inc., 1991). Excerpts reprinted by permission of the publisher.

Michael Hammer and James Champy, *Reengineering the Corporation: A Manifesto for Business Revolution* (New York: HarperBusiness, 1993). Copyright 1993 by Michael Hammer and James Champy. Excerpts reprinted by permission of HarperCollins Publishers, Inc.

Mack Hanan and Peter Karp, *Customer Satisfaction: How to Maximize, Measure, and Market Your Company's "Ultimate Product"* (New York, AMACOM, 1989). Copyright 1989 by Mack Hanan and Peter Karp. Published by AMACOM, a division of the American Management Association. All rights reserved. Excerpts reprinted with permission of the publisher.

James L. Heskett, W. Earl Sasser, Jr., and Christopher W. L. Hart, *Service Breakthroughs: Changing the Rules of the Game* (New York: The Free Press, 1990). Copyright 1990 by James L. Heskett, W. Earl Sasser, Jr., and Christopher W. L. Hart. Excerpts reprinted with the permission of The Free Press, a Division of Simon & Schuster.

Linda M. Lash, *The Complete Guide to Customer Service* (New York: John Wiley & Sons, 1989). Copyright 1989 by John Wiley & Sons, Inc. Excerpts reprinted by permission of John Wiley & Sons, Inc.

Michael LeBoeuf, Ph.D., *How to Win Customers and Keep Them for Life* (New York: Berkley Books, 1987). Copyright 1988 by Michael LeBoeuf, Ph.D. Excerpts reprinted by permission of the Putnam Publishing Group.

Kathleen H. J. Leibfried and C. J. McNair, *Benchmarking: A Tool for Continuous Improvement* (New York: HarperBusiness, 1992). Copyright 1992 by Kathleen H. J. Leibfried and C. J. McNair. Excerpt reprinted by permission of HarperCollins Publishers, Inc.

Milind M. Lele (with Jagdish N. Sheth), *The Customer is Key: Gaining an Unbeatable Advantage Through Customer Satisfaction* (New York: John Wiley & Sons, 1987). Copyright 1987 by Milind M. Lele and Jagdish N. Sheth. Excerpts reprinted by permission of John Wiley & Sons, Inc.

Donald R. Libey, *Libey on Customers* (Washington, D.C.: Libey Publishing Incorporated, 1992). Excerpts reprinted by permission of Libey Publishing, Potomac, Maryland.

Laura A. Liswood, *Serving Them Right: Innovative & Powerful Customer Retention Strategies* (New York: HarperBusiness, 1990). Copyright 1990 by Harper & Row Publishers, Inc. Excerpts reprinted by permission of HarperCollins Publishers, Inc.

Ron McCann (as told to Joe Vitale), *The Joy of Service!* (Stafford, Texas: Service Information Source Publications, 1989). Excerpt reprinted by permission of the publisher.

Rebecca L. Morgan, *Calming Upset Customers: Staying Effective During Unpleasant Situations* (San Francisco: Crisp Publications, Inc., 1989).

Ronald A. Nykiel, *You Can't Lose if the Customer Wins: Ten Steps to Service Success* (Stamford, Connecticut: Longmeadow Press, 1990).

Charles C. Poirier and William F. Houser, *Business Partnering for Continuous Improvement: How to Forge Enduring Alliances Among Employees, Suppliers & Customers* (San Francisco: Berrett-Koehler Publishers, 1993).

Hal F. Rosenbluth and Diane McFerrin Peters, *The Customer Comes Second: And Other Secrets of Exceptional Service* (New York: William Morrow and Company, Inc., 1992). Copyright 1992 by Hal F. Rosenbluth and Diane McFerrin. Excerpts reprinted by permission of William Morrow & Company, Inc.

Richard J. Schonberger, *Building a Chain of Customers: Linking Business Functions to Create the World Class Company* (New York: The Free Press, 1990).

Peter M. Senge, *The Fifth Discipline: The Art & Practice of The Learning Organization* (New York: Doubleday, 1990). Copyright 1990 by Peter M. Senge. Excerpts reprinted by permission of the publisher.

Carl Sewell and Paul B. Brown, *Customers for Life: How to Turn that One-Time Buyer into a Lifetime Customer* (New York: Doubleday, 1990). Copyright 1990 by Carl Sewell. Excerpts reprinted by permission of the publisher.

Terry G. Vavra, *Aftermarketing: How to Keep Customers for Life Through Relationship Marketing* (Homewood, Illinois: Business One Irwin, 1992). Excerpts reprinted by permission of Irwin Professional Publishing.

Richard C. Whiteley, *The Customer-Driven Company: Moving from Talk to Action* (Reading, Massachusetts: Addison-Wesley Publishing, Inc., 1991). Copyright 1993 by The Forum Corporation. Excerpts reprinted by permission of Addison-Wesley Publishing Company, Inc.

Valarie A. Zeithaml, A. Parasuraman, and Leonard L. Berry, *Delivering Quality Service: Balancing Customer Perceptions and Expectations* (New York: The Free Press, 1990). Copyright 1990 by The Free Press. Excerpts reprinted with the permission of The Free Press, a Division of Simon & Schuster.

Ron Zemke and Chip R. Bell, *Service Wisdom: Creating and Maintaining the Customer Service Edge* (Minneapolis: Lakewood Publications Inc., 1989). Copyright 1989 by Performance Research Associates, Inc. Excerpts reprinted by permission.

Ron Zemke (with Dick Schaaf), *The Service Edge: 101 Companies That Profit from Customer Care* (New York: PLUME, 1989). Copyright 1989 by Ron Zemke and Dick Schaaf. Excerpts used by permission of Dutton Signet, a division of Penguin Books USA Inc.

Other Service Books

The following books provided valuable background information for our understanding of the concept of customer service.

Joan Koob Cannie, *Keeping Customers for Life* (New York: AMACOM, 1991).

Clay Carr, *Front-Line Customer Service: 15 Keys to Customer Satisfaction* (New York: John Wiley & Sons, 1990).

Stephen R. Covey, *The 7 Habits of Highly Effective People: Restoring the Character Ethic* (New York: Simon & Schuster, Inc., 1989).

John A. Czepiel, Michael R. Solomon, and Carol F. Surprenant, *The Service Encounter: Managing Employee/Customer Interaction in Service Businesses* (Lexington, Massachusetts: Lexington Books, 1985).

Louis De Rose, *Value Selling* (New York: AMACOM, 1989).

Robert L. Desatnick, *Keep the Customer! Making Customer Service Your Competitive Edge* (Boston: Houghton Mifflin Company, 1987).

Masaaki Imai, *KAIZEN: The Key to Japan's Competitive Success* (New York: McGraw-Hill Publishing Company, 1986).

Robert C. Kausen, *Customer Satisfaction Guaranteed: A New Approach to Customer Service, Bedside Manner, and Relationship Ease* (Trinity Center, California: Life Education, Inc., 1988).

John Tschohl (with Steve Franzmeier), *Achieving Excellence Through Customer Service* (Englewood Cliffs, New Jersey: Prentice Hall, 1991).

Books on Real Estate Management

The following publications were used as resources on real estate trends.

Emerging Trends in Real Estate: 1995 (Chicago: Real Estate Research Corporation; and New York: Equitable Real Estate Investment Management, Inc., 1994).

Emerging Trends in Real Estate: 1994 (Chicago: Real Estate Research Corporation; and New York: Equitable Real Estate Investment Management, Inc., 1993).

IREM Foundation (prepared by Arthur Andersen Real Estate Services Group), *Managing the Future: Real Estate in the 1990s* (Chicago: Institute of Real Estate Management Foundation, 1991). Quoted material reprinted with permission of the publisher.

Articles on Commercial Tenant Retention

John N. Gallagher, "Managing Leases to Improve Tenant Relations," *Journal of Property Management* 52(6):60-61, November-December 1987.

Bary Graeler, "The Value of Indirect Marketing," *Journal of Property Management* 55(6):32-33, November-December 1990.

Chuck Kusbit and Joe Sutton, "Tenant Retention: Making It Hard to Leave," *Journal of Property Management* 56(1):18-20, January-February 1991.

Charles S. Madden, "Keeping Tenants Satisfied," *Journal of Property Management* 54(1):52-53, January-February 1989.

Sharon K. Mount, "Long-Term Space Planning as a Retention Tool" *Journal of Property Management* 56(2):48-51, March-April 1991.

Richard F. Muhlebach and James O. Wood, "Retaining Tenants with the Personal Touch," *Journal of Property Management* 54(1):50-52, January-February 1989.

William D. Norwell and Victoria A. Stevens, "Tracking Retention Efforts" *Journal of Property Management* 57(2):24-28, March-April, 1992.

Cathie Rategan, "Making the Most from Your Amenities, *Journal of Property Management* 56(2):22-26, March-April, 1991.

Ellen Romano, "Retaining Tenants Against the Odds," *Journal of Property Management* 57(4):32-35, July-August 1992.

Ray Timberlake, "Early Renewals Make Economic Sense," *Journal of Property Management* 55(6):22-25, November-December 1990.

Index